T0331298

'A timely and highly valuable addition to the discourse around smart specialisation and regional development.'

Louis Brennan, *Professor in Business Studies,*
Business & Administrative Studies, Trinity College Dublin, Ireland

The Empirical and Institutional Dimensions of Smart Specialisation

Smart specialisation is the new policy approach to the development of regional innovation systems across Europe and it involves fostering innovative and entrepreneurial initiatives which are well tailored to the local context. The different technologies, skills profiles, business activities, institutions and sectors which reflect a region's economic strengths and potential are to be fostered and encouraged to diversify in ways which also exploit the region's linkages with broader global value-chains.

Yet, the ideas contained in the smart specialisation agenda have until now been primarily conceptual in nature. *The Empirical and Institutional Dimensions of Smart Specialisation* draws together some of the leading regional economists and scientists in Europe to analyse how smart specialisation is working in practice. This book investigates different dimensions of the agenda as it is developing across parts of Europe from both quantitative and qualitative perspectives. The quantitative analysis examines the nature of the diversification processes undertaken by regions and the interplay between the chosen local regional development priorities and the wider global value-chain impacts of these choices. Meanwhile, the qualitative analysis examines the institutional opportunities and challenges facing policy makers and the key elements most likely to provide the underpinnings of a workable set of policy settings.

The book is aimed both at academic researchers interested in the interface between economic geography and regional innovation systems as well as at policy makers making public policy decisions related to regional development at the local, city, regional or national levels.

Philip McCann holds the University of Groningen Endowed Chair of Economic Geography at the University of Groningen and is also the Tagliaferri Research Fellow in the Department of Land Economy, University of Cambridge.

Frank van Oort is Professor of Urban and Regional Economics at Erasmus University Rotterdam and at Utrecht University. He is also the Academic Director of the Institute of Housing and Urban Development Studies at Erasmus University Rotterdam.

John Goddard is Emeritus Professor in the Centre for Urban and Regional Development Studies (CURDS) at Newcastle University. He is a co-author of the European Commission Guide to RIS3 Smart Specialisation and a member of the advisory group to the Smart Specialisation Platform at the European Joint Research Centre.

Regions and Cities

Series Editor in Chief
Susan M. Christopherson, *Cornell University, USA*

Editors
Maryann Feldman, *University of Georgia, USA*
Gernot Grabher, *HafenCity University Hamburg, Germany*
Ron Martin, *University of Cambridge, UK*
Kieran P. Donaghy, *Cornell University, USA*

In today's globalised, knowledge-driven and networked world, regions and cities have assumed heightened significance as the interconnected nodes of economic, social and cultural production, and as sites of new modes of economic and territorial governance and policy experimentation. This book series brings together incisive and critically engaged international and interdisciplinary research on this resurgence of regions and cities, and should be of interest to geographers, economists, sociologists, political scientists and cultural scholars, as well as to policymakers involved in regional and urban development.

For more information on the Regional Studies Association visit www.regional-studies.org

There is a **30% discount** available to RSA members on books in the **Regions and Cities** series, and other subject related Taylor and Francis books and e-books including Routledge titles. To order just e-mail Cara.Trevor@tandf.co.uk, or phone on +44 (0) 20 7017 6924 and declare your RSA membership. You can also visit www.routledge.com and use the discount code: **RSA0901**

The Empirical and Institutional Dimensions of Smart Specialisation

Edited by Philip McCann,
Frank van Oort and John Goddard

Routledge
Taylor & Francis Group

LONDON AND NEW YORK

First published 2017
by Routledge

2 Park Square, Milton Park, Abingdon, Oxfordshire OX14 4RN
52 Vanderbilt Avenue, New York, NY 10017

Routledge is an imprint of the Taylor & Francis Group, an informa business

First issued in paperback 2019

British Library Cataloguing in Publication Data
A catalogue record for this book is available from the British Library

Library of Congress Cataloging in Publication Data
Names: Goddard, J. B., editor. | McCann, Philip, 1964– editor. | Oort, Frank van, editor.
Title: The empirical and institutional dimensions of smart specialisation / edited by John Goddard, Philip McCann and Frank Van Oort.
Description: Abingdon, Oxon, New York, NY: Routledge, 2017. | Includes index.
Identifiers: LCCN 2016025445 | ISBN 9781138695757 (hardback) | ISBN 9781315526218 (ebook)
Subjects: LCSH: Regional economics–European Union countries. | Regional planning–European Union countries. | Economic specialization–European Union countries. | European Union countries–Economic conditions.
Classification: LCC HC240 .E459 2017 | DDC 330.94–dc23
LC record available at https://lccn.loc.gov/2016025445

ISBN: 978-1-138-69575-7 (hbk)
ISBN: 978-0-367-87871-9 (pbk)

Typeset in Times New Roman
by Deanta Global Publishing Services, Chennai, India

Contents

Figures

Tables

About the Authors

Martin Andersson is Professor of Industrial Economics at Blekinge Institute of Technology (BTH) and Professor of Innovation Studies at CIRCLE, Lund University. His research focuses on the interplay between innovation, technological change and business dynamics, and on the role of cities and local labour markets in fostering innovation and entrepreneurship.

Mari Jose Aranguren is Professor of Economics at the Deusto Business School, University of Deusto, and General Director of Orkestra–Basque Institute of Competitiveness, specialised in territorial strategies, policy analysis and clusters.

Ron Boschma is Professor in Regional Economics and Research Director at the Department of Human Geography and Planning at Utrecht University in the Netherlands. He is also Professor in Innovation Studies at CIRCLE (Centre for Innovation, Research and Competence in the Learning Economy) at Lund University in Sweden.

Nicola Cortinovis holds a PhD in Economic Geography from Utrecht University and currently work as Assistant Professor in Regional and Industrial Economics at Erasmus University in Rotterdam. He specializes in regional development, agglomeration economies and spatial and network relations.

Teodora Dogaru is specialized in urban and regional economic planning in Central Eastern Europe. She recently defended her PhD thesis (University of A Coruña, Spain) on the growth potential of second-tier cities in CEE space.

John Goddard is Emeritus Professor in the Centre for Urban and Regional Development Studies (CURDS) at Newcastle University. He is a co-author of the European Commission Guide to RIS3 Smart Specialisation and a member of the advisory group to the Smart Specialisation Platform at the European Joint Research Centre.

Robert Huggins is Professor of Economic Geography and director of the Centre for Economic Geography at Cardiff University, Wales, United Kingdom. His research focuses on international competitiveness and regional economic dynamics.

Olga Ivanova is senior researcher economics at PBL Netherlands Environmental Assessment Agency. She has a PhD in Economics from the University of Oslo and is specialized in macro-economic modelling and analysis, (dynamic) CGE modelling, regional-economic and transport modelling, and integrated impact assessment.

Sierdjan Koster is Assistant Professor in Economic Geography at the Faculty of Spatial Sciences at the University of Groningen. He specialises in issues around entrepreneurship, innovation and labour markets in relation to regional economic dynamics.

Maureen Lankhuizen is affiliated to the Department of Spatial Economics at the Free University (VU) of Amsterdam and also teaches at the University of Amsterdam. Her research interests include regional development, trade and commodity flows, foreign direct investment, and quantitative research including input–output analysis and integrating datasets.

Bart Los is Associate Professor at the University of Groningen. He has mainly published on topics related to structural change, productivity, innovation and international trade. He has also been one of the coordinators of the FP7-funded project in which the World Input-Output Database was constructed.

Philip McCann holds the University of Groningen Endowed Chair of Economic Geography at the University of Groningen and is also the Tagliaferri Research Fellow in the Department of Land Economy, University of Cambridge.

Mikel Navarro is Professor of Economics at the Deusto Business School, University of Deusto, and Senior Researcher at Orkestra-Basque Institute of Competitiveness, specialised in regional competitiveness and innovation systems.

Raquel Ortega-Argilés is the Rosalind Franklin Research Fellow in the Department of Global Economics and Management of the Faculty of Economics and Business at the University of Groningen. Her research focuses on innovation, entrepreneurship and productivity and the links between analysis and policy. Raquel is also a co-author of the official RIS3 Smart Specialisation Guide published by the European Commission.

Daniel Prokop is a Lecturer in International Business in International Business and Economics Research at Sheffield Business School, Sheffield Hallam University. He researches regional economic development with a particular interest in entrepreneurship and innovation.

Mark Thissen is a Senior Researcher Economics at the PBL Netherlands Environmental Assessment Agency. He has published on spatial Computable General Equilibrium modelling, the economic effects of infrastructure investment, interregional trade between European regions, and topics related to regional economic competitiveness and smart specialisation.

Paul Vallance is a Research Associate in the Centre for Urban and Regional Development Studies (CURDS) at Newcastle University. His research interests include universities, public research organisations, regional innovation policy, and evolutionary economic geography.

Frank van Oort is Professor of Urban and Regional Economics at Erasmus University Rotterdam and at Utrecht University. He is also the Academic Director of the Institute of Housing and Urban Development Studies at Erasmus University Rotterdam.

James R. Wilson is Senior Researcher at Orkestra–Basque Institute of Competitiveness and a faculty member at Deusto Business School, University of Deusto, Spain. His research is focused on territorial strategy, competitiveness policy, governance and the roles of universities in territorial economic development.

Foreword

The short life of Smart Specialisation has been nothing less than remarkable in the long history of regional policy. Within the space of a few years it has progressed from being an arcane concept at the margins of academic debate to being a central theme of EU Cohesion Policy, an astonishing career by any standards. However, this short lifespan means that Smart Specialisation was launched into the real world of regional development policy without the benefit of a pilot action to test its credentials and without a robust evidence base to assess its practical relevance to the public administrations that are responsible for implementing it. The lack of an empirical evidence base to justify the launch of Smart Specialisation makes it all the more imperative that theorists and policymakers scrutinise the ways in which the concept is being implemented. Although this book does not offer an evaluation of Smart Specialisation in practice – because it is far too early for such an exercise – it does aim to address the theoretical and policy implications of this remarkable regional innovation policy concept.

The book springs from one of the key work packages in the *SmartSpec* project, a research project funded under the EU's Seventh Framework Programme and coordinated by Cardiff University. The project involved a judicious mix of theorists, policymakers and reflexive practitioners, comprising eight universities working in concert with independent experts, two regional network organisations and ten regions.

The chapters in the book cover some of the major themes that have loomed large in the debates about innovation and regional development over the past 20 years or so, including the role of (formal and informal) institutions in fostering/frustrating economic development, the path dependent mechanisms through which urban and regional economies diversify into new or adjacent activities, the interplay of intra-regional and inter-regional learning, the uneven spatial effects of knowledge networks, the under-researched role of universities in innovation ecosystems, the position and performance of regions in international trade networks and, last but not least, the context-dependent nature of innovation and development.

This book – and the SmartSpec project on which it is based – addresses these themes in a theoretically-informed and empirically-sensitive manner. The authors are leading lights in their field and they prove that gifted individuals can work as a team in a project that was as stimulating as it was enjoyable. We thank all those involved for freely sharing their knowledge and their enthusiasm and we are especially grateful to the European Commission for funding the *SmartSpec* project.

Adrian Healy and Kevin Morgan
Cardiff University

1   Introduction to the Empirical and Institutional Dimensions of Smart Specialisation

Philip McCann, Frank van Oort and
John Goddard

There is a large literature emerging both from academic and policy circles on the concept and application of smart specialisation in European regions (Foray *et al.* 2012; Thissen *et al.* 2013; McCann and Ortega-Argilés 2015; Foray 2015; McCann 2015). Smart specialisation was introduced into the reformed EU Cohesion Policy as a method helping to prioritise investments in innovation and knowledge-related activities, and the overall format in which the approach is implemented in EU Cohesion Policy is under the heading of 'RIS3', the acronym for Research and Innovation Strategies for Smart Specialisation (Foray *et al.* 2012). The timeliness of RIS3 is underscored by the extremely tight budget conditions facing many EU regions and member states. Resource allocation decisions are always complex and challenging, and the influences on resource allocations decisions are multi-faceted in nature. However, in many parts of Europe the pressures on public policy resource allocation decisions have never been greater than they are now. Yet, as the Barca (2009) report explained, competing and diverse interests, many of which are political in nature, often lead to a lack of resource concentration on key priorities, thereby limiting the potential impacts of policy actions and interventions. As such, a policy prioritisation methodology which is amenable to different regional contexts and which is also consistent with the fundamental premises of Cohesion Policy was much-needed, and smart specialisation was identified as reflecting both of these key features (McCann and Ortega-Argilés 2013a, b). As such, the RIS3-smart specialisation agenda sits within the overall set of reforms to EU Cohesion Policy, and on various dimensions can be seen as one of the key aspects of the reforms. Yet, this is not a European issue per se, in that the thinking underpinning smart specialisation is consistent with the many recent world-wide developments in thinking regarding modern regional policy and regional innovation policy (McCann and Ortega-Argilés 2013c) across many different subjects, disciples and policy arenas which previously were largely scattered and fragmented (OECD 2013). This smart specialisation-type thinking builds on different lines of scientific enquiry including the related variety literature (Frenken *et al.* 2007; Neffke *et al.* 2011), the structure-competition-trade literature (Thissen *et al.* 2013), the connectivity and global value-chains literatures (Los *et al.* 2015, Timmer *et al.* 2013), the systems-of-innovation literature (Cooke *et al.* 2004), the Triple Helix-type literatures regarding university–industry linkages

(Ponds *et al.* 2010, Goddard *et al.* 2011), and also many of the institutions and governance literatures (Valdaliso and Wilson 2015) underpinning the learning region arguments (Morgan 1997). However, the smart specialisation approach puts an overall logical framework and discipline onto these different literatures and insights and as such, groups them into an integrated whole which ought to be amenable to policy debates and decision-making. The idea of smart specialisation is one of the most important EU's policy attentions focussing on the overcoming of fragmentation – fragmentation across countries and regions, all inhabiting small specialisations compared to US or Chinese economies, varying over institutions and cultures, embedded in relatively small cities within the EU countries. Smarts specialisation strives for excellence and newly developed, diversified niche markets and multilevel cooperative structures across industry, knowledge institutes and government as a potential catalyst for economic development after recent years of austerity, while simultaneously urban policies ('Urban Agenda') and corridor policies (TEN-T) strive for connectivity, complementarities and developing polycentric urban interaction for competitive, smart and inclusive growth, urgent cohesion and migration policies strive for redistribution and creation of economic and social opportunities, while networking policies on knowledge (ERA), trade (TTIP) and FDI are pursued for cross-regional economic linkages within and outside Europe. Yet, the identification and exploitation of regional endogenous development opportunities based on smart evolution, diversification and specialisation are at the core of this overcoming-fragmentation disadvantages process in Europe, as it potentially creates long-run and self-sustaining developments. Other policies, mostly based across various directorate generals in the European Commission, ideally should align.

Having said that, translating an academic idea of smart specialisation into a workable policy implementation tool involves many different steps and leads to many different challenges, and these steps and challenges can variously be technological, institutional, political or governance-related in nature. As such, following the progress of an academic idea into a workable policy schema involves charting many different policy-development trajectories, and many different experiences in different places. Policy cycles are hardly ever identical between different places and in particular across different countries, the arena over which EU Cohesion Policy operates. As such, while many features are likely to be common, at the same time a policy schema such as smart specialisation may exhibit rather different features in different contexts and display differing degrees of efficacy in different settings. Where they are evident, the reasons for these differences are likely to differ according to the context. However, identifying and distinguishing those policy-related features which are similar across regions from those which are different and specific to regions is an important role for policy analysis and policylearning. Similarly, identifying the nature and magnitude of any opportunities and challenges associated with innovation system successes or system failures, which are evident in different regional contexts, is also important for policy analysis. The reason is that the whole arena of policy prioritisation requires us to build up knowledge-bases, both of what works – when and where – and what does not; and in each case why, alongside a sense of relevant magnitudes of any impacts or blockages. Policymaking is always to some extent a step in the dark, with policy design based on observations of other cases and examples, alongside a certain degree of trial and error. However, good policy transfer mechanisms are always grounded on the lessons learned from examples of best-practice cases which are then tailored to local circumstances. Yet, even with solid policy transfer systems, the outcomes of specific policy actions are still uncertain, and therefore a major part of the institutional learning undertaken by regions is also one of knowledge sharing between different regions. As will be clear in the following chapters, the smart specialisation agenda has pushed forward the EU-wide sharing of knowledge, and as such, is helping to foster an improved climate of policy transfer across the EU.

The research undertaken for this book makes significant progress in identifying which aspects of smart specialisation are common and which are specific to the regional context, and also helps to provide ways of identifying the orders of magnitude associated with particular types of policy interventions in different contexts. Economic, technological, institutional and governance dimensions are discussed on the basis of different research lines, and as part of this agenda the research also uncovers different aspects and dimension of smart specialisation which can be articulated empirically in a manner which is helpful to policymakers. The research undertaken for each of the different chapters in this book has all been carried out as part of the Research Project *Smartspec – Smart Specialisation for Regional Innovation*, an international research project involving many partners in different European countries, coordinated by Cardiff University UK.[1] The project is funded through the EU's Seventh Framework Programme for research, technological development and demonstration under grant agreement number 320131. The chapters in this book reflect the work undertaken in work package 1 on empirical research aiming for identification of the economic and institutional mechanisms impacting on smart specialisation, the entrepreneurial search processes and network connectivity opportunities.

In Chapter 2 the broad intellectual themes underpinning the smart specialisation agenda are outlined and articulated by Philip McCann and Raquel Ortega-Argilés. The approach as adopted in EU Cohesion Policy (Foray *et al.* 2012), as already mentioned above, is comprised of the insights and ideas derived various different lines of enquiry which are have been moulded into a much more integrated system than was previously evident in the academic literature, and in a manner which makes it workable for policy makers. The approach as implemented is therefore underpinned both by strong intellectual foundations as well as also a need for a pragmatic and realistic methodology which can explicitly be adapted to the local context and circumstances. There are obviously many obstacles and difficulties associated with the implementation of the RIS3 agenda, but the early evidence is that is indeed being taken up seriously across Europe.

One of the key features of the smart specialisation type way of thinking concerns the idea of economic diversification and related variety. This is the principle that a significant part of the successful growth of regions is associated with the incremental branching out of existing core specialisations and competences, rather than leaps into skills and technologies which are unrelated to the region's prevailing industrial, technological and skills profile. In Chapter 3 Ron Boschma explains these principles and the evidence underpinning these arguments but also moves beyond a purely technical and technological argument to incorporate wide issues relating to institutions. While the related variety approach cannot yet provide specific policy advice in particular contexts, what it can do is outline key principles which need to be followed at the local level. Policy interventions should aim to help a region diversify by developing new linkages and crossovers between the region's existing sectors, activities, technologies and skills-sets, rather than seeking to import new sectors, activities or technologies which are largely unrelated to the existing regional industrial set-up.

One of the key themes of RIS3 relates to entrepreneurial search processes and the need for policysettings to encourage local entrepreneurs, firms and institutional actors such as universities to come up with proposals for policy-enhanced innovation initiatives. In Chapter 4 these ideas are further developed by Martin Andersson and Sierdjan Koster who aim to bring additional perspectives on the role industry structure plays in shaping the conditions and potential for renewal and growth of regional economies through entrepreneurship. They review recent literature on (1) the labour market origins of entrepreneurs and (2) the role of the social environment in encouraging individual entrepreneurial behaviours, and draw two important conclusions. The first is that it is critical that analyses of regional economies in a smart specialization context acknowledge the 'functional specialization' of local industries: the 'contents' of what workers do and the associated skills, experiences and capabilities they are likely to accumulate during their professional career. The nature of workers' jobs provides an important learning context, and influences the scope and direction for entrepreneurial discovery. Their second conclusion is that it is equally important that smart specialization policy acknowledges and craft strategies to cope with the broader social environment for entrepreneurship in a region. Various structuring types of social, or cultural, characteristics of regions are typically historically rooted and display significant inertia, and put constraints on as well as constitute a major challenge for policy.

The related variety and entrepreneurial search aspects of RIS3 are also heavily contingent on knowledge networks. Yet, while mobilising the local knowledgebase has to be the bedrock of RIS3, as is consistent with the whole place-based and learning region approach, the relevant knowledge networks facilitating and articulating the key knowledge flows are typically neither defined nor wholly constrained to within the local regional context. Indeed, as Robert Huggins and Daniel Prokop demonstrate in Chapter 5, not only are the knowledge networks which are critical for local regional development often widely dispersed across many regions, but also these knowledge networks impact differently on different regions, due to the differential positing of individual regions within the overall network architecture. The practical and data-based visualisation approach developed by Huggins and Prokop provides a methodology which can help regions to better understand their positioning in the networks and therefore to better identify those critical linkages which need to be fostered and bolstered.

Similar types of themes are taken up by Mark Thissen, Frank van Oort and Olga Ivanova in Chapter 6 who demonstrate a technique for decomposing the performance of individual regions according to their positioning and performance in international trade networks. In particular, the methodology that they outline allows regional policymakers to identify whether the performance of the region is primarily related to the sectors in which the region is specialised, the performance of these specialised sectors in general across all regions, or the performance of region's specialised sectors in comparison to the performance of those same sectors in other regions. Structural, local based growth is distinguished from demand-led growth, stemming from other regions. These aspects are important for profiling and understanding the underlying regional growth dynamics, and for distinguishing the extent to which region's performance in a global context is a matter of its structure and patterns of local specialisation (prone to local policy) or a question of the performance of those specialisations vis-à-vis other regions (prone to network policies).

The impacts of a region's structure and trade in the context of global value-chains are examined in Chapter 7 by Bart Los, Maureen Lankhuizen and Mark Thissen. This chapter develops measures of competitiveness for EU regions at NUTS2-level. Within European countries, transportation costs and transaction costs are relatively low due to exchange rate risks and legal and cultural differences, leading to situations in which small differences in comparative advantage across regions can lead to the relocation of stages of production from one region to another one. Participating in global value chains and upgrading to higher value added activities within these has become an essential aspect of regional development. This chapter presents a method for quantifying the success of European regions in doing so, and emphasizes the heterogeneity of regions within countries and in pre- and post-financial crises regimes in being successful. This has large policy implications for any place-based economic development strategy.

Chapter 8 by Paul Vallance explores the institutional challenges involved in engaging universities, research centres and other similar knowledge institutions to the wider arenas of the economy including the private, public and civil society sectors. Based on the evidence derived from key case studies in Finland and Northern Ireland, the chapter examines the types of governance issues and challenges which arise in driving forward a RIS3-type policy agenda. The reciprocal interactions between RIS3-types of initiatives and the institutional and societal context in which they are situated reflect a different but no-less-equally important notion of the embeddedness of the policy schema. In particular, and examination of certain healthcare and smart city initiatives points to the importance of users in the policy processes as well as providers, thereby suggesting that more 'quadruple' rather than 'triple helix' types of mechanisms may be operating, thereby both enriching and further complicating the policy processes.

Chapter 9 sets out the major challenges facing the RIS3 agenda in Central and Eastern European Countries (CEECs). As Teodora Dogaru, Frank van Oort and Nicola Cortinovis explain, the institutional, structural and governance challenges associated with enhancing the local and regional economic conditions are very real indeed. Translating the RIS3 ideas into workable policy actions in these contexts involves addressing various other challenges and difficulties, many of which are either not evident in other richer regions, or at least do not significantly constrain policy activities in many other regions. Given the scale of these challenges, the successful application of RIS3 in these countries will involve a further step-change in terms of all aspects of policy implementation, involving a consideration of all of the different issues raised in this book ranging from knowledge networks to global–local spillovers from foreign investment, through to skills provision, as well as well as major governance and institutional challenges. In particular, mobilising the second and third tier cities and regions in CEECs will involve new thinking around networks formation and institutional linkages.

Chapter 10 by Mari Jose Aranguren, Mikel Navarro, and James R. Wilson builds on the insights of the previous two chapters and explores the often-forgotten human element that is critical in moving the entrepreneurial discovery process forward from an abstract concept to practical reality. In particular, the shift from fixed government plans to flexible entrepreneurial discovery processes, which should involve a wide range of agents from the quadruple helix of business, government, research and civil society, generates particular governance and leadership demands. A review of literature on place leadership and territorial strategy identifies these demands, which are explored empirically through analysis of the distinct RIS3 processes in two neighbouring Spanish regions, namely the Basque Country and Navarra. The evidence arising suggests that the shift from planning to process requires policy leadership of a form which engages, includes, and motivates, but the actual required leadership mix will differ between regions depending on their economic, institutional, governance and geographical features.

Chapter 11 by Robert Huggins once again returns to the theme of networks as already discussed in Chapter 5, and which also connects in different ways with many of the issues arising from Chapters 3, 6, 7 and 9. Networks promote and mediate the relationships between entrepreneurship, innovation and regional economic outcomes, and promoting connectivity with intra-regional, inter-regional, and inter-national knowledge flows is a core theme of RIS3 agenda. As Huggins explains, fostering such connectivity also requires enhancing the network capital of entrepreneurs and firms. As also discussed in other chapter, this is an area where public policy may be able to play a constructive role, with key actors and institutions playing the role of bridge-builders between different stakeholders and constituencies. However, the enhancement of network capabilities also implies that the knowledge roles must be highly distributed, with no one actor establishing a gatekeeper role which leads to the development or strengthening of local monopoly or monopsony types of positions. RIS3 must be as open as possible, in order to foster open innovation processes based on the types of recombination opportunities examined earlier in Chapter 3 by Ron Boschma.

Note

1   http://www.cardiff.ac.uk/cplan/research/smartspec.

References

Barca, F. (2009), *An Agenda for A Reformed Cohesion Policy: A Place-Based Approach to Meeting European Union Challenges and Expectations*, European Commission, Brussels.

Cooke, P., Heidenreich, M., and Braczyk H.J. (2004), *Regional Innovation Systems. The Role of Governance in a Globalized World*. London: Routledge.

Foray, D. (2015), *Smart Specialization: Opportunities and Challenges Regional Innovation Policy*, Routledge, London.

Foray, D., Goddard, J., Morgan, K., Goenaga Beldarrain, X., Landabaso, M., Neuwelaars, C., and Ortega-Argilés, R. (2012), *Guide to Research and Innovation Strategies for Smart Specialisation (RIS 3)*, S3 Smart Specialisation Platform, IPTS Institute for Prospective Technological Studies, Joint Research Centre of the European Commission, Seville.

Frenken, K., Van Oort, F.G., and Verburg, T. (2007), 'Related Variety, Unrelated Variety and Regional Economic Growth', *Regional Studies*, 41 (5), 685–697.

Goddard, J., and Vallance, P. (2011), Universities and regional development. In Pike, A., Rodriguez-Pose, A., Tomaney, J, ed. *Handbook of Local and Regional Development*. London, UK: Routledge, 2011, 425–437.

Los, B., Timmer, M.P., and de Vries G.J. (2015), 'How Global Are Global Value Chains? A New Approach to Measure International Fragmentation', *Journal of Regional Science*, 55, 66–92.

McCann, P. (2015), *The Regional and Urban Policy of the European Union: Cohesion, Results-Orientation and Smart Specialisation*, Edward Elgar, Cheltenham.

McCann, P., and Ortega-Argilés, R. (2013a), 'Redesigning and Reforming European Regional Policy: The Reasons, the Logic and the Outcomes', *International Regional Science Review*, 36 (3), 424–445.

McCann, P., and Ortega-Argilés, R. (2013b), 'Transforming European Regional Policy: A Results-Driven Agenda and Smart Specialisation', *Oxford Review of Economic Policy*, 29 (2), 405–431.

McCann, P., and Ortega-Argilés, R. (2013c), 'Modern Regional Innovation Policy', *Cambridge Journal of Regions, Economy and Society*, 6 (2), 187–216.

McCann, P., and Ortega-Argilés, R. (2015), 'Smart Specialization, Regional Growth and Applications to EU Cohesion Policy', *Regional Studies*, 49 (8), 1291–1302.

Morgan, K. (1995), 'The Learning Region: Institutions, Innovation and Regional Renewal'. *Regional Studies*, 31, 491–503.

Neffke, F., Henning, M., and Boschma, R. (2011), 'How do Regions Diversify Over Time?', *Economic Geography*, 87 (3), 237–265.

OECD (2013), *Innovation Driven Growth in Regions: The Role of Smart Specialisation*, Organisation for Economic Cooperation and Development, Paris.

Ponds, R., van Oort, F.G., and Frenken, K. (2010), 'Innovation, Spillovers, and University-Industry Collaboration: An Extended Knowledge Production Function Approach'. *Journal of Economic Geography*, 10, 231–255.

Thissen, M., van Oort, F.G., Diodato, D., and Ruijs, A. (2013), *Regional Competitiveness and Smart Specialization in Europe: Place-Based Development in International Economic Networks*, Edward Elgar, Cheltenham.

Timmer, M.P., Los, B., Stehrer, R., and de Vries, G.J. (2013), 'Fragmentation, Incomes and Jobs: An Analysis of European Competitiveness', *Economic Policy*, 28, 613–661.

Valdaliso, J.M., and Wilson, J.R. (2015), *Strategies for Shaping Territorial Competitiveness*. London: Routledge.

2 The Intellectual and Practical Bases of the Application of RIS3 within EU Cohesion Policy

Philip McCann and Raquel Ortega-Argilés

2.1 Introduction

In recent years there has been much discussion in the European policy circles regarding the importance and workability of the ideas and principles of smart specialisation within EU regional policy, or more precisely, EU Cohesion Policy (McCann and Ortega-Argilés 2013a, b). The smart specialisation themes have been incorporated in the overall RIS3 agenda, whereby the acronym RIS3 refers to Regional Innovation Strategies for Smart Specialization. The incorporation of smart specialisation ideas within the overall regional innovation approach carries with it some clear and important clarifications. First, neither smart specialisation nor RIS3 define EU Cohesion Policy or even one particular stream of EU Cohesion Policy, namely the policy actions underpinned by the European Regional Development Fund. Rather, the principles and agenda set by smart specialisation and RIS3 sit within the smart growth strands of EU Cohesion Policy actions and interventions. Second, the innovation agenda being pursued within EU Cohesion Policy is not defined or confined to smart specialisation principles, but rather is framed in an overall innovation-systems understanding of regional development, of which smart specialisation is a key constituent part. Rather than an in-depth discussion of the EU Cohesion Policy architecture and the role of smart speciali-sation within this policy programming architecture, all of which is discussed in detail elsewhere (McCann 2015), the aim of this chapter is to discuss exactly how and where the RIS3 agenda sits within modern conceptual arguments regarding regional development. In order to examine these issues, the rest of the chapter is organised as follow. In Section 2.2 we discuss knowledge systems and the underlying intellectual basis for smart specialisation and RIS3 thinking. This allows us in Section 2.3 to discuss the analytical basis for RIS3 policy frameworks, and in Section 2.4 we discuss some of the institutional and governance challenges aris-ing out of the need to implement such an approach. Section 2.5 discusses the recent progress of the RIS3 agenda and Section 2.6 provides some brief conclusions.

2.2 Knowledge Systems Frameworks and RIS3

The original smart specialisation idea emerged from a knowledge-systems way of thinking about entrepreneurship, innovation and growth (Foray 2015). Moreover, many of the ideas and elements in the smart specialisation approach already existed in the literature, but were rather scattered across many different fields and lacking any framework for integration (OECD 2013). Smart specialisation provided a framework for thinking about these different insights from various fields in a consistent manner which was also well-suited to the prioritisation challenges faced by policy making. Therefore, in order to situate RIS3 within the broader conceptual arena it is first necessary to consider what we mean by a knowledge-systems way of thinking. The systems approach to innovation and entrepreneurship is based on the understanding that innovation is a result of complex linkages between different elements, and the strength of the system as a whole is only as strong as the weakest link between key elements (REDI 2013). Innovation-systems frameworks come in various types, including national innovation systems, sectoral innovation-systems, technological innovation-systems and regional innovation-systems approaches (Iammarino and McCann 2013). These approaches are neither strictly exclusive of each other, and nor are they contradictory to each other. Rather, different frameworks are used for different purposes, depending on the issues at hand and the specific questions being examined. For regional development matters, the regional innovation-system perspective is the most appropriate framework.

The regional innovation-systems framework considers local innovation performance to be a result of complex and varied knowledge interactions between different actors, be they firms, entrepreneurs, or brokers, or institutions such as universities, research centres, local government agencies, and civil society organisations. The flows of knowledge between institutions and actors, and the specific ways in which knowledge is generated, communicated and transmitted are regarding as being essential in order to understand regional spillovers and externalities. Standard urban economics arguments point to the importance of localised learning, sharing and matching (Duranton and Puga 2004) mechanisms for fostering growth. However, the innovation-systems approach treats these mechanisms in a more nuanced and detailed manner. We can learn about technologies, we can share technologies and we can match technologies; we can learn about human capital, we can share human capital and we can match human capital; we can learn about infrastructure, we can share infrastructure and we can match infrastructure; we can learn about research, we can share research and we can match research; we can learn about markets, we can share markets and we can match markets. Given the specific topic or issues at hand, these learning, sharing and matching mechanisms may be very different, and in addition may imply differences in the importance of proximity and geography in facilitating or inhibiting these mechanisms. The different specific mechanisms and the potentially different role of geography in facilitating these mechanisms are seen as being central to the innovation-systems approach to understanding regional development. Clues as to region's innovation and entrepreneurial performance are therefore to be found in the particular local characteristics and mechanisms displayed by a region. In addition, within the regional innovation-system the specific mapping of the relationships between the various different actors and institutions will be seen to differ between places, as will the relative monopoly or monopsony positions of key individuals, entities or institutions within the local schema. Yet, the innovation-system approach does not imply that all aspects of a region's entrepreneurial and innovation performance are internally driven. Nor does it imply that the regional innovation-system is understood as being an entirely closed framework. Rather, the regional innovation-system framework also perceives the region's innovation and entrepreneurial performance as being partly shaped by external factors. This is because the local actors and institutions themselves interact with the external firms, brokers and institutions which are located elsewhere, and these external linkages often also play a critical role in the functioning or the local internal linkages. The scale, importance and spatial extent of these external linkages is determined by many different factors including the region's economic geography, its industrial structure, its firm composition, its degree of sectoral disaggregation, the local presence of multinational establishments, and the region's connectivity to other places, and together these various influences shape the levels of interregional or international openness of the local economic system. Importantly, however, the regional innovation-system approach assumes that all regions differ from each other both internally and externally, and the innovation-systems approach argues that the internal and external specifics of each region hold many of the clues to the region's success in innovation-related activities, because these determine how knowledge flows both within and without the region.

In recent European debates regarding the innovation and entrepreneurial performance of EU regions, these systems-types of themes are explicitly understood as being central to the modelling and analysis of these issues (REDI 2013; Capello and Lenzi 2013). Moreover, these ideas are also well articulated in the North American and Asian arenas (OECD 2013). However, the fact that many of the clues as to the innovation and entrepreneurial performance of a region are to be found in its internal institutional dynamics as well as its external linkages, does not imply that more general patterns of innovation and entrepreneurial performance cannot be observed or identified across regions. While the specifics may vary in each case, there are certain patterns which appear to be evident in many different examples and situations, and the identification of these patterns has emerged in response to numerous empirical analyses and wide-ranging case study literature. One such pattern is that regions which are favourably situated at the core of large market areas, and thereby also exhibit high levels of market potential, tend to enjoy advantages for both entrepreneurship and innovation over more geographically peripheral regions, because the core regions offer greater market opportunities to risk-takers. At the same time, larger and more densely populated regions tend to exhibit greater local agglomeration advantages over smaller and more peripheral regions. These market potential and agglomeration arguments are basically different types of *scale*-related explanations regarding the ways in which knowledge and knowledge-flows acts as key determinants of regional economic growth.

At the same time, regions with *knowledge institutions* such as universities or scientific research institutes tend to exhibit local knowledge spillover advantages over other regions which do not enjoy the local presence of these types of institutions (Varga 2009). Similarly, nursery city type arguments (Duranton and Puga 2001) suggest that regions whose economies are characterised by a highly disaggregated firm base, and which are not overlydominated by a few monopoly or monopsony-type firms tend to offer greater entrepreneurial opportunities for new firm foundation and formation. Regions with highly skilled workforces exhibiting high levels of human capital also tend to exhibit higher levels of creativity, innovation and entrepreneurship, and regions with larger market potential also offer greater possibilities for entrepreneurship and innovation. The growth advantages associated with the sectoral structure of a region, and in particular the extent to which the region is specialised or diversified, is one which has been widely discussed since the seminal paper by Glaeser *et al.* (1992). While earlier analyses tended to advocate the advantages of regional sectoral diversity (Partridge *et al.* 2008; Desmet and Fafchamps 2005), more recent analyses based on the findings of numerous papers have tended to find that there is no clear-cut answer to this question, with both sectoral diversity and specialisation offering different advantages to different regions in different cases (de Groot *et al.* 2009; De Melo *et al.* 2009; Beaudry and Schiffauerova 2009). These arguments regarding firms and industries have also tended to be reflected in similar arguments relating to both technologies and institutions. Regions with a variety of different technologies are often argued to offer more advantageous growth conditions than regions dominated by specific technologies, as these are regarded as being more vulnerable to specific market shocks, whereas regions with more diverse technological profiles are seen as being better at adapting to changing circumstances. Similarly, regions with a broader range of knowledge or governance-related institutional and institutional types tend to be seen as offering more diverse pathways for knowledge flows than regions characterised by local governance structures with monopoly-type or monopsony-type institutions. More varied knowledge-flow pathways are widely understood as fostering both local entrepreneurship and innovation because both the sources of knowledge and the types of knowledge being transmitted are likely to be more varied. These various arguments are basically all different types of *structure*-related explanations about the ways in which knowledge and knowledge flows act as key determinants of regional economic growth.

Other lines of research also suggest that the extent to which these knowledge pathways also traverse regional, national or even intercontinental borders also influences the levels and the types of innovation being undertaken locally (Simonen and McCann 2008, 2010; Iammarino and McCann 2013). In particular, knowledge connections to certain key 'knowledge regions' appear to be especially important, rather than international connections per se, for fostering economic development. Yet, it is also likely that the key knowledge regions than a specific individual region ought to be well-connected to may also differ between regions, depending on the region's key technologies, sectors, and institutional features. Regions which are relatively specialised in advanced electronics or nano-technologies may well benefit far more from connections with world-leading knowledge regions in these sectors and technologies such as Silicon Valley and Taiwan, far more than connections with global cities such as New York or Hong Kong. Similarly, regions with strong financial services sectors may well find the connections with London to be far more important than those with San Francisco, while those in biosciences may find connections with Cambridge UK and Cambridge USA far more important than those with Paris. These arguments suggest that the interregional, international and intercontinental connections have a specific logic and polarity to their economic geography, driven by the local knowledge dynamics of the activities undertaken in the local region. Accessing external sources of knowledge is critical in areas which are complementary to the knowledge base of the region, and which help to expand and increase the region's internal knowledge base and knowledge assets. These ideas can also be extended to include access to external sources of human, physical and financial capital and all of these arguments are basically different versions of the role which *connectivity*-related features of the region play in facilitating the types of knowledge flows essential for its growth and development.

Taken together, all of these arguments provide us with three broad key sets of themes and features determining the ways in which knowledge and knowledge flows help to foster entrepreneurial and innovation performance of the region, namely the *scale*-related, the *structure*-related and the *connectivity*-related features of the region. These three themes also chime with the major features of the smart specialisation approach to regional policymaking, in that the smart specialisation approach also contends that good regional entrepreneurship and innovation policies must be based on a constructive and realistic engagement with the opportunities offered and challenges posed by each of these features of the region in question, so that the role which knowledge and knowledge flows may play in fostering regional growth is maximised.

Smart specialisation, in the sense in which it has been incorporated into EU Cohesion Policy, is in essence about the smart prioritisation of policy. Funding and policy resources are severely constrained in many countries, so the development emphasis on ensuring the best use of funds is paramount. Yet, even in situations where and when funding stream are not so severely constrained, the need to ensure the maximum effectiveness of policies and their funding streams remains critical, in order to maintain the credibility and workability of the policy. In many funding arenas, the prioritisation of policy funds has been based to a greater or lesser extent on allocation principles with an underlying political logic, and this logic often undermines the policy effectiveness and impact by militating against resource concentration on the most important priorities. The need to move away from this primarily political logic underpinning resource allocation to one which is more clearly based on the economic potential of a region has become critical, and particularly in the aftermath of the 2008 global financial crisis, and this was made explicit by the Barca (2009) critique. The challenge, however, is to develop a realistic and practical policy priortisation framework which is meaningful and workable in such a diverse and heterogeneous setting as the EU. Smart specialisation has emerged as just such a framework.

2.3 The Analytical Basis of RIS3 Policy Frameworks

The basic elements of the original non-spatial smart specialisation concept, namely a knowledge ecology framework in which entrepreneurial search processes operate across relevant economic domains characterised by both scale and connectedness, are already well-known and discussed in detail elsewhere (Foray *et al.* 2009; David *et al.* 2009; Foray 2015; McCann 2015). However, when translated into an explicitly geographical and regional setting these elements focus our attention on the importance of roles played by economic scale, embeddedness and connectivity in facilitating and enhancing the types of knowledge flows (McCann and Ortega-Argilés 2015; Foray *et al.* 2015) which are crucial for fostering entrepreneurial search processes. Yet, the explicit economic geography translation of the original non-spatial smart specialisation concept (McCann and Ortega-Argilés 2015) also brings to light the importance of providing for different pathways toward regional branching and diversification across technologies, activities, sectors and skills, rather than a narrowing towards a greater sectoral or technological specialisations. In policy terms smart specialisation is therefore about smart prioritisation, in which policy decisions are based on a set of key principles, but an important change of perspective provided by the smart specialisation logic is to think in terms of activities, tasks, roles, operations and initiatives, rather than just on sectors. This approach emerges naturally from the economics of knowledge (Foray 2006) and economics of technology (Foray 2009) literatures which traverse sectors, and instead focus on the nature, the generation, the sources and the pathways of knowledge through the economic system. In these literatures, classifications systems based on sectors (Pavitt 1984) are just one lens though which these phenomena are understood. As well as sectoral systems of classification, in the economics of knowledge literature there are technological systems of classification, and either of these classification systems can also be mapped onto regional or national schema. The focus on activities and initiatives within a knowledge ecology framework also moves the analytical focus point away from industry types and even firm types and towards the types of activities, actions and initiatives being undertaken by different firms and also the potential linkages between these different types of activities. This represents major twist on some of the standard place-based ways of thinking, which have not been without their critics (Olfert *et al.* 2014; Yu and Jackson 2011). Here, the basis of the smart specialisation logic demands that policy makers and analysts step away from sectoral classifications typically adopted by economic researchers and consider much more finely-grained frames of reference based on activities, actions and initiatives which also traverse sectoral classifications. As such, the smart specialisation approach requires much more of a programme-based and project-based way of thinking than simply an industry classification-based way of thinking. In order to think along these different lines of thinking, which may reflect either broader or more specific lines of enquiry than typical sectoral approaches imply depending on the issue in question, also requires us to build on insights from a range of different fields including those derived from engineering, environmental sciences, human resource models, and institutional arguments, as well as from more orthodox economics and economic geography types of arguments.

The related variety approach (Frenken *et al.* 2007; Boschma and Frenken 2011; Neffke *et al.* 2011a, b) is seen to be one of the most critical elements of smart specialisation, and in particular, the need to enable regions to diversity around their existing core specialisations, skills and technologies, is paramount in the RIS3 agenda. Regions generally grow and develop on the basis of their existing assets and competences, as these largely determine not only what is currently possible, but what is also most possible in terms of the potential steps forward that regions may take by adding to or complementing their existing skills, sectors or technologies. The related variety argument, which is also central to the RIS3 approach, provides an alternative and more nuanced way of think about the relationships between specialisation and diversification of earlier debates, which as we have already seen, were largely inconclusive. In contrast, the evidence on the related variety argument is growing, and as discussed below this type of growth is very relevant for public policy actions. As we see in other chapters in this book, there is also evidence of regional economic growth via unrelated variety, although unrelated variety is by definition, largely beyond the realms of public policy analysis and actions. Instead, innovations via unrelated variety and the management of the risks associated with such innovations are the prerogative of venture capitalists, private equity investors and other private sector institutional fund managers whose job it is to take on and manage such portfolio risks, whereas related variety is explicitly within the realms of public policy. The reason is that attempting to foster local growth by encouraging innovations building on related variety involves working with what is already evident in the region, in the sense of the local actors and institutions as well as the existing skills-sets, rather than on speculating with what is not currently there. Working with what is already present and aiming to enhance via related diversification what is already currently available in the region provides both realistic and reasonable policy objectives. In the past, too many regional policy actions attempted to build high technology clusters by importing firms in these sectors via the provision of location subsidies, but often these policy actions took place in situations where the region had little or no pre-existing capabilities in the particular sector or the technology. All too often therefore the firms therefore failed to develop any real embeddedness in the region and once the subsidies had ceased the firms relocated elsewhere (Glaeser and Gottlieb, 2008). These types of policy actions represented discredited approaches to fostering growth via the promotion of unrelated variety, and such approaches have come in for much criticism from many quarters as they embeddedness or synergies between the immigrant firms and the host technologies, local supply chains and regional labour force capabilities. In contrast, policy built around related variety-type principles forces policy makers to develop a strong awareness of their local skills-sets, the technological competences of local firms, and the institutional capabilities of the local governance actors, and to design policy actions and interventions explicitly with these factors in mind. Such locally-tailored approaches also raise the changes that local actors will actively engage with the policy process as private sector actors, in particular, are much more likely to see the policies as being meaningful and credible and cognisant of their own challenges and possibilities. All of these features relate directly to the embeddedness, domain and relevant scale dimensions of the explicitly geographical translation of the smart specialisation concept (McCann and Ortega-Argilés 2015).

This related variety principle, whereby a region's growth potential is not entirely constrained or pre-determined, but is still heavily shaped by its current trajectory, is also reflected in the insights derived from network analyses of regions. Network models imply that that a region's positioning in an interregional and international network system of flows (of knowledge, people, goods and services) also critically determines the particular pattern of knowledge and resource linkages on which the region may draw to aid its development. Network models demonstrate that scale effects do operate, but the exact positioning of a region within a network or within networks is also essential for determining the region's growth potential. A region's positioning in global networks is a result of numerous factors over a long period of time, but the knowledge capabilities of the local firms and institutions is the paramount arbiter of such positioning. Regional policy frameworks or schema which are in part constructed with these networks ideas in mind require both the policy makers and also the potential beneficiaries or recipients of the policy to consider their current positioning and also how such positioning may wish to be improved, enhanced or altered by the policy. These network dimensions of RIS3 link directly to the connectivity aspect of smart specialisation (McCann and Ortega-Argilés 2015).

As well as the related variety and network frameworks, smart specialisation also benefits from and builds on insights from the competitiveness approaches (Thissen *et al.* 2013). Competiveness approaches have been developed by Thissen *et al.* (2013) which links performance of sectors to their trade patterns and also the geography of their input and output markets. Traditional approaches to benchmarking competitiveness typically compare sectors with each other (Porter 1980, 1985), or compare the performance of specific sectors across different regions (Porter 1990) in the context of clustering patterns (McCann and Ortega-Argilés 2016a). However, these approaches often fail to incorporate the broader positioning of local firms and sectors in wider interregional, international and global trade and value-chain systems, which will heavily impinge on their performance possibilities As such, an alternative to this primarily sectoral approach to competiveness is to consider the performance of firms and sectors not only in their own regions, but also in the geographical and product-type spaces in which the firms compete nationally and internationally (Thissen *et al.* 2013). It has long been understood that analytically the concepts of geographical space and product space developed in parallel and as such display large overlaps (McCann 2013). Therefore, building on these analytical parallels and exploiting these conceptual overlaps allows us to develop another and subtler understanding of competitiveness in which competition in both geographical and product space can be modelled simultaneously (Thissen *et al.* 2013). This line of research demonstrates that neither local sectoral comparisons, nor even cross-regional comparisons of similar sectors, are always the most insightful or useful ways of understanding the competiveness performance of local firms and industries. Rather, the performance of a region's firms and industries in the specific markets in which they source their inputs and also in which they sell their outputs, is far more instructive than specifically local observations. As such, this modified and novel competitiveness approach, along with the network approach, both emphasise that the external linkages of the region and the region's positioning within wider networks and global value-chains have critical implications for the performance of a region's local actors. Again, these approaches force policy makers to consider local performance in the context of wider interregional and international settings, and link directly to the connectivity aspects of smart specialisation and RIS3 (Sörvik *et al.* 2016).

Taken together, these various features of smart specialisation and RIS3 all link directly to the main policy themes of the need to foster greater embeddedness, greater diversification and upgrading around the region's core capabilities, and also the need to develop enhanced network linkages and positioning. Moreover, the data and analytical toolkits at our disposal aimed at helping policy makers to better design and position their policy actions and interventions should slowly over time, step by step, allow for more nuanced policy making.

2.4 Institutional and Governance Challenges in RIS3

Good local and regional policy, however, is not simply a matter of accessing better data and models, although these are very welcome additions to the policy maker's toolkit. The reason is that policy making is also inherently a process activity, involving engagements with multiple and diverse stakeholders, each with different interests and incentives, and with differing perceptions regarding the potential role that policies can play in their activities and they in turn, can play in the policy's activities. Indeed, a major challenge associated with the introduction of a new bottom-up and more modern regional policy (McCann and Ortega-Argilés 2013c) schema such as RIS3 is that it is often introduced in the context of regions which have in many cases been operating primarily traditional approaches to regional policy in which subsidies are typically allocated to regions primarily on a top-down and sectoral logic (OECD 2009, 2011). Moving to a more nuanced and bottom-up activity-based, technology-based, or project-based logic, as is consistent with more modern approaches regional development approaches, is a very difficult task, which at least in the short run, often involves grafting new ideas and systems onto existing governance systems and structures, rather than a wholesale and immediate transformation of the local institutional system (McCann and Ortega-Argilés 2014a, b). Such an incremental approach can, on the one hand, be seen as posing a major a major weakness and limitation of the RIS3 approach, inhibiting any genuine transformation of the policy system. Alternatively, given political economy realities, incrementalist and gradualist change may in some cases result in a more long-term and fundamental reorientation of policy systems than rather rapid attempts at transforming governance systems. Ironically, this may be an advantage in some situations where the relations between different stakeholders are required to change as a result of the new policy framework. Resistance to change may increase where many new demands are placed on stakeholders, so while in some cases rapid and wholesale institutional changes can help to mobilise actions by a range of stakeholders who perceive that the existing governance order is evolving, in other cases the uncertainty generated by such changes may lead firms to be conservative and reticent to engage with policy set-up, at least for a period. These things cannot be known in advance, and policy makers have to adapt to the realities as they emerge in a pragmatic manner in order to ensure that policies can be workable.

The need for a pragmatic approach is essential because the combining, merging and the building upon of knowledge emerging from different fields which is implied by the RIS3 embodiment of the smart specialisation approach also explicitly implies the coordination and cooperation between different types of stakeholders. In order to assist with this the RIS3 agenda also both traverses and incorporates various other narratives and research programmes (Lakatos 1970) into its umbrella schema, including the 'Triple Helix' research programme (Leydesdorff and Etzkowitz 1996), various aspects of the competitiveness or clusters approaches (Ketels 2013), as well as different approaches adopting network types of analyses (Gulati 2007). Indeed, the hybrid nature of the RIS3 schema is explicit in the official documentation emerging from the European Commission (Foray *et al.* 2012), which is largely silent on which particular strategy or school of thought to adopt, but which also encourages local and regional policy makers to decide which policy approaches are the most appropriate for their particular policy challenges they face (McCann 2015). Indeed, this rather more eclectic approach to tailored policy making also implies that data and knowledge will need to be acquired from different sources depending both on the development context and also the challenges being addressed. In many cases, this will also require rather new ways of thinking about the production and generation of data. In principle, all RIS3 programmes and projects should be data-generating exercises in their own right (McCann 2015), but the types of data to be generated, collected and analysed depends critically on exactly what the project was intended to achieve. In many cases bespoke data produced by the policy interventions would be the most appropriate for monitoring and analysing the effects of the RIS3 policy interventions, rather than off-the-shelf secondary data, which typically is far too removed from the particular policy context or the specific policy intentions to be of much use.

The exact data chosen to be generated, collected and analysed depend critically on the intended outcomes and results of the policy project, action or intervention, and the definition of these data depends on the specific objective-based challenges which the project is intended to respond to, and the likely timeframe over which these responses are expected to occur. The life cycle of the policy project also implies that the policy effects, as revealed in the data generated, are also likely to differ over time, so different staging markers or mileposts with possibly different data, are required in order to best capture the expected evolution of the policy effects. Some of these data will be quantitative and some will be qualitative in nature, and the balance between these two may also differ during the lifetime of the project. A mixture of both sorts of data is likely to be most successful in most cases, as these different types of data can be used for different purposes and to throw light on different issues, and different types of data will be required for different types of interventions (Barca and McCann 2011a, b, c). Where RIS3 projects and actions interface or traverse different sectors, different themes, different technologies, different scientific disciplines or even different geographical boundaries, then newer or move novel forms of data will need to be employed. In particular, wherever possible, programme or project data will need to be able to capture aspects of related variety, market and competitive spaces, network arrangements, and institutional and governance set-ups. These ideas are not specific or particular to RIS3, but represent a broadly-based consensus from many parts of the world in a variety of different policy arenas (McCann and Ortega-Argilés 2016b). Yet, exactly how this is to be achieved depends on the individual project, the project design and the intended outcomes or results of the project (McCann and Ortega-Argilés 2016b). But good policy programming implies that these elements should as far as possible be incorporated in the project design from the outset, although whether this takes place in a rapidly-evolving governance setting or an incrementalist and gradualist institutional setting remains to be seen. In reality, however, the extent to which RIS3 ideas are genuinely being incorporated into EU Cohesion Policy making can only be determined by observation of activities on the ground.

2.5 Evidence on the Early Progress of RIS3

Although it is relatively recent since the new EU Cohesion Policy logic was introduced in the programming period 2014–2020, it is possible to get a sense of how the new RIS3 policy approach is being adopted and embodied within the overall Cohesion Policy logic and architecture from various surveys and data-sources. McCann and Ortega-Argilés (2016c) examine the evidence emerging from the thematic programming choices made by different regions and member states in their ERDF Operational Programmes. What is apparent is that there is a great deal of diversity in thematic priorities chosen by managing authorities, and this diversity does not display any simple north–south or east–west logic to it, but rather reflects a great deal of heterogeneity both across the EU and also within particular parts of Europe. This is a positive sign, and suggests that regions are not simply copying each other in their decisions, but rather making specific decisions for their own contexts. In addition, evidence from three surveys by Fraunhofer ISI also suggest that the implementation of RIS3 has been broadly well-received (McCann and Ortega-Argilés 2016c) although there are differences across Europe. Many northern European regions have to a large extent grafted RIS3 onto their existing policy systems and structures, while more fundamental shifts have been evident in various southern European regions. The differences here may in part reflect prior differences in the quality of institutions (Charron *et al.* 2013, 2014) but may also reflect a greater sense of urgency and need for good policy making in the wake of the 2008 economic crisis. On the other hand, regions in central and eastern Europe appear to face the most significant challenges in designing and implementing RIS3 strategies, and this may relate to their less diverse (knowledge) asset base and greater quality shortfalls in their governance systems. Whatever, the reason for the implementation differences across Europe, the RIS3 agenda appears to have been taken up seriously in many parts of Europe, in a manner which is not entirely different from what was intended or anticipated, although this done not imply that in the long-run the policy will be seen as a success. There are no guarantees of success, but the adoption and implementation of the RIS3 approach itself is likely to foster constructive governance institutional changes, and this is important as these are generally seen to constitute the most difficult challenges facing economically weaker regions (Garcilazo and Rodríguez-Pose 2015).

2.6 Conclusions

This chapter has examined the intellectual basis for the RIS3 approach and argued that it is grounded on a longstanding and well-rehearsed systems tradition of thinking about innovation and entrepreneurship. Such a tradition perceives of local factors as playing a critical part in the regional development story, and in particular the interactions between local actors and institutions, and in turn the interactions between local and external actors and institutions. At the same time, the institutional and governance challenges involved in adopting and implementing a smart specialisation-type way of thinking are very real, although the early evidence on the take-up of these approaches does provide some grounds for optimism. However, it will be several years before we can really determine the extent to which such RIS3 approaches have been successful in enhancing the innovation-related capabilities of regions which most need these capability improvements.

References

Barca, F., 2009, *An Agenda for A Reformed Cohesion Policy: A place-based approach to meeting European Union challenges and expectations*, Independent Report Prepared at the Request of the European Commissioner for Regional Policy, Danuta Hübner, European Commission, Brussels.

Barca, F., and McCann, P., 2011a, 'Outcome Indicators and Targets – Towards a new system of monitoring and evaluation in EU cohesion policy', 2011, *DGRegio Website*, July. Available at: http://ec.europa.eu/regional_policy/information/evaluations/guidance_en.cfm#1, http://ec.europa.eu/regional_policy/sources/docgener/evaluation/doc/performance/outcome_indicators_en.pdf.

Barca, F., and McCann, F., 2011b, 'Complementary Note 1: Outcome indicators for the thematic priorities addressing the Europe 2020 objective "Improving the conditions for innovation, research and development. Examples"', *DGRegio Website*. Available at: http://ec.europa.eu/regional_policy/sources/docgener/evaluation/doc/performance/improve_inno_resear_en.pdf.

Barca, F., and McCann, P., 2011c, 'Complementary Note 2: Outcome indicators for the thematic priorities addressing the Europe 2020 objective "Meeting Climate Change and

Energy Objectives"', *DGRegio Website*. Available at: http://ec.europa.eu/regional_policy/ sources/docgener/evaluation/doc/performance/climate_obj_en.pdf.

Beaudry, C., and Schiffauerova, A., 2009, 'Who's Right, Marshall or Jacobs? The Localization versus Urbanization Debate', *Research Policy*, 38, 318–337.

Boschma, R., and Frenken, K., 2011, 'Technological Relatedness and Regional Branching', in Bathelt, H., Feldman, M. P., and Kogler, D. F., (eds.), *Dynamic Geographies of Knowledge Creation and Innovation*, Taylor and Francis, Routledge, London, Forthcoming.

Capello R. and Lenzi C., 2013, (eds.) *Territorial Patterns of Innovation. An inquiry on the knowledge economy in European regions*, Routledge, London.

Charron, N., Lapuente, V., and Rothstein, B., 2013, *Quality of Government and Corruption from a European Perspective: A comparative study of good governance in EU regions*, Edward Elgar, Cheltenham.

Charron, N., Dijkstra, L., and Lapuente, V., 2014, 'Mapping the Regional Divide in Europe: A measure for assessing quality of government in 206 European regions', *Social Indicators Research*, 122, 315–346.

David, P., Foray, D., and Hall, B., 2009, *Measuring Smart Specialisation: The Concept and the need for indicators,* Knowledge for Growth Expert Group, See: http://cemi. epfl.ch/files/content/sites/cemi/files/users/178044/public/Measuring%20smart%20 specialisation.doc.

De Groot, H.L.F., Poot, J., and Smit, M., 2009, 'Agglomeration Externalities, Innovation and Regional Growth: Theoretical perspectives and meta-analysis', in Capello, R., and Nijkamp, P., *Handbook of Regional Growth and Development Theories*, Edward Elgar, Cheltenham.

De Melo, P., Graham, D., and Noland, R., 2009, 'A Meta-Analysis of Estimates of Urban Agglomeration Economies', *Regional Science and Urban Economics*, 39 (3), 332–342.

Desmet, K., and Fafchamps, M., 2005, 'Changes in the Spatial Concentration of Employment across US countries: A sectoral analysis 1972–2000', *Journal of Economic Geography*, 5 (3), 261–284.

Duranton, G., and Puga, D., 2001, 'Nursery Cities: Urban diversity, process innovation, and the life cycle of products', *American Economic Review*, 91 (5), 1454–1477.

Duranton, G., and Puga, D., 2004, 'Micro-Foundations of Urban Agglomeration Economies', in Henderson, J.V., and Thisse, J.-F., (eds.), *Handbook of Regional and Urban Economics, Vol IV: Economic Geography*, Elsevier, Amsterdam.

Frenken, K., Van Oort, F.G., and Verburg, T., 2007, 'Related Variety, Unrelated Variety and Regional Economic Growth', *Regional Studies*, 41 (5), 685–697.

Foray, D., 2006, *The Economics of Knowledge*, MIT Press, Cambridge MA.

Foray, D., 2009, (ed.), *The New Economics of Technology Policy*, Edward Elgar, Cheltenham.

Foray, D., 2015, *Smart Specialization: Opportunities and challenges regional innovation policy*, Routledge, London.

Foray, D., David, P., and Hall, B., 2009, 'Smart Specialisation – The Concept' Knowledge Economists Policy Brief No. 9, June 2009.

Foray, D., Goddard, J., Morgan, K., Goenaga Beldarrain, X., Landabaso, M., Neuwelaars, C., and Ortega-Argilés, R., 2012, *Guide to Research and Innovation Strategies for Smart Specialisation (RIS 3)*, S3 Smart Specialisation Platform, IPTS Institute for Prospective Technological Studies, Joint Research Centre of the European Commission, Seville. See: http://s3platform.jrc.ec.europa.eu/-/guide-on-research-and-innovation-strategies-for-smart-specialisation-ris3-guide-?inheritRedirect=true&redirect=%2Fcommission-guides.

Foray, D., McCann, P., and Ortega-Argilés, R., 2015, 'Smart Specialization and European Regional Development Policy', in Audretsch, D.B., Link, A., and Walshok, M., (eds.), *Oxford Handbook of Local Competitiveness*, Oxford University Press, Oxford.

Garcilazo, E., and Rodriguez-Pose, A., 2015, 'Quality of Government and the Returns of Investment: Examining the Impact of Cohesion Expenditure in European Regions', *Regional Studies*, 49 (8), 1274–1290.

Glaeser, E.L., and Gottlieb, J.D., 2008, 'The Economics of Place-Making Policies', *Brookings papers on Economic Activity*, 1, 155–253.

Glaeser, E.L., Kallal, H.D., Scheinkman, J.A., and Shleifer, A., 1992, 'Growth in Cities', *Journal of Political Economy*, 100, 1126–1152.

Gulati, R., 2007, *Managing Network Resources: Alliances, affiliations, and other relational assets*, Oxford University Press, Oxford.

Iammarino S., and McCann, P., 2013, *Multinationals and Economic Geography: Location, technology and innovation*, Edward Elgar, Cheltenham.

Ketels, C., 2013, 'Recent Research on Competitiveness and Clusters: What are the implications for regional policy?', *Cambridge Journal of Regions, Economy and Society*, 6 (2), 269–284.

Lakatos, I., 1970, 'Falsification and the Methodology of Scientific Research Programmes', in Lakatos, I., and Musgrave, A., (eds.), *Criticism and the Growth of Knowledge*, Cambridge University Press, Cambridge.

Leydesdorff, L., and Etzkowitz, H., 1996, 'Emergence of a Triple Helix of university-industry-government relations', *Science and Public Policy*, 23 (5), 279–286.

McCann, P., 2013, *Modern Urban and Regional Economics*, 2013, Oxford University Press, Oxford.

McCann, P., 2015, *The Regional and Urban Policy of the European Union: Cohesion, results-orientation and smart specialisation*, Edward Elgar, Cheltenham.

McCann, P., and Ortega-Argilés, R., 2013a, 'Redesigning and Reforming European Regional Policy: The reasons, the logic and the outcomes', *International Regional Science Review*, 36 (3), 424–445.

McCann, P., and Ortega-Argilés, R., 2013b, 'Transforming European Regional Policy: A results-driven agenda and smart specialisation', *Oxford Review of Economic Policy*, 29 (2), 405–431.

McCann, P., and Ortega-Argilés, R., 2013c, 'Modern Regional Innovation Policy', *Cambridge Journal of Regions, Economy and Society*, 6 (2), 187–216.

McCann, P., and Ortega-Argilés, R., 2014a, 'Smart Specialisation in European Regions: Issues of strategy, institutions and implementation', *European Journal of Innovation Management*, 17 (4), 409–427.

McCann, P., and Ortega-Argilés, R., 2014b, 'The Role of the Smart Specialisation Agenda in a Reformed EU Cohesion Policy', *Italian Journal of Regional Science*, 13 (1), 15–32.

McCann, P., and Ortega-Argilés, R., 2015, 'Smart Specialization, Regional Growth and Applications to EU Cohesion Policy', *Regional Studies*, 49 (8), 1291–1302.

McCann, P., and Ortega-Argilés, R., 2016a, 'Regional Competitiveness, Policy Transfer and Smart Specialization', 2016, in Huggins, R., and Thompson, P., (eds.), *Handbook of Regions and Competitiveness: Contemporary theories and perspectives on economic development*, Edward Elgar, Cheltenham.

McCann, P., and Ortega-Argilés, R., 2016b, 'Smart Specialisation, Entrepreneurship and SMEs: Issues and challenges for a results-oriented EU regional policy', *Small Business Economics*, 46 (4), 537–552.

McCann, P., and Ortega-Argilés, R., 2016c, 'The Early Experience of Smart Specialisation Implementation in EU Cohesion Policy', *European Planning Studies*, Forthcoming, doi:10.1080/09654313.2016.1166177.

Neffke, F., Henning, M., and Boschma, R., 2011a, 'The Impact of Aging and Technological Relatedness on Agglomeration Externalities: A survival analysis', *Journal of Economic Geography*, 12 (2), 485–517.

Neffke, F., Henning, M., and Boschma, R., 2011b, 'How do Regions Diversify Over Time?', *Economic Geography*, 87 (3), 237–265.

OECD, 2009, *Regions Matter: Economic Recovery, Innovation and Sustainable Growth*, Organisation for Economic Growth and Development, Paris.

OECD, 2011, *OECD Regional Outlook 2011*, Organisation for Economic Development and Cooperation, Paris.

OECD, 2013, *Innovation Driven Growth in Regions: The role of smart specialisation*, Organisation for Economic Cooperation and Development, Paris. See: http://www. oecd.org/innovation/inno/smart-specialisation.pdf.

Olfert, M. R., Partridge, M.D., Berdegué, J., Escobal, J., Jara, B., and Modrego, F., 2014, 'Places for Place-Based Policy', *Development Policy Review*, 32 (1), 5–32.

Partridge, M.D., Rickman, D.S. and Olfert, M.R., 2008. 'Employment Growth in the American Urban Hierarchy: Long Live Distance'. *The BE Journal of Macroeconomics: contributions to macroeconomics*, 8 (1), 1–38.

Pavitt, K., 1984. 'Sectoral Patterns of Technical Change: Towards a taxonomy and a theory', *Research Policy*, 13, 343–373.

Porter, M.E., 1980, *Competitive Strategy*, Free Press, New York.

Porter, M.E., 1985, *Competitive Advantage: Creating and sustaining superior performance*, Free Press, New York.

Porter, M.E., 1990, *The Competitive Advantage of Nations*, Free Press, New York.

Regional Entrepreneurship Development Index (REDI). See: http://bookshop.europa.eu/ en/redi-the-regional-entrepreneurship-and-development-index-pbKN0214462/?Catalog CategoryID=cKYKABsttvUAAAEjrpAY4e5L

Simonen, J., and McCann, P., 2008, 'Firm Innovation: The influence of R&D cooperation and the geography of human capital inputs', *Journal of Urban Economics*, 64 (1), 146–154.

Simonen, J., and McCann, P., 2010, 'Knowledge Transfers and Innovation: The role of labour markets and R&D cooperation between agents and institutions', *Papers in Regional Science*, 89 (2), 295–309.

Sörvik, J., Midtkandal, I., Marzocchi, C., and Uyarra, E., 2016, 'How Outward Looking is Smart Specialisation: Results from a survey on inter-regional collaboration in smart specialisation strategies (RIS3)', *S3 Policy Brief Series, No. 16/2016*, JRC Technical Reports, Smart Specialisation Platform, Joint Research Centre IPTS, Seville, Spain.

Thissen, M., van Oort, F.G., Diodato, D., and Ruijs, A., 2013, *Regional Competitiveness and Smart Specialization in Europe: Place-based development in international economic networks*, Edward Elgar, Cheltenham.

Varga, A., 2009, (ed.), *Universities, Knowledge Transfer and Regional Development: Geography, Entrepreneurship and Policy*, Edward Elgar, Cheltenham.

Yu, J., and Jackson, R., 2011, 'Regional Innovation Clusters: A critical review', *Growth and Change*, 42 (2), 111–124.

3 Regional Diversification and Smart Specialization Policy

Ron Boschma

3.1 Introduction

Serious concerns have been raised about the feasibility of smart specialization policy, not the least by the leading proponents of the smart specialization policy concept (Foray 2014). It would run ahead of theory, it was not entirely clear what specialization meant in the context of smart specialization, it lacked geographical wisdom (Hassink 2015), it would run the risk going against the objectives of regional cohesion policy (McCann and Ortega-Argilés 2015), and some of its claims were not backed by systematic empirical evidence. In other words, it was felt among many scholars that smart specialization policy had been introduced far too early.

There is increasing recognition that smart specialization policy is about developing new specializations in regions, instead of strengthening existing specializations. However, this requires a basic understanding of how new specializations in regions occur, what conditions favour diversification, and to what extent regional innovation policy can be effective and make a difference. This chapter will report about some of the progress that has been made recently in the empirical literature on how regions diversify (Boschma 2016), but we will also argue there are still some notable gaps in our knowledge of how new specializations come about, and how to conduct effective smart specialization strategies.

We report about the main drivers of regional diversification that have been found in recent studies (Neffke *et al.* 2011). In Section 3.2, we discuss the relationship between regional diversification, relatedness and related variety (Xiao *et al.* 2016), which are looked upon to an increasing extent as key ingredients of a smart specialization policy (Boschma 2014). Section 3.3 devotes attention to the importance of non-regional factors for regional diversification, such as inter-regional links (Thissen *et al.* 2013), the effect of neighbouring regions (Boschma *et al.* 2016) and the role of non-regional actors (Neffke *et al.* 2015). Section 3.4 looks at the role of institutions, both at the national (Boschma and Capone 2015) and regional scale (Cortinovis *et al.* 2016). Section 3.5 briefly discusses some implications for smart specialization policy and Section 3.6 provides some brief conclusions.

3.2 Relatedness, Complexity and Regional Diversification

Smart specialization is about the development of new specializations in regions, not intended simply to strengthen existing specializations in regions (Boschma 2014; McCann and Ortega-Argilés 2015). This implies that the huge literature on regional specializations is of less relevance (Maskell and Malmberg1999) for our discussions here. Rather, it requires a better understanding of how new specializations come about, not of why specializations exist once they are in place. In other words, it requires a historical, evolutionary perspective that accounts for the dynamics of new specializations and how these emerged in highly uncertain circumstances, rather than making long lists of local features such as the supply of infrastructure or a specialized labour markets that miraculously fit the regional specialization case (Scott 1988). Instead, our analysis should focus on questions of why a certain specialization emerged there, and not elsewhere, and fully account for fundamental uncertainties that are part and parcel of any new growth path development in space.

When focusing on new specializations in a smart specialization framework, it is important to notice that building new specializations in regions is almost never about radical breakthroughs that reflect a sharp break with the past. History always matters in some way or another to a smaller or larger extent, and geography also plays a crucial part in this respect for at least three reasons.

First, new specializations are generally not about new activities that are new to the world. For most regions it might not be a good idea to work on something radical that is completely new and disruptive, and which also requires a long-time horizon to develop. The overwhelming majority of regions, if not all regions (as there is no compelling reason why Silicon Valley would be an exception) are not in such position, as their own history sets serious limits. Nevertheless, regions can still target an upgrade of their local economy, given their current local situation in which their own history also defines their opportunity space to construct new regional competitive advantages. So, it matters in which direction regions diversify: regions that diversify into new sectors that reduce the complexity of their local economy would face more competition and run the risk of getting trapped into a low return-economy that is not sustainable in the long-run. So, smart specialization is about upgrading the regional economy, not downgrading it. Hausmann and Hidalgo (2010) developed this idea further, looking at the economic complexity of countries. In their framework, the economic complexity of countries is proxied by looking at the number of export products and the average ubiquity of export products in each country (Hidalgo 2015). By comparing the economic complexity of countries with their respective GDP levels per capita, they identify whether countries have the potential to increase their GDP given their current level of economic complexity. This turns out to be a good predictor of which countries grow faster in the long run (though not in the short run), meaning over periods of ten to fifteen years (Hidalgo 2015).

Second, new specializations are not about new sectors or technologies that start from scratch and can thus be considered to be historical accidents or random events. On the contrary, there is much evidence that local assets provide opportunities for new combinations that give birth to new technologies, industries or products in regions. What comes out of these studies is that if regions do not possess the capabilities (such as knowledge, skills, institutions, etc.) required for a new technology, industry or product, it is unlikely that these will be developed fully, as local related externalities are missing. Many activities cannot be meaningfully combined: variety must be related, as this increases the scope for knowledge spillovers and learning (Nooteboom 2000; Frenken *et al.* 2007; Van Oort *et al.* 2013). Recombinations are more likely to emerge from technologies or industries that share similar knowledge bases: the more variety of related technologies or sectors in a region, the more learning opportunities, and the higher the potential for recombinations across local technologies or industries.

Therefore, one expects regions to have a higher probability to diversify into new activities that are related to existing local activities (Fornahl and Guenther 2010; Neffke *et al.* 2011). This branching process is regarded as a central feature of long-term regional development (Frenken and Boschma 2007). Hidalgo *et al.* (2007) found evidence of such branching showing that building comparative advantage in export products that are new to countries is possible then these are related to their existing export products. Hausmann and Klinger (2007) demonstrated that countries that have a wide range of related export products have more options to diversify, as their capabilities can be redeployed in a higher number of new export products. Neffke *et al.* (2011) systematically investigated the diversification of regions in industries that are new to the region. They found that an industry is more likely to enter a region when it is technologically related to local industries. Follow-up studies on industrial diversification of regions have also come to similar conclusions (e.g. Boschma *et al.* 2013; Essletzbichler 2015; He and Rigby 2015). In addition, other studies found evidence of occupational diversification to be driven by relatedness: the emergence of new occupations in regions is determined by the degree of relatedness with existing local occupations (Muneepeerakul *et al.* 2013; Brachert 2016). Similar results have been found for technological diversification: technologies that are related to local existing technologies had a higher probability to enter that region (Rigby 2015). This finding of relatedness driving technological diversification in regions has since been replicated in other studies (Kogler *et al.* 2013; Boschma *et al.* 2015; Van den Berge and Weterings 2014; Tanner 2016; Colombelli *et al.* 2014; Heimeriks and Boschma 2014; Feldman *et al.* 2015; Quatraro and Montresor 2015).

Third, new specializations are not about new sectors or technologies that start from scratch but arise by combining local capabilities across sectors or technologies. When doing so, these new recombinations may reflect combinations that have not been combined before. Indeed, it is rather common to define radical breakthroughs as making combinations between unrelated fields that become related when successfully combined (Arts and Veugelers 2015). The development of self-driving cars is a prime example: it will revolutionize and disrupt the automotive industry because it connects disparate technological fields like automotives, sensor-based safety systems, communication-based systems and high-resolution mapping that have not been combined before (Wallace and Silberg 2012). These recombinations may be referred to as radical, but they still build on (evolving) capabilities that come from various knowledge domains. Having said that, there is still little understanding of the origins of such breakthroughs (Barbosa *et al.* 2013). Arts and Veugelers (2015) claim that 'despite their importance, we know relatively little about the evolutionary origins of breakthroughs and the search process governing their discovery … What characteristics of the search process are more likely to lead to big inventive successes?' (p. 2).

Jacobs (1969) claimed that variety in regions conditions the scope for such recombinant breakthroughs: the more variety, the higher the potential to make new recombinations. Castaldi *et al.* (2015) claimed that regions with unrelated variety are more likely to produce technological breakthroughs, as they provide local opportunities to recombine previously unrelated knowledge domains. Their arguments also imply that, instead, incremental innovations are believed to benefit from related variety in a region, as these would arise out of recombinations of more closely related knowledge domains along well-defined paths. This focus on radical breakthroughs and unrelated variety can be linked to so-called mission-oriented policies, as advocated by Mazzucato (2013), that target specific pre-defined Grand Societal Challenges in which many domains need to be brought together in a fundamental explorative search process.

3.3 Relatedness, Non-Local Capabilities and Regional Diversification

In Section 3.2, local capabilities are considered to be important ingredients for regional diversification, as new industries or technologies demand access to local capabilities. This is because capabilities are locally sticky and hard to copy by other regions, and thus having local access is rather critical (Markusen 1996). Therefore, it comes as no surprise that studies show that related diversification in regions is the rule, in which new industries or technologies draw on and recombine local capabilities that are related to theirs. However, this almost complete reliance on local capabilities leaves unanswered the question to what extent regions also rely on non-local capabilities and non-local actors to trigger diversification and the development of new industrial growth paths (Trippl 2013; Trippl *et al.* 2015; Boschma 2016).

A key finding in the literature on the geography of innovation is that spillovers are geographically bounded (Feldman 1994; Audretsch and Feldman 1996). So, if spillovers occur between regions, it is most likely to occur between neighbouring regions. Little attention has been paid to the role of spillovers from neighbouring regions for industrial diversification. Nor has the role of network interactions with neighbouring regions on regional diversification been investigated systematically. Following Bahar *et al.* (2014) who found that export baskets of neighbouring countries look more similar, Boschma *et al.* (2016) found that an US state had a higher probability of developing a comparative advantage in a new industry if a neighbouring US state was specialized in that industry, and when it had local capabilities related to that industry. Neighbouring US states also turned out to display more similar export structures, as compared to the (lower) export similarity between non-neighbouring states. This export similarity across states was especially high when neighbouring US states were connected through bilateral migration patterns. Apparently, therefore, the spread of capabilities is constrained by geographical distance and it is more likely to occur between regions that are geographically nearby, and this is affects their diversification patterns. As such, spillovers occur more likely within regions, and between regions that are geographically close than between regions that are geographically far, and this tends to be reflected in the nature of the diversification process in regions. There is also increasing recognition that the role of non-regional linkages is key to avoiding 'lock-in' in regions (Asheim and Isaksen 2002; Moodysson 2008; Dahl Fitjar and Rodríguez-Pose 2011; Andersson *et al.* 2013). Thissen *et al.* (2016) have pointed to the importance of inter-regional trade linkages, as regions have demand-led growth relations with other regions. However, it is still unclear to what extent inter-regional network linkages matter for the development of new specializations in regions.

Non-local players such as relocating firms or migrants (Trippl 2013) are also increasingly considered to have a major impact on the diversification in regions, and this has implications for any smart specialization policy that currently focuses almost entirely on local stakeholders. Neffke *et al.* (2015) found that new plants from outside the region tend to induce structural change in regions, that is, they tend to weaken the regional capability base by being active in industries that are less related to existing local industries. Start-ups induce most structural change in the short run, but their survival depends on the presence of related activities in the region, and this implies that new start-ups rely on local related industries, and therefore will induce less structural change in the long-run. This stands in contrast to the effects of new subsidiaries of non-local firms, which induce the most structural change in their host region in the long run, because they can rely on inter-regional parent-subsidiary networks within the same organization, and therefore new subsidiaries are less dependent on a supportive local environment with related industries. This is in line with our understanding of the role of multinational firms that may shift specializations in their host regions (Cantwell and Iammarino 2003). However, we still need a better understanding of how investment strategies of multinational firms influence regional diversification, and to what extent they may shift the capability base of regions (Iammarino and McCann 2013). So, while related diversification is the rule, preliminary findings also suggest that structural change in regions predominantly depends on non-local firms. It seems that the inter-regional mobility of entrepreneurs and subsidiaries make regions diversify in less related activities, but more systematic evidence is needed to substantiate such a claim.

3.4 Relatedness, Institutions and Regional Diversification

Related local capabilities are a driving force behind regional diversification, and some types of non-local actors also have an effect on regional diversification, especially on less related diversification. Another factor that might influence the process of regional diversification is the role of institutions which, so far, has attracted relatively little attention in the regional diversification literature (Boschma and Capone 2015; Boschma 2016). In the smart specialization literature, institutions have recently been discussed as potential facilitators or bottlenecks. Yet, local knowledge is not regarded as being entirely sufficient for regional development, because institutions are required to turn technological capabilities into innovation and economic development (Rodríguez-Pose and Crescenzi 2008; Fagerberg *et al.* 2014). In the regional diversification literature, institutions may be referred to as social capabilities that facilitate interactions, crossovers and coordination between different actors and communities and, thus, enable recombinations between sectors that are regarded as crucial for the diversification process, as outlined in Section 3.2. Few empirical studies exist that explore the role of institutions on diversification processes in countries, and the role of national and regional institutions on diversification patterns and processes in regions (Boschma and Capone 2015). This requires insights in how institutions matter for regional development, and for regional diversification in particular, and which types of institutions (such as formal and informal institutions) are relevant for regional diversification, and at what spatial scale (such as national and regional).

While the role of institutions on growth and innovation in countries has been widely studied (Acemoglu and Robinson 2012), as well as their effects on regional development (Beugelsdijk and Van Schaik 2005; Arbia *et al.* 2010; Tabellini 2010; Crescenzi *et al.* 2013; Echebarria and Barrutia 2013; Rodríguez-Pose 2013), the effects of institutions on regional diversification have remained largely unexplored. The potential relevance of institutions affecting diversification came from a study of Boschma and Capone (2016) who found a remarkable difference between Western European and Eastern European countries. The former countries tended to diversify in more unrelated industries on average, while the latter countries turned out to be engaged in more related diversification, that is, they were more inclined to stay close to their existing industries in terms of relatedness. Though the role of institutions was not directly measured, it showed the relevance of different spatial regimes that prevail in the two main European heartlands (Cortinovis and Van Oort 2015). A more direct sign of the relevance of institutions came from Boschma and Capone (2015) who tested whether institutions matter for the type of diversification that prevail in countries. Drawing on the literature on Varieties of Capitalism (Hal and Soskice 2001), they demonstrated that institutions associated with 'liberal market economies' (i.e. institutions that regulate less tightly labour, capital and product markets) gave countries more freedom to diversify in new directions. This stood in contrast to national institutions that coordinate more tightly market relations ('coordinated market economies') which made countries to be more engaged in related diversification: their national institutions almost forced countries to stick more close to their existing specializations when diversifying.

Cortinovis *et al.* (2016) explored the effect of different sorts of regional institutions on the diversification process in European regions, following the literature on institutions (Olson 1982; Putnam *et al*. 1993; Fukuyama 1995). Recent studies show there are big differences between regions in terms of their quality of government (Charron *et al*. 2014), but Cortinovis *et al*. (2016) found no direct effect of such formal institutions on the probability of a region to diversify into new industries. However, there was an indirect effect in that formal institutions increased the effect of relatedness on regional diversification. This latter finding suggests that relatedness becomes a stronger driving force in regions with high quality of government. Informal institutions such as norms and cultural values, are often associated with trust and social capital, and sometimes a distinction is made between bonding and bridging social capital (Putnam 2001). Cortinovis *et al*. (2016) showed that the predominant type of social capital in a region is quite critical, and that bridging social capital had a positive effect on regional diversification but bonding social capital a negative effect on regional diversification. Bridging social capital had an even stronger positive effect in regions with a low quality of government, while the negative effect of bonding social capital disappeared in regions with a high quality of government. These findings suggest that institutions relevant for regional diversification are predominantly informal rather than formal, and are related to bridging rather than bonding capital.

The institutional literature discussed here has focused almost entirely on the structure of institutions at the national and regional level as enabling or constraining factors for regional diversification. This has led to new important insights, as outlined above, but it also takes the role of institutions as given, as if institutions do not change, and ignores the role of agents. Yet, the evolutionary literature has pointed to the need for institutional change to enable the emergence and growth of new industries (Nelson 1994). This makes very relevant the question as to how local agents engage in collective action in order to mobilize knowledge, resources and public opinion so as to create new, or adapt existing, institutions to enable new industry formation (Battilana *et al*. 2009; Strambach 2010; Sotarauta and Pulkkinen 2011). New industries and technologies are often contested (Aldrich and Fiol 1994), that is, there is resistance from all kinds of players and groups that need to be accommodated, and some regions might have better capabilities to do so. There is still little understanding of which institutional actors make a difference, what types of institutional change can be identified and work best under what conditions, and which regions are better capable of making the required institutional transformation. Therefore, a better understanding of the complex interplay between institutional agents and their surrounding institutional and governance structures is considered as being crucial for the design and implementation of smart specialization policy.

3.5　Regional Diversification and Smart Specialization Policy

As outlined above, despite some considerable progress, the empirical literature on regional diversification is still full of gaps. Moreover, no systematic attempt has yet been made to assess the effect of smart specialization policy (intentional or not) on regional diversification. This rather bleak current state-of-affairs is a clear limitation that should make us cautious about jumping into strong policy implications too quickly. It is just too premature to come up with strong policy suggestions. All what can be done now is to discuss some policy suggestions that are in line with some of the facts that have so far come out of the empirical literature on regional diversification.

First, it has become clear that in general new regional specializations do not come out of the blue, except in a few rare cases. Building new specializations in regions is generally about making crossovers and recombinations between various activities (Boschma and Gianelle 2013). Accordingly, smart specialization policy should incorporate a network approach in which different activities are brought together with the aim of developing new specializations in regions.

Second, a key observation from studies is that regional diversification is driven mostly, but not exclusively, by local capabilities that are combined and thereby result in new specializations in regions. This implies that the local structure should be taken as point of departure (Valdaliso *et al.* 2014), and regarded as providing a potential pool of opportunities to make new recombinations, so as to avoid copying examples such as Silicon Valley in places where no such regional potential exists. 'One-size-fits-all' policy should also be avoided at all costs, if only because it would save a lot of waste in public spending (see Tödtling and Trippl 2005 for an excellent critique on such regional policy).

Third, studies show that related diversification is predominant in regions, although unrelated diversification also occurs now and then (Zhu *et al.* 2015; Boschma 2016). The big question is how to incorporate such a finding in smart specialization policy? This actually goes back to the critical question in the smart specialization policy agenda, regarding which activities should be prioritized and targeted in smart specialization policy, and if so, which local activities? Foray *et al.* (2011) claimed that smart specialization is about making a selection of fields or areas concerning the future specialization in regions, and that these should be identified through the entrepreneurial discovery process, but that these should also be embedded in the existing capabilities of regions. Note that this bottom-up policy is different from a 'picking-the-winner-policy' which would simply impose new specializations on regions from a top-down perspective.

It is quite likely that in practice, the entrepreneurial discovery process will take advantage of a wide range of related activities in which the region is already specialized (Boschma 2014). As outlined before, making combinations is not a random process in which every activity can just be combined with any other activity, but one which is often guided and constrained by the degree of related-ness between local activities. Though still risky, it is more likely to be successful because new entrepreneurial initiatives can build on and exploit related externali-ties in the region. However, it would be too restrictive for smart specialization policy to include only local activities that have been predefined as related on the basis of techniques discussed earlier, as the entrepreneurial discovery process should be demand-driven, not supply-driven, and also give room to unexpected connections between formerly unrelated local activities. It is important to note that this latter type of diversification is more risky and uncertain, which policy makers might want to avoid. Such a policy approach is more radical in nature but still demand-led, and it builds on local assets and exploits connections between local activities that have not been connected and exploited before. And in the end, smart specialization policy will always be about experimentation, and which itself involves both trial-and-error and learning-by-failure, a policy environment in which things might go wrong because the future is unknown and for which no blueprints are readily available. Nevertheless, the risks of policy failure are higher in case of unrelated as compared to related diversification.

Fourth, evidence is accumulating that non-local interactions and non-local agents are also crucial for developing new specialization in regions. Thissen *et al.* (2016) argue that smart specialization policy in regions should account for inter-regional linkages, as these may have a large impact on the competitiveness of regions, as well as local characteristics. While EU smart specialization policy primarily focuses on the latter, they argue that policy is rather silent on the impact of demand-led growth and learning relationships between regions. Due to the strong emphasis on the entrepreneurial discovery process, local actors are also considered to be the crucial players in a smart specialization agenda that determines which potentials to target, and in which directions the regions might go. However, more than once, it has been argued that there is a potential danger of involving local actors in the design and implementation of smart specialization policy, as this could lead to local rent-seeking behaviour, corruption and lock-in (Rodrik 2004; Boschma 2014). Local players do have certain interests, and they can be quite dominant players, with tight links to other local public agents, especially in more peripheral regions (Hassink 2015). There is increasing awareness that non-local actors should be made part of smart specialization policy in regions, but it remains a challenge to implement that in practice.

Fifth, smart specialization policy requires the involvement of new players, possibly together with the involvement of vested players, but only if vested players are committed to contribute to the development of new specializations in the region. This is a tricky and sensitive issue, as smart specialization policy always runs the risk of including local stakeholders that will conduct rent-seeking behaviour and will be engaged in blocking strategies. This risk is higher when the targeted new developments pose a serious threat to dominant players in the regions. In the transition literature, there is a lot of attention on new 'clean' technologies that challenge the overarching high-carbon regime, but few studies concentrate on the spatial dimension of such tensions and conflicts (Truffer and Coenen 2012). Little research exists that has systematically assessed whether new industries or technologies fail to emerge in regions where they contest the locally-dominant players.

Sixth, evidence is accumulating that it makes sense for regions to diversify into more complex industries or technologies, given their current complexity levels. When the objective is to upgrade the local economy (instead of downgrading the local economy through diversification in less complex activities), it could be useful to expose local policy makers to information on all activities that might be feasible for development but are not yet present in their region. This information should contain the complexity level of all these activities, and to what extent related activities are already present in the region that might support the development of such new specializations in a region. So, one could focus on new activities that are related to other local activities (to reduce the risk of failure as much as possible) but also add complexity to the local economy at the same time (but not too much so as to avoid jumping from bananas to computers). Recently, progress has been made in measuring the relatedness and complexity of activities, but it is also fair to say that it remains a challenge to develop more sophisticated measures of complexity of industries or technologies. Moreover, as yet there is little evidence showing that adding more complexity in the way it is measured now matters for regional economic development in the long run. In that respect, we have to be cautious about drawing strong policy lessons.

Seventh, we are beginning to understand better how institutions at various spatial scales have a direct impact on the intensity and nature of regional diversification. Having said that, more evidence is still needed to substantiate this claim. There is also increasing awareness that regions differ in their capacity to intervene in the entrepreneurial discovery process, as formal institutions like governance structures (such as the degree of autonomy, or the quality of government) and informal institutions like social capital differ between regions (Fritsch and Stephan 2005; Charron *et al*. 2010; McCann and Ortega-Argilés 2014). As Cortinovis *et al*. (2016) showed, the positive impact of social capital on regional diversification is stronger where formal institutions are poor, and this effect weakens when the quality of government in a region increases. This suggests that regions with lower formal institutional capabilities but high levels of social capital might still be able to successfully diversify into new industries. However, low levels of both formal and informal institutions make it very difficult for regions to pursue an effective smart specialization policy. Surely more evidence is needed here before we can make strong policy recommendations. Also, studies on institutions and regional diversification so far have not even come close to making an explicit assessment of the role of public policy for regional diversification (Morgan 2013; Dawley *et al*. 2015), so it remains premature to make strong policy implications at this stage.

3.6 Conclusions

This chapter has made an attempt to outline some of the most recent findings from the growing body of literature on regional diversification that has relevance for smart specialization policies. We discussed the role of local related activities, the importance of network linkages with other regions, the role of non-local actors, the effects of national and regional institutions, including both formal and informal institutions, and we reported about the latest empirical findings concerning these topics wherever possible. We have also identified a number of gaps in our understanding of regional diversification that need to be taken up in future research.

Having said that, we also discussed a number of implications for smart specialization policy that can be derived from this literature so far, some of which can already be clearly formulated, while other issues require some more elaboration and empirical proof. We suggested a network view on smart specialization is important, in which various activities are brought together and combined to develop new specializations in regions. In this context, the local structure in a region could be regarded as a pool of opportunities to make new combinations (both in terms of relatedness and complexity), and on which the entrepreneurial discovery process could draw. The degree of relatedness and complexity of existing activities in regions should be taken as a point of departure, to avoid regions making big technological jumps that have a high probability of failing. A less risky policy is a smart specialization strategy that supports new entrepreneurial initiatives that build on and exploit related local externalities. However, the entrepreneurial discovery process should also be given room to build on local activities that have not been combined before. Moreover, despite its reliance on local capabilities, we also made the claim that smart specialization policy is bound to fail if it does not consider the role of non-local capabilities. In other words, if a policy fails to involve both new local players as well as non-local agents, it is much less likely to be successful because these are both considered to be crucial for the development of new specializations in regions.

Finally, institutions should be given more consideration in the design and implementation of smart specialization policy. Regions differ in their institutional capacity to activate a successful entrepreneurial discovery process, as they are embedded in institutions such as governance structures and social capital at various spatial scales. These provide opportunities for some advanced regions but also set limits for regional diversification in general, and limits to what the entrepreneurial discovery process can potentially achieve in regions that are characterized by low levels of formal and informal institutional capacity. Having said that, we still have little understanding of how institutions at various spatial scales may impact on the intensity and nature of regional diversification, and nor are there any existing studies on institutions and regional diversification that have systematically assessed the role of public policy.

In sum, while general principles can indeed be articulated, it is still premature to derive any strong or specific implications for smart specialization policy on the basis of the current body of literature on regional diversification. While progress has surely been made, and relevant evidence on regional diversification is accumulating, it is still just too early to tell.

References

Acemoglu, D., and Robinson, J. A. (2012) *Why Nations Fail: The origins of power, prosperity and poverty*. New York: Random House.

Aldrich, H. E. and Fiol, C. M. (1994) Fools Rush In? The institutional context of industry creation, *Academy of Management Review*, 19 (4), 645–670.

Andersson, M., Bjerke, L. and Karlsson, C. (2013) Import Flows: Extraregional linkages stimulating renewal of regional sectors? *Environment and Planning A*, 45, 2999–3017.

Arbia, G., Battisti, M., and Di Vaio, G. (2010) Institutions and Geography: Empirical test of spatial growth models for European regions. *Economic Modelling*, Elsevier, vol. 27 (1), 12–21, January.

Arts, S. and Veugelers, R. (2015) Technology Familiarity, Recombinant Novelty, and Breakthrough Invention, *Industrial and Corporate Change*, 24 (6), 1215–1246.

Asheim, B. T. and Isaksen, A. (2002) Regional Innovation Systems. The integration of local 'sticky' and global 'ubiquitous' knowledge, *Journal of Technology Transfer*, 27, 77–86.

Audretsch, D. B. and Feldman, M. P. (1996) Innovative clusters and the industry life cycle, *Review of Industrial Organization*, 11, 253–273.

Bahar, D., Hausmann, R. and Hidalgo, C. A. (2014) Neighbors and the Evolution of the Comparative Advantage of Nations: Evidence of international knowledge difussion?, *Journal of International Economics*, 92 (1), 111–123.

Barbosa, N., Faria, A. P. and Eiriz, V. (2013) Industry- and Firm-Specific Factors of Innovation Novelty, *Industrial and Corporate Change*, 23 (3), 865–902.

Battilana, J., Leca, B. and Boxenbaum, E. (2009) How Actors Change Institutions: Towards a theory of institutional entrepreneurship, *The Academy of Management Annals*, 3, 65–107.

Berge, M. van den, and Weterings, A. (2014) Relatedness in Eco-Technological Development in European Regions, The Hague: Planbureau voor Leefomgeving.

Beugelsdijk, S. and van Schaik, T. (2005) Social Capital and Growth in European Regions: An empirical test. *European Journal of Political Economy*, 21, 301–324.

Boschma, R. (2014) Constructing Regional Advantage and Smart Specialization: Comparisons of two European policy concepts, *Italian Journal of Regional Science*, 13 (1), 51–68.

Boschma, R. (2016) Relatedness as Driver Behind Regional Diversification: A research agenda, *Regional Studies*, forthcoming.

Boschma, R., Balland, P. A. and Kogler, D. F. (2015) Relatedness and Technological Change in Cities: The rise and fall of technological knowledge in U.S. metropolitan areas from 1981 to 2010, *Industrial and Corporate Change*, 24 (1), 223–250.

Boschma, R. and Capone, G. (2015) Institutions and Diversification: Related versus unrelated diversification in a varieties of capitalism framework, *Research Policy*, 44, 1902–1914.

Boschma, R. and Capone, G. (2016) Relatedness and Diversification in the European Union (EU-27) and European Neigbourhood Policy countries, *Environment and Planning C: Government and Policy*, 34, 617–637.

Boschma, R. and Gianelle, C. (2013), Regional Branching and Smart Specialization Policy, Policy Note IPTS, Seville, November 2013, 35 pp.

Boschma, R., Martin V. and Minondo A. (2016) Neighbour Regions as the Source of New Industries, *Papers in Regional Science*, doi:10.1111/pirs.12215.

Boschma, R., Minondo, A. and Navarro, M. (2013) The Emergence of New Industries at the Regional Level in Spain: A proximity approach based on product relatedness. *Economic Geography*, 89 (1), 29–51.

Brachert, M. (2016) The Rise and Fall of Occupational Specializations in German Regions from 1992 to 2010. Relatedness as driving force of human capital dynamics, working paper.

Cantwell, J. A. and Iammarino, S. (2003) *Multinational Corporations and European Regional systems of Innovation*, London/New York: Routledge.

Castaldi, C., Frenken, K. and Los, B. (2015) Related Variety, Unrelated Variety and Technological Breakthroughs. An analysis of US state-level patenting, *Regional Studies*, 49 (5), 767–781.

Charron, N., Dijkstra L. and Lapuente V. (2014) Regional Governance Matters: Quality of government within European Union member states. *Regional Studies*, 48 (1), 68–90.

Charron N., Lapuente V., Rothstein B., Varraish A., Hernandez M., Kazemi Veisari L., Dinescu M., Popovski D., Håkanssson J., Jonsson S., Morgado T., Borcan O. (2010)

Measuring the Quality of Government and Subnational Variation. Report prepared for European Commission, DG Regional Policy and Directorate Policy Development by the research team at the Quality of Government Institute, Department of Political Science, University of Gothenburg, Sweden.

Colombelli, A., Krafft, J. and Quatraro, F. (2014) The Emergence of New Technology-Based Sectors in European Regions: A proximity-based analysis of nanotechnology, *Research Policy*, 43, 1681–1696.

Cortinovis, N. and van Oort, F. (2015) Variety, Economic Growth and Knowledge Intensity of European Regions: A spatial panel analysis. *The Annals of Regional Science*, 55, 7–32.

Cortinovis, N., Xiao, J., Boschma, R. and Van Oort, F. (2016) Formal and Informal Institutions as Drivers of Regional Economic Diversification, PEEG working paper.

Crescenzi R., Gagliardi, L. and Percoco, M. (2013) Social Capital and the Innovative Performance Of Italian Provinces. *Environment and Planning A*, 45, 908–929.

Dahl Fitjar R. and Rodríguez-Pose A. (2011) When Local Interaction Does Not Suffice; Sources of firm innovation in urban Norway. *Environment and Planning A*, 43 (6), 1248–67.

Dawley, S., MacKinnon, D., Cumbers, A. and Pike, A. (2015) Policy Activism and Regional Path Creation: The promotion of offshore wind in North East England and Scotland, *Cambridge Journal of Regions, Economy and Society*, 8, 257–272.

Echebarria, C. and Barrutia J. (2013) Limits of Social Capital as a Driver of Innovation: An empirical analysis in the contest of European regions. *Regional Studies*, 47, 1001–1017.

Esslezbichler, J. (2015) Relatedness, Industrial Branching and Technological Cohesion in US Metropolitan Areas, *Regional Studies*, 49 (5), 752–766.

Fagerberg, J., Feldman, M. and Srholec, M. (2014) Technological Dynamics and Social Capability: US states and European nations, *Journal of Economic Geography*, 14, 313–337.

Feldman, M. P. (1994) *The Geography of Innovation.* Boston, MA: Kluwer Academic Publishers.

Feldman, M. P., Kogler, D. F. and Rigby, D. L. (2015) rKnowledge: The spatial diffusion and adoption of rDNA methods, *Regional Studies*, 49 (5), 798–817.

Foray D. and David P., Hall B. H. (2011) Smart Specialization: From academic idea to political instrument, the surprising career of a concept and the difficulties involved in its implementation. Lausanne: École Polytechnique Fédérale de Lausanne, *MTEI Working Paper* n. 2011.001.

Foray, D. (2014) From Smart Specialisation to Smart Specialisation Policy, *European Journal of Innovation Management*, 17 (4), 492–507.

Fornahl, D. and Guenther, C. (2010) Persistence and Change of Regional Industrial Activities. The impact of diversification in the German machine tool industry, *European Planning Studies*, 18 (12), 1911–1936.

Frenken K. and Boschma R. A. (2007) A Theoretical Framework for Evolutionary Economic Geography: Industrial dynamics and urban growth as a branching process, *Journal of Economic Geography*, 7 (5), 635–649.

Frenken, K. Van Oort, F. G. and Verburg, T. (2007) Related Variety, Unrelated Variety and Regional Economic Growth *Regional Studies*, 41 (5), 685–697.

Fritsch M., and Stephan A. (2005), Regionalization of Innovation Policy. Introduction to the special issue. *Research Policy*, 34 (8), 1123–1127.

Fukuyama, F. (1995) Social Capital and the Global Economy. *Foreign Affairs*, 74, 89–103.

Hall, P. A. and Soskice, D. (eds.) (2001) *Varieties of Capitalism. The institutional foundations of comparative advantage*, New York: Oxford University Press.

Hassink, R. (2015) Smart Specialization. A constructive critique, paper presented at RIP conference, Karlsruhe, 16 October 2015.

Hausmann, R. and Hidalgo, C. A. (2010) Country Diversification, Product Ubiquity, and Economic Divergence. Working Paper No. 201. Cambridge, MA: Center for International Department, Havard University.

Hausmann, R. and Klinger, B., (2007) The Structure of the Product Space and the Evolution of Comparative Advantage. Working paper no. 146. Cambridge, MA: Center for International Development, Harvard University.

He, C. and Rigby, D. (2015) Regional Industrial Evolution in China: Path dependence or path creation?, working paper.

Heimeriks, G. and Boschma, R. (2014) The path- and Place-Dependent Nature of Scientific Knowledge Production in Biotech 1986–2008, *Journal of Economic Geography*, 14, 339–364.

Hidalgo, C. (2015) *Why Information Grows. The evolution of order, from atoms to economics*, London: Allen Lane.

Hidalgo, C. A., Klinger, B., Barabási A.-L. and Hausmann R. (2007) The Product Space Conditions the Development of Nations. *Science*, 317(5837), 482–487.

Iammarino, S. and McCann, P. (2013) *Multinationals and Economic Geography*, Cheltenham: Edward Elgar.

Jacobs, J. (1969) *The Economy of Cities*. New York: Vintage Books.

Kogler, D. F., Rigby, D. L. and Tucker, I. (2013) Mapping Knowledge Space and Technological Relatedness in US Cities, *European Planning Studies*, 21 (9), 1374–1391.

Markusen, A. (1996) Sticky Places in Slippery Space: A typology of industrial districts. *Economic Geography*, 72 (3), 293–313.

Maskell, P., Malmberg, A. (1999) Localised Learning and Industrial Competitiveness. *Cambridge Journal of Economics*, 23 (2), 167–186.

Mazzucato, M. (2013) *The Entrepreneurial State: Debunking public vs private sector myths*, Anthem Press.

McCann, P., Ortega-Argilés, R. (2014) Smart Specialisation in European Regions: Issues of strategy, institutions and implementation, *European Journal of Innovation Management*, 17 (4), 409–427.

McCann P., Ortega-Argilés, R. (2015) Smart Specialisation, Regional Growth and Applications to EU Cohesion Policy. *Regional Studies*, 49 (8), 1291–1302.

Moodysson, J. (2008) Principles and Practices of Knowledge Creation: On the organization of 'buzz' and 'pipelines' in life science communities. *Economic Geography*, 84 (4), 449–69.

Morgan K. (2013) The Regional State in the Era of Smart Specialisation. *Ekonomiaz*, 83, 103–126.

Muneepeerakul, R., Lobo, J., Shutters, S. T., Gomez-Lievano, A. and Qubbaj, M. R. (2013) Urban Economies and Occupation Space: Can they get 'there' from 'here'?, *PLoS ONE* 8 (9), e73676. doi:10.1371/journal.pone.0073676.

Neffke, F., Hartog, M., Boschma, R. and Henning, M. (2015) Agents of Structural Change. The role of firms and entrepreneurs in regional diversification, Papers in Evolutionary Economic Geography, Utrecht University.

Neffke, F., Henning, M. and Boschma, R. (2011) How Do Regions Diversify Over Time? Industry relatedness and the development of new growth paths in regions. *Economic Geography*, 87 (3), 237–265.

Nelson, R. R. (1994) The Co-evolution of Technology, Industrial Structure and Supporting Institutions. *Industrial and Corporate Change*, 3 (1), 47–63.

Nooteboom, B. (2000) *Learning and Innovation in Organizations and Economies*, Oxford, Oxford University Press.

Olson, M. (1982) *The Rise and Decline of Nations*, New Haven, CT, Yale University Press.

Putnam R. (2001) *Bowling Alone*, Touchstone Books by Simon & Schuster, New York.

Putnam, R., Leonardi, R., and Nanetti, R. (1993) *Making Democracy Work*. Princeton University Press, Princeton, NJ.

Quatraro, F. and Montresor, S. (2015) Key Enabling Technologies and Smart Specialization Strategies. Regional evidence from European patent data, DRUID working paper, Rome.

Rigby, D. (2015) Technological Relatedness and Knowledge Space. Entry and exit of US cities from patent classes, *Regional Studies*, 49 (11), 1922–1937.

Rodríguez-Pose, A. (2013) Do Institutions Matter for Regional Development? *Regional Studies*, 47, 1034–1047.

Rodríguez-Pose, A. and Crescenzi, R. (2008) R&D, Spillovers, Innovation Systems and the Genesis of Regional Growth in Europe. *Regional Studies*, 41, 51–67.

Rodrik, D., Subramanian, A. and Trebbi, F. (2004) Institutions Rule: The primacy of institutions over geography and integration in economic development. *Journal of Economic Growth*, 9, 131–165.

Scott, A. J. (1988) *New Industrial Spaces. Flexible production organization and regional development in north America and western Europe*, London: Pion.

Sotarauta, M. and Pulkkinen, R. (2011) Institutional Entrepreneurship for Knowledge Regions: In search of a fresh set of questions for regional innovation studies, *Environment and Planning C*, 29, 96–112.

Strambach, S. (2010) Path Dependency and Path Plasticity. The co-evolution of institutions and innovation – the German customized business software industry, in: R. A. Boschma, R. Martin (eds.), *Handbook of Evolutionary Economic Geography*. Cheltenham: Edward Elgar, 406–431.

Tabellini, G. (2010) Culture and Institutions: Economic development in the regions of Europe. *Journal of the European Economic Association*, 8 (4), 677–716.

Tanner, A. N. (2016) The Emergence of New Technology-Based Industries: The case of fuel cells and its technological relatedness to regional knowledge bases. *Journal of Economic Geography*, 16 (3), 611–635.

Thissen, M., van Oort, F., Diodato, D. and Ruijs, A. (2013) *Regional Competitiveness and Smart Specialization in Europe. Place-based development in international economic networks*. Cheltenham: Edward Elgar.

Thissen, M. F., de Graaff, T. and van Oort, F. (2016) Competitive Network Positions in Trade and Structural Economic Growth: A geographically weighted regression analysis for European regions, *Papers in Regional Science*, forthcoming, doi:10.1111/pirs.12224.

Tödtling F., Trippl M. (2005) One Size Fits All? Towards a Differentiated Regional Innovation Policy Approach. *Research Policy*, 34, 1203–1219.

Trippl, M. (2013) Scientific Mobility and Knowledge Transfer at the Interregional and Intraregional Level. *Regional Studies*, 47 (10), 1653–1667.

Trippl, M., Grillitsch, M. and Isaksen, A. (2015) External 'Energy' for Regional Industrial Change: Attraction and absorption of non-local knowledge for new path development, Papers in Innovation Studies, no. 2015/47, CIRCLE, Lund University. Lund.

Truffer, B. and Coenen, L. (2012) Environmental Innovation and Sustainability Transitions in Regional Studies, *Regional Studies*, 46 (1), 1–21.

Valdaliso, J. M., Magro, E., Navarro, M., Aranguren, M. J. and Wilson, J. R. (2014) Path Dependence in Policies Supporting Smart Specialisation Strategies, *European Journal of Innovation Management*, 17 (4), 390–408.

Van Oort, F., de Geus, S. and Dogaru, T. (2013) Related Variety and Regional Economic Growth in A Cross-Section of European Urban Regions. *European Planning Studies*, 23, 1110–1127.

Wallace, R. and Silberg, G. (2012) Self-Driving Cars: The next revolution, Center for Automotive Research, Transportation Systems Analysis Group.

Xiao, J., Boschma, R. and Andersson, M. (2016) Regional Diversification: The differentiated role of industry relatedness over sectors and regions, working paper.

Zhu, S., He, C. and Zhou, Y. (2015), How to jump further? Path dependent and path breaking in an uneven industry space, Papers in Evolutionary Economic Geography, no. 15.24, Utrecht University, Utrecht.

4 Local Industry Structure as a Resource-Base for Entrepreneurship

Implications for Smart Specialization Strategies

Martin Andersson and Sierdjan Koster

4.1 Introduction

Entrepreneurial discovery is a key element in the Smart Specialization policy concept (Foray 2009, McCann and Ortega-Argiles, 2016). It is advanced as a main mechanism, or driving force, through which development is instigated, and it is motivated with reference to Schumpeterian ideas of recombinations of local resources for innovation (Schumpeter 1912, Frenken and Boschma 2007). Smart specialization is meant to develop regional economies by stimulating diversification and expansion of industry. This involves entrepreneurship and scaling up of Small and Medium-sized Enterprises (SMEs) through experimentation, for example by entering new market niches, as well as embeddedness in (global) value chains.

Another key argument underlying the smart specialization framework is that policy must prioritize; not so much because of scarce resources, but primarily because not all potential alternatives are realistic: 'policy resources must be prioritized on those activities, technologies or sectors where a region has the most realistic chances to develop wide-ranging and large-scale impacts' (McCann and Ortega-Argiles 2016, p. 538). The emphasis on priorities and realistic alternatives has two implications. First, it implies that any smart specialization strategy must build on a careful analysis of existing regional resources, industry specializations and production structures in order to identify pertinent priority areas. Second, almost by definition, it implies that smart specialization policy strategies not only embrace, but also enforce path-dependence. The reason is that what is deemed realistic will be tightly connected to how it links up to existing regional industry activities. In fact, McCann and Ortega-Argiles (2016, p. 538) are explicit about this and argue that smart specialization policy; 'requires that many of these activities and technologies to be prioritized are already partly embedded in the region's existing industrial fabric and that as many local actors and institutions are engaged in the policy design and delivery process'.

In discussions of where to look for regional priority areas in smart specialization policy, the existing industrial structure is often put in center stage. One rationale for this comes from recent analyses taking an evolutionary economic geography perspective on how regional diversification and growth processes, sometimes referred to as branching (Frenken and Boschma 2007) associate with relatedness.

This literature holds that regional growth is significantly influenced by relatedness structures between industries in regions. Industries have better prospects of growth if they are embedded in regions that have similar or related industries (Neffke *et al.* 2011, Frenken *et al.* 2007), because the labor market for suitable employees is likely to be thicker, relevant input–output relations may be easier to establish and productive knowledge spillovers are more likely to occur.

This chapter aims to bring additional perspectives on the role industry structure plays in shaping the conditions and potential for renewal and growth of regional economies through entrepreneurship. It contributes to the debate about what conceptual underpinnings, and what aspects of a regional economy, discussions of policy priorities in smart specialization contexts should be based on. We review recent literature on (1) the labor market origins of entrepreneurs and (2) the role of the social environment in encouraging individual entrepreneurial behaviors, and make two claims.

The first is that it is critical that analyses of regional economies in a smart specialization context acknowledge the 'functional specialization' of local industries (cf. Duranton and Puga 2005, Wixe and Andersson 2015). With this we mean the 'contents' of what workers do and the associated skills, experiences and capabilities they are likely to accumulate during their professional career. A main reason for this is that new firms are started by individuals who capitalize on their accumulated experiences and skills. The nature of their jobs provides an important learning context, and influences the scope and direction for entrepreneurial discovery. Shane (2003), for example, observes how the recognition of business opportunities is significantly influenced by the environment in which entrepreneurs work. In view of this, we argue that:

- a region's industry structure may be described as a 'resource base for entrepreneurship'. Discussions of priorities in smart specialization contexts will benefit from recognizing this and should be based on empirical assessments of the links between the (current) regional economic structure including the available skills for entrepreneurship and the subsequent manifestations of entrepreneurship.

The second claim is that it is equally important that smart specialization policy acknowledges and crafts strategies to cope with the broader social environment for entrepreneurship in a region. We present and discuss recent research on how individuals' inclination to act on entrepreneurial opportunities are significantly influenced by the general level of social acceptance and encouragement of entrepreneurs and their activities in a region. Such types of social, or cultural, characteristics of regions are typically historically rooted and display significant inertia, and put constraints on as well as constitute a major challenge for policy. Our argument is that:

- there are often important links between industry structures and regional entrepreneurship cultures (cf. Chinitz 1961). Smart specialization policy strategies have much to gain by identifying these and adapt to and cope with such long-lasting regional social characteristics

In summary, our arguments lead to the conclusion that, while local industry structure certainly is important to consider in discussions of priorities in smart specialization strategies, the center of attention should not be on the industry composition as such. We claim that it is instead what a region's industry composition implies for the local skill composition and the social environment for entrepreneurship that ought to guide priorities. This is because it is those underlying structures that reflect conditions and potential for entrepreneurial discovery, for example through new firms or SMEs that diversify the local economy.

The rest of this chapter is organized as follows: Section 4.2 provides the conceptual underpinnings for the argument that the local industry structures may be conceived of as a resource base for entrepreneurship, and it reviews the empirical evidence. Section 4.3 discusses recent literature linking entrepreneurship outcomes in regions to local entrepreneurship cultures and makes the case that at least part of such cultures may be linked to the industry structure, and elaborates what this means for smart specialization strategies. Section 4.4 concludes.

4.2 The Local Industry Structure as a 'Resource Base' For Entrepreneurship

Regarding the region as a holder of resources that guide the manifestations of entrepreneurship, has a strong parallel to the resource-based view of the firm as discussed by Barney (1991). This parallel is a particularly interesting starting point in the context of smart specialization strategies as it automatically opens up the discussion about what are the relevant resources for entrepreneurial discovery. Although focused on the firm level, the main tenets of the resource-based framework translate well to the regional context: (1) Firms are heterogeneous with respect to the strategic resources they control and (2) these resources are not perfectly mobile across firms and as such the heterogeneity can be long lasting (ibid, p. 101). Indeed, the idea that regional development paths are highly dependent on regional conditions is central in the smart specialization strategy and more broadly the main departure point in endogenous growth theories of the region (Lucas 1988; Romer 1989).

The spatial inertia of the resource holders – people and firms – supports the parallel perspective in the resource-based view. As an illustration, Weterings and Knoben (2013) show that yearly only 3.1% of all establishments relocate in the Netherlands. If relocations are required to cross municipal boundaries, the share drops to 1.2%. Given, that the Netherlands is a small country with good infrastructure, it is relatively easy to relocate without losing access to the main market and suppliers. Even under these circumstances, the costs and risks of relocating a business, particularly across larger distances, appear substantial and firm owners refrain from relocating. In addition, there may be other reasons related to family formation and social networks that keep business owners and by proxy their businesses anchored in place (Koster and Venhorst 2014).

Even though migration rates for people are higher than for firms, most people are relatively inert in space. Even in the heydays of migration in the USA, a country with traditionally dynamic migration patterns and flexible labour markets, the cross-county migration rate hovered around 6% (Partridge *et al.* 2012). During the crisis, migration rates fell to under 4% (ibid). Though small in numbers on a yearly basis, the cumulative numbers of migrants can be large over time. If, on a yearly basis 4% of the population moves, then in 10 years, potentially 40% of the population has changed in a certain region, unless many of these migrants are repeat migrants. Yet, migration is selective both in terms of origins and destinations and in characteristics of the people involved. As a result, over time regions tend to attract people with similar characteristics. Likewise, emigration tends to be selective for certain groups in a given region. Student cities are prime examples of this mechanism; students flock in to attend college and leave the city after graduation (Venhorst *et al.* 2011). Famously, Fielding (1992) shows how South East England acts as a social escalator through the career opportunities it offers to ambitious young adults. They subsequently tend to leave the region – step of the escalator – later in their careers. Importantly, the selectivity of migration processes implies that even though there are dynamics in the population, the regional skill structure is much more stable over time. Within the framework of a smart specialization policy strategy then, even though there may be dynamics in the people and firms in a region, the underlying resources that make up the opportunity set for development and entrepreneurial discovery can be regarded as slowly changing.

4.2.1 Skills, industry structure and entrepreneurship

A key question then becomes how to identify and characterize the opportunity set for entrepreneurial discovery in a region. In other words, how can the available resources for entrepreneurial discovery be identified? Though relevant in conceptual terms, it is particularly significant in the practical translation of smart specialization strategies which revolves around the idea of developing the most promising elements in a regional economy.

The industrial structure, particularly, has been foregrounded as conditioning the path dependent growth potential of regions. Industries have better prospects of growth if they are embedded in regions with similar or related industries (Neffke *et al.* 2011). The focus on the industry structure as a backdrop for regional economic growth and related policies has an important empirical basis. More practically, the existing industry structure offers policy makers a tangible and well-defined framework within which policy priorities, for example as part of a smart specialization strategy, can be defined.

Indeed, also in entrepreneurship research, the industry structure has been shown to importantly condition the possibilities and the direction of entrepreneurial endeavors. Shane (2003) and Eckhardt and Shane (2003) demonstrate how the recognition of viable entrepreneurial opportunities is shaped by the context in which entrepreneurs have worked. Industry tenure is an important aspect of this context. Possibly reflecting the enhanced potential of recognizing business opportunities, having industry experience is an important indicator of future success of the firm

(Sørensen and Phillips 2011; Iversen *et al.* 2010). This stylized fact also reflects how entrepreneurship is a method to capitalize on context-specific learning (Becker 1964). Not only the business opportunity may be better if staying in the same sector (positive selection of business opportunities), but also the skills, networks and experience that the entrepreneur brings to the table may be more relevant within the same industry. It has for example been shown that spin-offs, i.e. new firms started by prior employees of established businesses in the same industry, outperform other types of new firms in terms of survival and employment growth, and that spin-offs gain their advantage from the experiences and knowledge that founders have acquired in their parent organizations (Andersson and Klepper 2013). This has important regional implications as well. As it is costly or risky to pursue entrepreneurial endeavors outside the known industry, entrepreneurship tends to follow and reiterate the regional industry structure. Klepper (2002), following the above arguments, shows how through repeated industry-specific entrepreneurship one industry can eventually grow to dominate the regional industry structure. A large share of the Detroit automotive industry can be traced back to one or two pioneer firms that spawned dozens of smaller and larger firms in the automotive industry.

The existing evidence on entrepreneurial discovery suggests that it is importantly guided by the existing industry structure. This implies that a smart specialization strategy that overly relies on targeting specific industries may run the risk of being redundant in the sense that there are inherently strong incentives for entrepreneurs to be active in the main regional industries. In the worst case, such an industry-focused policy translation of the Smart Specialization concept may stifle entrepreneurial progress and the development of new industries through entrepreneurial discovery.

The industry structure is thus a key aspect of the economic context in which entrepreneurial discovery takes place, but it only partially informs the development potential of a region. In a sense, the industry structure is the current sublimation of the available technological assets and human capital available in a region and too large a focus on the status-quo may hide potential avenues for development. Similarly, the resource-based view of the firm does not consider the products as the main competitive advantage, but rather the resources that can be directed either to a current product or a new product. At the regional level, industry structure significantly conditions the path dependent development potential of regions, but also aspects related to demographic characteristics, the available skill set in the labour market, educational attainment and the institutional context importantly shape the regional entrepreneurial discovery process and may perhaps be more fundamental to the opportunities for development, while the industry structure actually reflects the current state of affairs. A heads-on approach to try and identify the skills available in a region as well as how they relate to entrepreneurial discovery is worthwhile Lucas (1978 p. 510) already hinted at an approach that acknowledges the task specificity of skills rather than the industry specificity:

As a preliminary matter, it is necessary to decide whether to follow Viner and develop a model at the industry level, or to theorize at an economy-wide level. The former would be appropriate if managerial ability were industry-specific, as a result of 'nature' or of the accumulation of industry-specific expertise. There is no doubt that these considerations matter, at some level, but the multi-product of at least the largest modern firms and the mobility of top managers across industries suggest that, if one is choosing between these extremes, it is best to attack the problem at an economy-wide level.

As a specific example, consider an IT-specialist who works in a large bank. Part of his or her skill set is related to the processes that are specific to the bank or financial services in more general. However, the functional skill set of the specialist is likely more related to the occupation or position that the IT specialist currently holds. The specific skill set can also have important merit outside financing. Given that tasks are increasingly specific and fragmented, it is likely that the industry context and the actual functional specialization – or skills – of employees become increasingly divorced. At the regional level, the industry structure may cloud significant underlying heterogeneity in the skills and tasks that people perform and that in fact make up the regional resource base for entrepreneurial discovery. What then is the relationship between industry structure and skills development, specifically in the context of entrepreneurship?

4.2.2 Empirical illustrations

In a number of earlier studies, both at the individual and the regional level, we have illustrated how the industry structure relates to the actual skill set available to entrepreneurs.[1] We reappraise the results within the context of smart specialization strategies. Figure 4.1, on the basis of a survey among 250 Dutch entrepreneurs (see further, Koster 2006), shows self-reported skills that entrepreneurs used in the set-up of their new firms. The answers are split between entrepreneurs with and without same-industry experience.

The results in Figure 4.1 illustrate the transferability of skills across industries. In line with Becker's (1964) distinction between generic and specific learning,

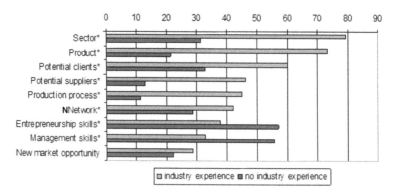

Figure 4.1 Nature of skills used in founding process depending on industry experience (N = 250).

* indicates significant differences p < 0.05.

entrepreneurs who switch industries are likely to do so on the basis of generic skills related to entrepreneurship and management. In contrast, specific skills, related to products, production and the relevant networks, are more valuable within the same industry. Further to this, entrepreneurs with same-industry experience report a higher number of skills and experiences from the previous job that served as relevant inputs for the new firm (4.4 versus 2.8 out of the possible 9). This then supports the relevance of the industry as a 'container' of relevant skills and resources for entrepreneurship. At the same time, the cross-industry transfer of specific skills is significant as well. Particularly skills concerning the business case (product and clients) of an entrepreneurial endeavor appear relatively transferable between industries. The inputs for production (suppliers and process) are more closely tied to the industry. In general, however, entrepreneurs appear inspired mostly by the envisioned product and clients than by the inputs needed for production. The figure shows that industry background is indeed a significant context for learning. It is clear, however, that relevant skill development, both generic and specific, also occurs outside of industry-specific contexts.

A promising approach to empirically addressing the underlying skill heterogeneity within industries is the occupational career of entrepreneurs. An occupation can be seen as the compilation of the different tasks someone performs and as such, it also holds information on the skill build-up by employees. Kambourov and Manovskii (2009) show that occupational tenure, even more so than firm tenure or industry tenure, significantly contributes to wage development. This corresponds to the idea that occupations are relevant learning arenas for development later in the career, either as an employee or in entrepreneurship. In a general sense, it is well established that certain occupations prepare for entrepreneurship. Particularly employees in occupations related to organizational skills (managers) have a higher propensity of entering into entrepreneurship. Managers experience many aspects of the daily practice of running a business and their jack-of-all-trades skill set prepares them well for entrepreneurship (Lazear, 2004). In the context of Becker's human capital framework, certain occupations instill generic skills which can be used in many different contexts. Indeed, the results in Figure 4.1 show that organizational skills transfer well across industries. In addition, however, certain occupations may also prepare for entrepreneurship in particular contexts or industries. Recall the IT-specialist working in a bank. If he or she decides to enter into entrepreneurship, it will most likely take place in the IT-industry. Expanding the argument to a wider context, it follows that not only the industry-structure conditions possibilities for industrial restructuring and branching into new industries, but also the occupational structure within the industries may be important.

Koster and Andersson (2014) identify specific occupation-industry transitions and assess to what extent they hold information on the skill structure of the entrepreneurs involved in addition to their industry experience. Using Swedish employers-employee data, the most common transition to an industry given a certain occupation is identified. The intuition of the approach is that entrepreneurs will enter an industry that is most likely to value the skills they learned in their previous occupation. For each occupation, we thus identify the most popular destination industry and these advantageous occupation-industry pairs are coined occupational spin-offs. They are cross tabulated with a spin-off that are based on the commonly used definition of same-industry experience to specify the complementarity of the two measures of relevant skill development (Table 4.1).

The sample includes 3615 unique transitions from employment in the year 2004 to entrepreneurship in 2005. A majority of the entrepreneurs (61%) remains active in the same 2-digit industry as is indeed the stylized fact.[2] The most common occupation-industry transitions describe 45% of the entrepreneurial entries. Most interestingly, however, is the overlap between the two different definitions. The on-diagonal shares show the correspondence between the two measures and sum to 59%. The off-diagonal shares describe 41% of the entrepreneurial entries and this indicates, as in Figure 4.1, that industry is important in describing the underlying skill structure for entrepreneurial discovery. It offers, however, only a partial account.

An important question in the context of smart specialization policies is to what extent a skills-approach to entrepreneurship translates to the regional context. Does it provide complementary information to understand regional differences in entrepreneurial discovery opportunities? For this, we rehearse, in Tables 4.2 and 4.3, empirical results from Andersson *et al.* (2016). Table 4.2 presents a break-down of the Swedish universe of start-ups for the years 2008–2012. The

Table 4.1 Same industry spin-offs and occupational spin-offs

	Same industry spin-off	*Other*	*Total*
Occupational spin-off	1185 (33%)	454 (13%)	1639 (45%)
Other	1029 (28%)	947 (26%)	1976 (55%)
Total	2214 (61%)	1401 (39%)	3615

Table 4.2 Industry distribution of start-ups along the urban hierarchy (N = 352,509)

Sector/Region	*Metropolitan*	*Urban*	*Countryside*	*Remote countryside*	*Total*
HighTech Manu	0.4%	0.5%	0.5%	0.4%	0.5%
LowTech Manu	2.5%	3.4%	4.4%	4.6%	3.4%
HighTech KIS	8.0%	4.7%	2.3%	1.5%	5.2%
MediumTech KIS	23.6%	16.1%	9.9%	6.7%	17.0%
KI Financial Services	0.9%	0.5%	0.3%	0.2%	0.6%
Other KIS	13.3%	9.1%	6.4%	5.0%	9.9%
Other Services	32.2%	33.0%	29.0%	24.5%	31.1%
Other Industries	19.1%	32.8%	47.2%	57.3%	32.5%
Total	100%	100%	100%	100%	100%

Note: KIS stands for Knowledge Intensive Services, data from Sweden for the years 2008–2012.

Table 4.3 Share of employees with a university education by industry

Region/Sector	HTM	LTM	HTKIS	MKIS	KIFS	OKIS	OS	OI	Total
Metropolitan	40.8%	30.1%	65.0%	62.5%	60.8%	63.9%	28.0%	27.2%	42.9%
Urban	32.5%	21.8%	62.8%	56.6%	49.7%	56.7%	21.4%	21.7%	32.0%
Countryside	21.7%	17.5%	51.9%	48.1%	40.3%	49.2%	18.2%	17.3%	23.5%
Remote countryside	23.2%	16.3%	44.7%	43.4%	12.5%	44.5%	15.9%	15.5%	19.5%

Note: HTM and LTM stands for High-tech and Low-tech manufacturing. HTKIS, MKIS and KIFS refer to High-tech knowledge intensive services, knowledge intensive market services, and knowledge intensive financial services. OKIS is other knowledge intensive services. OS is other services and OI is other industries.

start-ups are classified on the basis of knowledge intensity in manufacturing and business services, following the Eurostat industry classification based on knowledge intensity.[3] The resulting classification is then aggregated along the urban hierarchy which runs from metropolitan areas (Stockholm, Malmö and Göteborg) to areas that are characterized as remote countryside. Table 4.2 shows, for each region type, the distribution of start-ups across the industry structure and it gives a first indication of the differences in skill structure, in terms of knowledge input, along the urban hierarchy. Not surprisingly, the distribution of start-ups is clearly different depending on the type of region. Because of spatial sorting and benefits from agglomeration, the urban and metropolitan regions have a higher share in Knowledge Intensive Services. Manufacturing, high and low tech, is much more evenly distributed along the urban hierarchy.

Table 4.3, however, shows that industry classifications tell an important but partial story about the skill structure and entrepreneurial discovery processes. The table documents the number of highly educated employees (including owners) within the different industries. It becomes clear that for each of the different industries, the knowledge intensity (measured by educational level) neatly follows the urban hierarchy. These findings are in line with Bacolod *et al.* (2009) who show significant differences in the skill structure along the urban hierarchy. Particularly people with well-developed cognitive skills cluster in cities where their skills are also better valued. Motor skills, for example, are more important in regions lower in the urban hierarchy.

4.3 The Social Environment and Individual Action

The previous section makes the argument that it is critical to assess a region's industry structure in terms of workers' skills and experiences. A main reason for this is that new firms are started by individuals (alone or in teams) who capitalize on their accumulated experiences and skills that they acquire during their professional career. It follows that to understand the conditions and potential for entrepreneurship in a region, it is necessary to study what workers in a region do, i.e. the 'contents' of their work, and what it means for their potential to develop a new business. Entrepreneurship is indeed often conceptualized as a result of individual action in response to perceived opportunities (Shane 2003). Work experience and the nature of the tasks/functions associated with an individual's work are likely to have a large influence on his/her perception of opportunities and business ideas.

Perception of an opportunity, however, is no guarantee that individual actions lead to the formation of new firms influencing the diversification and expansion of a local economy. One stream of the recent research literature on the 'geography of entrepreneurship' shows for example that the regional environment in which individuals operate can to a large extent influence individual action, i.e. the likelihood that an individual in fact acts on an opportunity and realizes a business idea. This research strand holds that the broader institutional environment of a region – comprising both formal (e.g. taxes, regulations, stringency of enforcement) and informal (e.g. attitudes, social legitimacy) institutions – is an important aspect to consider in crafting policy strategies involving entrepreneurship (cf. Andersson and Henrekson 2015).[4]

Acs *et al.* (2008) argue that there is a twofold effect of the local institutional environment. First, there is a *direct effect* through the impact that institutions have on the incentives and returns to entrepreneurship. Second, there is also an *indirect effect* reflecting that the institutional environment may influence the supply of entrepreneurs, for example through spatial sorting. Figure 4.2 is from Andersson and Henrekson (2015) and summarizes the two-pronged effect of the institutional environment. We will here focus on the role of informal institutions, and in particular the role that the social environment plays in influencing peoples' inclination to engage in entrepreneurship.

4.3.1 What is the social environment and how does it matter?

It is often argued that every region has locally embedded values and attitudes towards entrepreneurship, which exert a strong influence on the rate

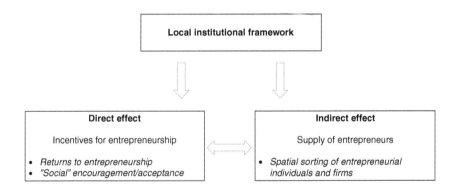

Figure 4.2 Direct and indirect effects of the local institutional environment on entrepreneurship (Andersson and Henrekson 2015).

of entrepreneurial activity in regions. For example, Etzioni (1987) argues that the extent to which entrepreneurship is legitimized in a society is crucial for entrepreneurship:

> The extent to which entrepreneurship is legitimate, the demand for it is higher; the supply of entrepreneurship is higher; and more resources are allocated to the entrepreneurial function. (*ibid.*, p. 175), [...] In the terms used by economists, legitimation is a key factor which affects the preferences, the constraints', and the resource allocation simultaneously.
>
> (*ibid.*, p. 185)

Many researchers use the concept of 'entrepreneurship culture' as a generic term to capture such a phenomenon. The term is usually employed to refer in a general sense to the level of social acceptance and encouragement of entrepreneurs and their activities in a region (Fritsch and Wyrwich 2013, Andersson and Koster 2011, Westlund *et al.* 2014). Beugelsdijk (2007), for example, discusses an entrepreneurship culture as a 'positive collective programming of the mind'. These types of social characteristics of regions typically change slowly and have long-lasting effects. They are durable, spatially 'sticky', maintained and spread through social networks and inherited across generations. Therefore, they put constraints on, as well as constitute, a major challenge for policy.

4.3.2 How does it influence entrepreneurship?

The effects of a local entrepreneurship culture on entrepreneurship run through two broad channels. The first channel comprises social interaction effects. The basic argument is that being embedded in an environment where one's 'neighbours' have a positive attitude towards entrepreneurship provide stimuli and support to individuals to engage in entrepreneurship. For example, in regions with a strong entrepreneurship culture, entrepreneurs may have a high social status, and this could trigger entrepreneurial endeavors (Casson 1995). A strong entrepreneurship culture in a region is also likely to imply that there is a large presence of people who are (or have been) entrepreneurs. This could induce motivation and self-confidence, e.g. 'if they can do it, I can too' (Sorenson and Audia 2000). Density of such role models also implies a breeding ground for learning the practice of entrepreneurship and may reduce uncertainties with the start-up process (e.g. Minniti 2005, Guiso and Schivardi 2011).

The second channel is more indirect and works through the formal institutional environment. Williamson (2000) argues that informal institutions, comprising culture, put significant constraints on the more formal institutions, i.e. the formal rules of the game like tax systems, business policy and employment regulations. In the context of regional entrepreneurship cultures, this means that regions with a strong entrepreneurship culture are more likely to develop a more favorable institutional environment in terms of not only the design of local regulations, but also the stringency of enforcement of national institutions (Andersson and Henrekson

2015). Examples of the latter include the speed with which local authorities deal with permits and how 'business friendly' various national regulations are interpreted and enforced at the local level. More business-friendly regulations could in turn stimulate and facilitate entrepreneurship.

4.3.3 Some empirical evidence

An often-cited study that provides suggestive evidence of the role that entrepreneurship cultures play is Saxenian's (1994) comparison of Silicon Valley and Route 128. While both regions had a historically strong concentration of knowledge- and technology-intensive sectors and bright prospects, the regions developed along different trajectories after the crisis period in the mid-1980s. Silicon Valley continued to flourish, in particular through a high rate of idea-driven and technology-based entrepreneurship that diversified the local economy, whereas Route 128 declined. Saxenian maintains that one important explanation for the divergent performance of the regions is rooted in differences in regional entrepreneurship culture. The following quote from an entrepreneur with experience from both regions serves as a case in point (Saxenian 1994, p 63):

> In Boston, if I said I was starting a company, people would look at me and say: 'Are you sure you want to take the risk? You are so well established. Why would you give up a good job as vice president at a big company?' In California, I became a folk hero when I decided to start a company. It wasn't just my colleagues. My insurance man, my water deliverer – everyone was excited. It's a different culture out here.

Another set of evidence comes from analyzes of the historical persistence of start-ups rates in regions. Fritsch and Wyrwich (2013) show that differences in self-employment and new firm formation across regions in Germany are not only substantial, but have endured over periods as long as 80 years. They find that the self-employment rate in 1925 in German regions is a highly robust determinant of entrepreneurial activity in 2005. Since this is a time period covering several disruptive changes in the German economy, they interpret this as reflecting a long-lasting influence of slowly changing locally embedded entrepreneurship cultures.

In addition, a large literature shows that individuals' inclination to engage in entrepreneurship is indeed higher if they operate in a local environment where there is a high density of established entrepreneurs around them or have people that are (or have been) entrepreneurs in their social networks. For example, it has been shown that the decision to become an entrepreneur is positively associated with having entrepreneurs in one's social network (Kim and Aldrich 2005, Klyver *et al.* 2007), and that entrepreneurial behaviors of school, workplace and neighborhood peers influence entrepreneurial behavior (Falck *et al.* 2012, Nanda and Sorensen 2010, Andersson and Larsson 2016).

In sum, there are robust empirical regularities that are consistent with the arguments that a regions' social environment, or culture of entrepreneurship, is important in influencing individuals' inclination to engage in entrepreneurship.

4.3.4 Where does it come from? – Coming back to the role of the local industry structure

The sources of entrepreneurship culture are difficult to pin down, since they are often unintended consequences of past events or historical (unplanned) circumstances. Williamson's (2000) argues that informal institutions '... have mainly spontaneous origins – which is to say that deliberative choice of a calculative kind is minimally implicated. Given these evolutionary origins, they are 'adopted' and thereafter display a great deal of inertia'. Likewise, Minniti (2005) claims that 'the social environment is not the planned outcome of the decisions of purposeful actors; rather it emerges as the unintended consequence of a sequence of decisions taken by individuals and serves as a conduit for information'.

What is established in the literature, however, is that local entrepreneurship cultures are linked to historical industry structures of regions. This brings us back to local industry structures, but this time not in terms of acquisition of skills and entrepreneurial discovery. The focus here is instead on how it may influence the social environment in terms of legitimacy and the social encouragement of entrepreneurship.

Regions that historically have been characterized by a wide set of small and medium-sized firms rather than a few large firms appear to be significantly more likely to be entrepreneurial from the perspective of generating high levels of start-up rates over extended periods of time. For example, Chinitz (1961, p. 284) claimed that the supply of entrepreneurship of an area is influenced by 'certain traditions and elements of the social structure which are heavily influenced by the character of the area's historic specializations'. He then went on to discuss the differences between steel and apparel industries, where the former is historically more tied to large firms and latter to small-scale businesses. A larger density of small-scale industries, he claimed, is more likely to produce a social environment conducive for entrepreneurship. He saw the social environment being linked to ease of entry and hypothesized that 'there is an aura of second-class citizenship attached to the small businessman in an environment dominated by big businesses' and that 'the ease of entry, to borrow a concept from industrial organization, is considerably greater in an environment dominated – not dominated to be more exact – by small firm industries' (ibid. p. 285).

The modern research literature provides evidence in support of this hypothesis. For example, average firms size of local industries in regions have been shown to have a negative influence on the overall start-up rates of regions and as well as their employment growth (e.g. Glaeser *et al.* 2010). Regions with a history of dependence on one or a few large employers, such as large-scale manufacturing like mines and shipyards, which are thus likely to have developed a culture of labor rather than entrepreneurs, appear to be less entrepreneurial even in modern times (Glaeser *et al.* 2015, Larsson 2016). Furthermore, there also appears to be an effect of employer size. A robust finding in many empirical analyses of the determinants of individuals' decision to leave employment for entrepreneurship is that the size of the firm they work at has a negative influence (e.g. Hyytinen and Maliranta, 2008; Elfenbein *et al.* 2010). One argument is that employees of smaller firms are exposed to the whole business process including customers, making them better equipped to start a firm.

4.3.5 Policy implications

What the argument of regional entrepreneurship cultures suggests is that two regions with similar skill sets available for entrepreneurship may show very different rates of experimentation and realizations of new business ideas due to the fact that they provide different entrepreneurship cultures. One region may have a social environment which is supportive for trying out new ideas: Entrepreneurship spurred by leaving a stable employer to try a new idea is socially legitimate and encouraged, whereas another region may have a more inhibiting culture, for example because of a historically larger dependence on large employers.

This is a significant policy challenge for two simple reasons. First, policy cannot change a region's history. Historically rooted and embedded phenomena, such as entrepreneurship cultures, must be perceived as 'gifts from the past' (Andersson 2012). Policy should yet be based on recognition of the role played by historical and cultural factors and be adapted to the circumstances in different regions. Accepting entrepreneurship cultures means for example that the (local) effects of the same policy measures may be quite different depending on the region in which they are implemented. This thus reinforces the argument of the importance of solid regional analyses prior the development smart specialization strategies (cf. McCann and Ortega-Argiles 2016). What the discussion here adds is that the analyses of a regional economy that serve as groundworks for smart specialization strategies must account for the social environment and try to assess the entrepreneurship culture of a region. Entrepreneurship and development of small and medium-sized businesses are after all key elements of smart specialization. Second, historically rooted phenomenon like entrepreneurship cultures change in slow processes. This means that policies for regions with a weak entrepreneurship culture, for example rooted in historical concentrations of large-scale manufacturing like mining, have a difficult task. Short-term policies are likely to be of little help in altering path-dependent development trajectories of regions. Instead, it calls for long-terms and catalytic policies.

4.4 Summary and Conclusions

In this chapter, we have presented a conceptual discussion and summarized empirical evidence on the role that industry structure plays in shaping the conditions and potential for the renewal and growth of regional economies through entrepreneurship. We reviewed recent literature on the labor market origins of entrepreneurs and the role of the social environment in encouraging individual entrepreneurial behaviors, and used this as a backdrop to discuss what conceptual underpinnings and what aspects of a regional economy, discussions of the policy priorities in smart specialization contexts may focus on.

Our conclusion is that, while local industry structure certainly is important to consider in discussions of the priorities in smart specialization strategies, the centre of attention should not be on the industry composition as such. We claim that it is instead what a region's industry composition implies for the local skill composition and the social environment for entrepreneurship that defines the scope for regional economic development. This is because it is those underlying structures that reflect the conditions and potential for entrepreneurship, for example through new firms or SMEs that diversify the local economy. In terms of agenda setting in smart specialization strategies it is these underlying structures that fundamentally define the activities that offer the most promising development path for regions.

One implication is that analyses of industry structures in a smart specialization context have a lot to gain by going beyond industry presence, and should study the skills and competencies of the workforce as well as the type of firms involved in different industries, for example by studying education profiles and occupational structure and firm size distributions. After all, the literature on functional specialization illustrates that the same type of industry may look very different in different places (e.g. Duranton and Puga 2005), and this means that conditions for entrepreneurship may also be very different across places even though they show similar overall industry structures. This also means that different places, despite similar industry structures, may need quite different policy priorities in a smart specialization context.

Notes

1 The empirical examples importantly draw from Koster (2007), Andersson, Koster and Lavesson (2016) and Koster and Andersson (2014).
2 Koster (2007), on the basis of a survey for the North of the Netherlands, finds 64% the start-ups to be same-industry spin-offs.
3 http://ec.europa.eu/eurostat/cache/metadata/Annexes/htec_esms_an3.pdf.
4 The discussion of local entrepreneurship cultures in this section draws on Andersson and Henrekson (2015), Andersson and Larsson (2016) and Andersson (2012).

References

Acs, Zoltan J., Edward L. Glaeser, Robert E. Litan, Lee Fleming, Stephan J. Goetz, William R. Kerr, Steven Klepper, Stuart S. Rosenthal, Olav Sorenson and William C. Strange (2008), 'Entrepreneurship and Urban Success: Toward a Policy Consensus'. *Economics Faculty Scholarship*, Paper No. 61, Syracuse University. Available online: http://surface.syr.edu/ecn/61 (accessed January 20, 2014).

Andersson, Martin (2012), 'Startup Rates, Entrepreneurship Culture and the Business Cycle', In Pontus Braunerhjelm, ed., *Entrepreneurship, Norms and the Business Cycle: The Swedish Economic Forum Report 2012*. Stockholm: Swedish Economic Forum.

Andersson, M. and J. P. Larsson (2016), 'Local Entrepreneurship Clusters in Cities' *Journal of Economic Geography*, 16 (1), 39–66.

Andersson, M. and M. Henrekson (2015), 'Local Competitiveness Fostered through Local Institutions for Entrepreneurship', in Audretsch, David B., Albert N Link and Mary Walshok (eds.), *Oxford Handbook of Local Competitiveness*, Oxford University Press, Oxford.

Andersson, Martin, and Steven Klepper (2013), 'Characteristics and Performance of New Firms and Spinoffs in Sweden'. *Industrial and Corporate Change*, 22 (1), 245–280.

Andersson, Martin, and Sierdjan Koster (2011), 'Source of Persistence in Regional Startup Rates: Evidence from Sweden'. *Journal of Economic Geography*, 11 (1), 179–201.

Andersson, M., S. Koster, and N. Lavesson (2016). 'Are Start-Ups the Same Everywhere?: The Urban–Rural Skill Gap in Swedish Entrepreneurship'. In: Mack, E. A., & Qian, H. (eds.). (2016). *Geographies of Entrepreneurship.*Routledge.

Bacolod, M., B. S. Blum, and W. C. Strange (2009). 'Skills in The City'. *Journal of Urban Economics*, 65 (2), 136–153.

Barney, J. (1991). 'Firm Resources and Sustained Competitive Advantage'. *Journal of Management*, 17 (1), 99–120.

Becker, G. S. (1964). *Human Capital: A Theoretical and Empirical Analysis, with Special Reference to Education.*University of Chicago Press.

Beugelsdijk, S. (2007), 'Entrepreneurial Culture, Regional Innovativeness and Economic Growth'. *Journal of Evolutionary Economics*17 (1), 187–210.

Casson, M. C. (1995), *Entrepreneurship and Business Culture*, Aldershot, UK and Brookfield, MA: Edward Elgar.

Chinitz, B. J. (1961), 'Contrasts in agglomeration: New York and Pittsburgh', *American Economic Review*, 51 (2), 279–289.

Duranton, G. and D. Puga (2005), 'From Sectoral to Functional Urban Specialization', *Journal of Urban Economics*, 57, 343–370.

Eckhardt, J. T., and S. A. Shane (2003), 'Opportunities and Entrepreneurship'. *Journal of management*, 2(3), 333–349.

Elfenbein, D. W., B. H. Hamilton, and T. R. Zenger (2010), 'The Small Firm Effect and the Entrepreneurial Spawning of Scientists and Engineers'. *Management Science*, 56: 659–681.

Etzioni, Amitai (1987), 'Entrepreneurship, Adaption and Legitimation: A Macro-Behavioral Perspective'. *Journal of Economic Behavior and Organization*, 8 (2), 175–189.

Falck, Oliver, Stephan Heblich and Erik Luedemann (2012), 'Identity and Entrepreneurship: Do School Peers Shape Entrepreneurial Intentions?' *Small Business Economics*, 39 (1), 39–59.

Fielding, A. J. (1992), 'Migration and Social mobility: South East England as an Escalator Region'. *Regional studies*, 26 (1), 1–15.

Foray, D. (2009). 'Understanding Smart Specialisation. The Question of R&D Specialisation', *JRC*, European Commission, Directoral General for Research, Brussels, 19–28.

Frenken K. and R. Boschma (2007), 'A Theoretical Framework for Evolutionary Economic Geography: Industrial Dynamics and Urban Growth as a Branching Process', *Journal of Economic Geography*, 7 (5), 635–649.

Frenken, K., F. van Oort, and T. Verburg (2007), 'Related Variety, Unrelated Variety and Regional Economic Growth', *Regional Studies*, 41 (5), 685–697.

Fritsch, Michael, and Michael Wyrwich (2013), 'The Long Persistence of Regional Levels of Entrepreneurship: Germany, 1925–2005'. *Regional Studies*, 48, 939–954.

Glaeser, E., S. P. Kerr, and W. Kerr (2015), 'Entrepreneurship and Urban Growth: An Empirical Assessment with Historical Mines', *Review of Economics and Statistics*, 97 (2), 498–520.

Glaeser, E., W. Kerr, and G. Ponzetto (2010), 'Clusters of Entrepreneurship', *Journal of Urban Economics*, 67 (1), 150–168.

Guiso, Luigi, and Fabiano Schivardi (2011), 'What Determines Entrepreneurial Clusters?' *Journal of the European Economic Association*, 9 (1), 61–86.

Hyytinen, A., and M. Maliranta (2008) 'When Do Employees Leave Their Job for Entrepreneurship?', *Scandinavian Journal of Economics*, 110, 1–21.

Iversen, J., N. Malchow-Møller, and A. Sorensen (2010). 'Returns to Schooling in Self-Employment'. *Economics Letters*, 109 (3), 179–182.

Kambourov, G., and I. Manovskii (2009), 'Occupational Specificity of Human Capital', *International Economic Review*, 50 (1), 63–115.

Kim, Philip H., and Howard E. Aldrich (2005), 'Social Capital and Entrepreneurship'. *Foundations and Trends in Entrepreneurship* and 1 (2), 55–104.

Klyver, Kim, Kevin Hindle, and Thomas Schøtt (2007), 'Who Will Be an Entrepreneur? How Cultural Mechanisms and Social Network Structure Together Influence Entrepreneurial Participation'. *Frontiers of Entrepreneurship Research*, 27 (7), 305–320.

Klepper, S. (2002), 'The Capabilities of New Firms and the Evolution of the US Automobile Industry', *Industrial and Corporate Change*, 11 (4), 645–666.

Koster, S. (2006), *Whose Child?: How Existing Firms Foster New Firm Formation: Individual Start-Ups, Spin-Outs and Spin-Offs* (Doctoral dissertation, University of Groningen).

Koster S. and M. Andersson (2014), *When is your experience valuable? Occupation – industry transitions and self-employment success*. Mimeo, presented at the ERSA-conference 2014 in Saint Petersburg.

Koster, S., and V. A. Venhorst (2014), 'Moving Shop: Residential and Business Relocation by the Highly Educated Self-Employed'. *Spatial Economic Analysis*, 9 (4), 436–464.

Larsson, J. P. (2016), *Det smittsamma entreprenörskapet – från bruksmentalitet till Gnosjöanda*, Regionalpolitiskt Forum Rapport #2, Swedish Entrepreneurship Forum, Stockholm.

Lazear, E. P. (2004), Balanced Skills and Entrepreneurship'. *The American Economic Review*, 94 (2), 208–211.

Lucas Jr, R. E. (1978), 'On the Size Distribution of Business Firms'. *The Bell Journal of Economics*, 508–523.

Lucas, R. E. (1988), 'On the Mechanics of Economic Development'. *Journal of monetary economics*, 22 (1), 3–42.

McCann, P. and R. Ortega-Argiles (2016), 'Smart Specialization, Entrepreneurship and Smes: Issues and Challenges for a Results-Oriented EU Regional Policy', *Small Business Economics*, 46, 537–552.

Minniti, Maria (2005), 'Entrepreneurship and Network Externalities'. *Journal of Economic Behavior and Organization*, 57 (1), 1–27.

Nanda, Ramana, and Jesper B. Sorensen (2010), 'Workplace Peers and Entrepreneurship'. *Management Science*, 56 (7), 1116–1126.

Neffke, F., M. Henning, and R. Boschma (2011), 'How Do Regions Diversify Over Time? Industry Relatedness and the Development of New Growth Paths in Regions'. *Economic Geography*, 87 (3), 237–265.

Partridge, M. D., D. S. Rickman, M. R. Olfert, and K. Ali (2012), 'Dwindling US internal migration: Evidence of Spatial Equilibrium or Structural Shifts in Local Labor Markets?' *Regional Science and Urban Economics*, 42 (1), 375–388.

Romer, P. (1989), 'Endogenous Technological Change' (No. w3210). National Bureau of Economic Research.

Saxenian, AnnaLee (1994), *Regional Advantage: Culture and Competition in Silicon Valley and Route 128*. Cambridge, MA: Harvard University Press.

Schumpeter, J. A. (1912). *Theorie der wirtschaftlichen Entwicklung*. Leipzig: Duncker & Humblot.

Shane, Scott (2003), *A General Theory of Entrepreneurship: The Individual–Opportunity Nexus*. Cheltenham, UK and Northampton, MA: Edward Elgar.

Sorenson, Olav, and Pino G. Audia (2000), 'The Social Structure of Entrepreneurial Activity: Geographic Concentration of Footwear Production in the United States, 1940–1989'. *American Journal of Sociology*, 106 (2), 424–462.

Sørensen, J. B., and D. J. Phillips (2011), 'Competence and Commitment: Employer Size and Entrepreneurial Endurance'. *Industrial and Corporate Change*, 20 (5), 1277–1304.

Venhorst, V., J. Van Dijk, and L. Van Wissen (2011). 'An Analysis of Trends in Spatial Mobility of Dutch Graduates', *Spatial Economic Analysis*, 6 (1), 57–82.

Westlund, Hans, Johan P. Larsson and Amy Rader Olsson (2014), 'Startups and Local Entrepreneurial Social Capital in the Municipalities of Sweden'. *Regional Studies*, 48, 974–994.

Weterings, A., and J. Knoben (2013), 'Footloose: An Analysis of the Drivers of Firm Relocations Over Different Distances'. *Papers in Regional Science*, 92 (4), 791–809.

Williamson, Oliver E. (2000), 'The New Institutional Economics – Taking Stock and Looking Ahead'. *Journal of Economic Literature*, 38 (3), 595–661.

Wixe, S and M. Andersson (2015), 'Which Types of Relatedness Matter in Regional Growth?' *Regional Studies*, X (X), doi:10.1080/00343404.2015.1112369.

5 Regional Innovation and the Network Structure of University–Industry Links

Robert Huggins and Daniel Prokop

5.1 Introduction

In recent years, the emergence of the network paradigm has led to a growing interest and recognition in understanding the influence of network structures in the context of spatial analyses (Balland, 2012; Broekel and Hartog, 2013; Boschma *et al.* 2014), in particular understanding network structures pertaining to knowledge flows and patterns of innovation (Capello and Camilla, 2013; Sebestyén and Varga, 2013). This chapter seeks to build upon this research by exploring the relationship between the structure of the knowledge networks stemming from links between universities and other actors, principally firms. Conceptually, it is situated in a network theory discourse, whereby network structures are considered a means of helping to explain other phenomena (Glückler, 2013), in this case patterns of regional innovation and development.

Based upon an exploratory network analysis of the knowledge-based ties held by universities across the regions of the UK, this chapter seeks to address whether or not it is the structural position of actors within inter-organisational knowledge networks associated with the innovation and economic development performance of the region in which they are geographically situated which matters for development. It further examines and discusses the likely key determinants of the centrality of regions within knowledge networks, as well as extent to which the architecture of regional networks, especially the 'openness' and 'thickness' of network ties, associated with rates of regional innovation are important for regional development. The results of the empirical network analysis are utilised to establish a theoretical model for considering the relationships between regional knowledge network structures and regional innovation.

5.2 Networks and Innovation

This chapter is positioned within the 'capitalisation' of networks discourse, whereby networks are considered to potentially offer benefits to network actors in terms of the resources they are able to access (Glückler, 2013). Specifically, it draws on the notion of network capital, which refers to the value actors gain from the knowledge they are able to access from their networks as a means of innovating and enhancing economic returns (Huggins and Thompson, 2014; 2015). Although much research has concentrated on the capitalisation aspects of networks with regard to the strength of ties, or relational embeddedness, of networks (Rivera *et al.* 2010), the analysis undertaken here is concerned more with the structural embeddedness of ties and the advantages accrued based on the structural position of actors within a knowledge network, or what can be termed their *structural network capital.*

It is generally accepted that the networks underpinning innovation processes allow firms to access knowledge that they do not, or cannot, generate internally based on their own capabilities (Bergenholtz and Waldstrøm, 2011). Knowledge sourcing from external actors has long been acknowledged as a significant factor in successful innovation (Langrish *et al.* 1972; Rothwell *et al.* 1974), with innovation increasingly viewed as a systemic undertaking requiring knowledge sourcing between firms and other actors, i.e. firms are no longer seen to innovate in isolation but through a complex set of interactions with external actors (Roper *et al.* 2008). In particular, firms often utilise considerably more knowledge than that which they have themselves created, and a key reason underlying inter-organisational knowledge flows is the search for 'lacking knowledge' (Storper, 2000).

According to Quatraro (2010), knowledge is the outcome of a combinatorial search activity carried out across a technological space in which combinable elements reside. In this sense, the term network covers a wide range of interactions, and, as noted by Contractor and Lorange (2002), may be either horizontal or vertical. Alongside customers, suppliers, and members of professional networks, other potential actors with which firms may engage in innovation related networks include rival firms, private and public sector knowledge providers, and universities. Inter-organisational networks, therefore, can be defined as consisting of the interactions and relationships which organisations (principally firms) utilise to access knowledge beyond their market relationships (Huggins *et al.* 2012). In other words, these networks consist of the means by which knowledge flows across organisations beyond transactions.

The existence of established knowledge networks has become viewed as one of the most important factors determining why some regions throughout the world have become or remained more competitive than others (Moreno and Miguélez, 2012). In general, modern competitive regional economies exhibit a highly networked regional business culture, rich in 'untraded interdependencies' (Storper 1995; Rutten and Boekema 2007). These networks are important in providing feedback loops between actors and, as a result, perpetuate high levels of innovation among members (Ter Wal and Boschma, 2011).

Although there is a generally accepted view that networks provide the means for knowledge flows, there have been few attempts to incorporate the role of such networks within regional innovation growth models, with the regional growth literature continuing to focus on one-way spillovers of knowledge rather than that flowing in multiple directions through inter-organizational networks. As Asheim and Gertler (2005) indicate, knowledge does not flow uni-directionally, but multi-directionally through networks. It has been suggested that a key determinant of regional innovation differentials is the capability and capacity of firms within regions to establish the network capital required to innovate in an increasingly open environment (Huggins and Thompson, 2014).

Furthermore, competitive regions generally have a higher number of knowledge-based firms as well as higher levels of R&D expenditure, and are typically populated by research intensive universities engaged in world leading research (Howells *et al.* 2012). In contrast, uncompetitive regions tend to be organisationally and institutionally 'thin', with a lack of innovation-driven public or private sector entities, coupled with a high dependence on small and medium enterprises exhibiting low growth trajectories and operating within only fragmented connections to external sources of knowledge (Ponds *et al.* 2007).

5.3 Network Structure and Geography

Our understanding of the performance of organisations, such as firms and universities, has made significant advances in recent years through studies of the networks in which those organisations are embedded. In particular, it has been argued that the network space occupied by actors, defined by the nature of the relationships, interactions and ties, may be equally, if not more important, than the geographic space within which actors are located and interact (Huggins *et al.* 2012). The network space of actors – be it firms or universities – can be usefully analysed by studying their position within a particular network structure through the use of social network analysis techniques. Social network analysis, as developed by sociologists, maintains a key behavioural assumption that any actor typically participates in a network system involving other actors who are significant reference points in decision-making (Knoke and Kuklinski, 1982). The nature of the relationships a given actor has with other system members may, therefore, affect the focal actor's actions. In recent years, social network analysis has been increasingly applied to examinations of the flow of knowledge across organisations and the knowledge networks these organisations utilise to facilitate innovation (Varga and Parag, 2009; Zaheer *et al.* 2010).

There is a growing school of research focused on analysing the impact of knowledge network structures on innovation outcomes (Whittington *et al.* 2009). In particular, research has drawn on network structure conceptions such as 'small worlds', whereby dense clusters of network actors are linked to other clusters via a relatively small number of bridging links (Gulati *et al.* 2012). Similarly, research drawing on Burt's (2005) notion of structural holes, whereby actors who link previously unconnected actors within a network are considered to occupy privileged and central positions, has been applied to innovation studies (Zaheer and Soda, 2009). These studies all tend to identify network actor centrality as a determinant of innovation outcomes, as well as the extent to which actors are embedded within either closed or open network structures (Cassi and Plunket, 2013). The vast majority of research, however, has focused on innovation returns for particular firms and organisations, rather than the regions in which they are located. The notable exception here is Fleming *et al.*'s (2007) study that found some evidence of an association between network structure and regional innovation productivity. Despite this, there is still little known with regard to the association between network and geographic spaces (Boschma and Frenken, 2010).

Some scholarly research suggests that the nature of networks is related to underlying patterns of knowledge flows (Clifton *et al.* 2010). The position of an actor within networks is found to be correlated with relative power, which refers to a set of resources that an actor (could) mobilise through its existing set of relationships, in this case: knowledge (Ahuja *et al.* 2012). At the individual level, these resources are usually considered to take the form of social capital, consisting of the benefits accruing from interpersonal networks (Coleman, 1988; Putnam, 2000).

Alongside the importance of the structural position of an actor with a network, its spatial and geographic position clearly remains of considerable relevance in terms of understanding patterns of regional innovation. Indeed, in debates concerning inter-organisational networks, the roles of space are recognised as increasingly important features of network structure and operation (Molina-Morales and Expósito-Langa, 2012). A key feature of this discourse has long concerned the role of networks of spatially proximate and co-located external organisations, such as universities, R&D labs, and other firms or individuals, within the innovation process (Mattes, 2012).

Implicit in the argument stemming from observations of advanced regional economies is that the skills gained through local interactions in such knowledge-rich environments better prepare firms for obtaining knowledge from distant sources, allowing them to benefit more from overseas knowledge (Ter Wal and Boschma, 2011). Indeed, alongside the recognised role of spatial proximity to network development, there is an increasing emphasis on the importance of understanding networks and knowledge flows in an environment that is simultaneously intra and inter-regional (D'Este *et al.* 2013). In general, the constraining effect of distance on knowledge flow and transfer is considered by some to be gradually diminishing, and there is increasing evidence of the heightened role being played by non-local knowledge sourcing networks in many places across the globe (Saxenian, 2005). Many firms do not acquire their knowledge from within geographically proximate areas, particularly those firms based upon innovation-driven growth where knowledge is often sourced extra-regionally (Davenport, 2005). If applicable knowledge is available locally, firms and other organisations will attempt to source it; if not they will look elsewhere (Drejer and Lund Vinding, 2007).

The key aspect of these developments is that the knowledge base of the world's most advanced local and regional economies is no longer necessarily local, but also positioned within more global knowledge networks (Fitjar and Rodríguez-Pose, 2011). There is also a growing school of thought that non-proximate actors are often equally, if not better, able to transfer strategically relevant and valuable knowledge across such spatial boundaries providing a high performing network structure is in place (Torré, 2008).

The differing spatial dynamics of knowledge sourcing activity therefore suggests that there is potentially some interdependency between intra and inter-regional networks. In particular, successful connectivity in global spaces is often considered to be the outcome of an initial system of localised interaction, whereby it is the knowledge crossing hallways and streets that initially catalyses intellectual exchange and knowledge transfer across oceans and continents (Glaeser *et al*. 1992). This phased transition is necessitated by the risk of firms becoming rigid and outdated when local networks fail to keep abreast of knowledge emerging outside of their respective region (Bathelt *et al*. 2004). However, not all firms may participate in the transition from local to extra-regional interactions. Whereas firms with less resources and lower absorptive capacity (Cohen and Levinthal, 1990) may tend to continue to network mainly locally, those with greater resources and higher absorptive capacity are likely to be more connected to inter-regional networks (Drejer and Lund Vinding, 2007). Indeed, emerging research suggests that differences in regional growth rates can be explained by differences in knowledge accessibility within and across regions (Andersson and Karlsson, 2007). This has led some to question the view that knowledge transfer is confined to local milieux, arguing that firms source knowledge from selected providers located outside the local milieu by investing in the building of new channels of communication (Fitjar and Rodriguez-Pose, 2011).

5.4 University–Industry Links and Knowledge Networks

Universities are increasingly portrayed as core knowledge-producing entities that can play an enhanced role in driving innovation and development processes by providing knowledge for business and industry (Huggins *et al*. 2008). Rather than just the knowledge possessed or generated by individual firms and organisations, knowledge sourced from external providers such as universities is considered to be a key factor within modern innovation processes and the formulation of innovation systems (Lawton Smith and Bagchi-Sen 2006).

Firms making the best use of the academic knowledge created within universities form an important element of well-functioning knowledge networks, which to a large extent drive development and prosperity (Fritsch and Slavtchev, 2008). Intense interactions between universities and external organisations are clearly not confined to one single type of organisation, but may span a number of actors and processes (Huggins *et al*. 2008), and the utilisation of university knowledge is likely to be influenced by the characteristics of firms such as size and sector (Santoro and Chakrabarti, 2002; Schartinger *et al*. 2002).

Extant research on university–industry ties has produced some evidence suggesting that the co-location of research intensive firms and universities in the same region facilitates interactions leading to innovative collaboration (D'Este *et al*. 2013). Given the current evidence base, it can be suggested that universities located in core regions with greater pools of large R&D-intensive firms may have better opportunities to forge links with large R&D players than their counterparts in more peripheral regions (Crescenzi *et al*. 2013).

Successful and competitive regional economies are typically populated by research-intensive universities engaged in world-leading research (Lawton Smith *et al.* 2014). Often these universities play an important role in a region's innovation and competitiveness culture, for example Cambridge University and the biotechnology and IT clusters in the local area (Hughes and Kitson, 2012) and Stanford University within Silicon Valley (Saxenian 1994). Whilst a world-leading research-intensive university does not necessarily create a high-technology economy (Feldman and Desrochers 2003), universities undertaking world-leading research in competitive regions are also more likely to be members of national or global knowledge pipelines (Bathelt *et al.* 2004).

The discourse on the role of universities as knowledge transfer institutions and key nodes in regional innovation systems is largely reliant on empirical work from exemplar regions; that is, those regions which are among the most competitive in the world in terms of economic growth rates, workforce qualifications and the number of large, international firms based in new or high-technology sectors (Garnsey and Heffernan 2005). However, for every successful region, there exist many more 'ordinary' and uncompetitive regions (Doloreux and Dionne 2008).

Rising levels of national and transnational academic–industry partnerships demonstrate that neither firms nor universities consider knowledge flows to be necessarily spatially constrained (Varga and Parag, 2009). The increased reliance on wider spatial knowledge pipelines is reflected by the growing number of firms choosing to work with the best universities regardless of location in order to take advantage of high talent pools, favourable intellectual property rules and government incentives for joint industry-university research (D'Este *et al.* 2013).

There are often considerable differences in the capability of universities to effectively transfer their knowledge, and of firms to effectively absorb such knowledge (Hewitt-Dundas, 2011; 2013; Huggins and Kitagawa, 2012). The quality and characteristics of university knowledge transfer practices and activities will necessarily be a determining factor of outputs. In the first instance, the knowledge creation capability of a university will be required to be of a quality and type that lends itself to potential transfer (Ponds *et al.* 2010). Furthermore, the capacity to effectively engage in knowledge transfer forms part of the wider capabilities of the institution, as well as the capabilities of respective knowledge or technology transfer offices (Chapple *et al.* 2005). External networking capability may also rely on the prestige and reputation of the institution (Shane and Cable, 2002). More established universities tend to be more research focused, especially in a UK context, and may have a greater attraction for external organisations looking to exploit the knowledge generated by this research for commercial purposes, with newer universities often being weaker in terms of research output (Wellings, 2008).

Finally, larger and smaller firms may both utilise knowledge generated within universities for innovation, but in smaller firms this knowledge may be of greater importance due to the fact they possess fewer knowledge resources internally (Acs *et al.* 1994). However, larger firms are likely to possess more resources – in the form of human, research and financial capital – as well the capability to engage in wider spatial knowledge networks. Therefore, intense interactions with larger organisations, which are not always spatially proximate to the universities with which they interact, are likely to be of greater benefit and value to universities.

5.5 Methodology

Empirically, the network analysis presented in following sections is based upon links between universities and firms and other organisations within and across the regions of the UK. In this case, the 'region' is taken to be one of the 12 UK NUTS 1 regions of the UK. According to the UK Competitiveness Index (Huggins 2003; Huggins and Thompson 2013), of these 12 regions, the most competitive regions of the UK consist of Eastern England, London and South East England, as these are the only ones performing above the UK average in terms of a broad number of economic indicators, such as gross value added per capita, productivity, R&D expenditure and unemployment. The remaining nine regions are classed as relatively 'uncompetitive' as they lag behind the UK average in terms of the same economic indicators, as well as knowledge-based indicators such as innovation, patenting and densities of knowledge-intensive firms.

Table 5.1 confirms that GVA per capita is highest in the most competitive regions. Also, it shows that based on the European Union's Summary Regional Innovation Index (Hollanders *et al.* 2014), the most competitive regions are generally also the most innovative. It is the association between the pattern of regional innovation and network structure that is the basis for the empirical analysis. At the time when the data for the study was collected there were 158 universities across the UK, with approximately one quarter of these located in London. South East England has the second highest number of institutions, followed by Scotland and North West England (Table 5.1).

The analysis is based on data concerning the interaction between firms and universities in the UK via knowledge transfer activities in the form of

Table 5.1 Summary Regional Innovation Index (2014), Gross Value Added (GVA) per capita and number of Universities by region

Region	Summary Regional Innovation Index 2014	Rank (Regional Innovation)	GVA per Head 2012 (£)	Rank (GVA per Head)	Number of Universities
East Midlands	0.45	6	17,448	8	9
East of England	0.54	1	19,658	4	9
London	0.47	4	37,232	1	39
North East	0.43	8	16,091	11	5
North West	0.46	5	18,438	6	14
Northern Ireland	0.37	12	16,127	10	2
Scotland	0.45	7	20,013	3	15
South East	0.53	2	23,221	2	17
South West	0.48	3	19,023	5	13
Wales	0.42	10	15,401	12	12
West Midlands	0.43	9	17,429	9	12
Yorkshire and The Humber	0.41	11	17,556	7	11

collaborative research, contract research and consultancy. Using social network analysis, it produces a range of network graphs as well as calculating the *betweenness* centrality of actors, which is generally considered to be one of the most robust measures of central positioning and attempts to quantify the *importance* or *prominence* of an individual actor in a network (Borgatti, 2005; Everett and Borgatti, 2005).

Overall, 137 of UK's universities were identified as having at least one tie with a firm or other organisation involving one or more of the forms of interaction indicated above. In total, 8,479 organisations were identified, with the large majority (86.5%) concerning private sectors firms. A further 5.1% of organisations are government establishments (principally, departments, agencies, executives, councils, the police force, and the National Health Service), and another 8.4% social enterprises, non-for-profit concerns and charities (within the analysis non-private sector firms are referred to as 'other organisations'). Across the private sector 7,334 establishments are represented, covering 8,335 links, with the majority of the firms being small in size (61.2%). A further 1,567 links are identified for the other organisations with which universities interact, resulting in the network as a whole consisting of a total of 9,902 links. As may be expected, a significant proportion of the links with other organisations (31.2%) concern those located in London, with the South East, South West and Scotland having the next highest number of representative organisations.

5.6 Network Structure and Centrality

Figure 5.1 presents the network as a whole, with the black nodes representing university actors and the grey nodes firms and other organisations. It is clear that there a number of universities that occupy highly central positions within the network, based on their links with a number of firms and other organisations that are themselves in positions of high centrality. Beyond this, the network forms a structure of loose concentricity as universities, firms and other organisations more relationally distant from the centre of the network are generally less connected to the network. In order to assess in more detail the key actors at the centre of the network, Figure 5.2 presents an illustration of the core sub-network, highlighting the principal universities and firms constituting the network, in particular those with the highest betweenness centrality.

From the university perspective, those actors at the centre of the network are the University of Cambridge (betweenness centrality (BC) score = 0.18), University College London (BC = 0.12), Imperial College London (BC = 0.10), the University of Birmingham BC = 0.10, and the University of Bath (BC = 0.08). These universities also represent leading and highly research-focused institutions, with an onus on high rates of knowledge creation and production (Huggins and Johnston, 2009). In this case, it is noticeable that the University of Cambridge possesses a considerably more influential and central position within the network than all the other universities represented. Furthermore, the most established universities (those institutions existing as universities prior to 1992) have, on average,

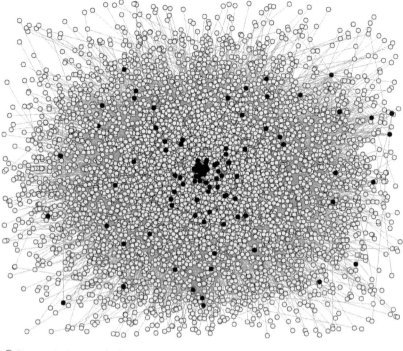

○ Firms and other organisations

● Universities

Figure 5.1 University links with firms and other organisations – the full network.

a betweenness centrality score that is 3.7 times higher than those institutions that were granted university status in the post-1992 period.

From the perspective of firms within the network, the most influential actor is Rolls-Royce (BC = 0.066), followed by GlaxoSmithKline (BC = 0.045), BP (BC = 0.031), BAE Systems (BC = 0.030), BT (BC = 0.030), and Pfizer (BC = 0.029). In general, these firms consist of large establishments that are amongst the UK's most R&D-intensive private sector companies (BIS, 2010). Along with the universities with the highest betweenness centrality, these firms are at the top of the hierarchy of the ecology of the network, and through their structurally central position they are the most important bridging and connecting agents of the knowledge flowing through the network.

In general, across the firms represented in the network the betweenness centrality of large firms is more than fifteen times higher than that of small firms and more five times higher than that of medium sized firms. This indicates that more established and economically significant firms are likely to hold more central positions within the network. Furthermore, on average, firms operating in the following industries are found to possess the highest rates of betweenness

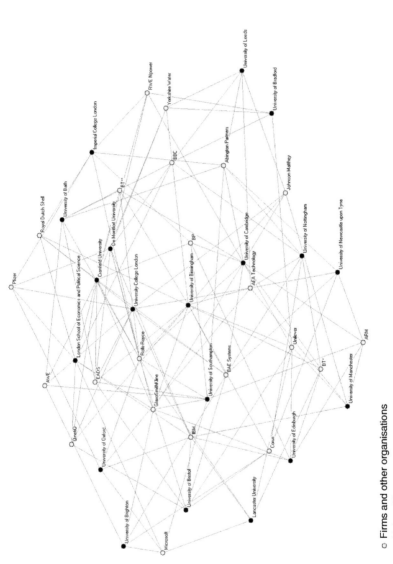

○ Firms and other organisations

● Universities

Figure 5.2 University links with firms and other organisations – the core sub-network.

centrality: the manufacture of transport equipment; the manufacture of chemicals and fuels; electricity, gas and water supply, and recycling; the manufacture of machinery and equipment. This indicates that knowledge relating to innovation within these sectors forms an important component of the flow of knowledge across the network.

In Figures 5.3–5.5 the regional structure of the networks is illustrated from the perspective of the links possessed by the firms and organisations located in each region. The regions have been grouped to represent to their regional innovation ranking based on the European Union's Regional Innovation Index (Hollanders *et al.* 2014). Therefore, Figure 5.3 illustrates the networks of the four highest ranked regions, termed here as the 'leading regions', Figure 5.4 depicts the four middle ranked regions, termed 'moderate regions', and Figure 5.5 illustrates the bottom four regions, termed 'lagging regions'. In each of the illustrations, the light grey nodes represent firms and organisations located in the regions, the dark

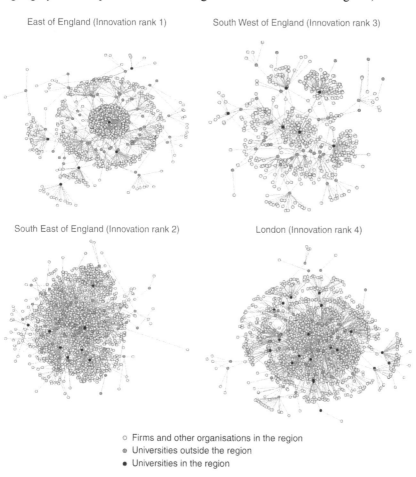

Figure 5.3 Networks of firms and organisations in leading innovation regions.

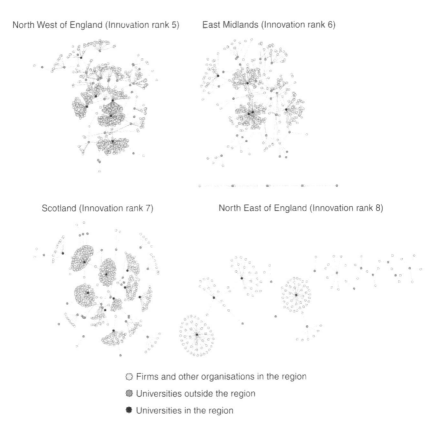

North West of England (Innovation rank 5)   East Midlands (Innovation rank 6)

Scotland (Innovation rank 7)   North East of England (Innovation rank 8)

○ Firms and other organisations in the region
◉ Universities outside the region
● Universities in the region

Figure 5.4 Networks of firms and organisations in moderate innovation regions.

grey nodes represent universities located outside the region, and the black nodes represent university actors located within the region.

Among the four leading regions, the network structure of firms and organisations located in the South East is the thickest, possessing the most aggregate links overall, and with links with universities across regions. It is quite tightly clustered with the edge of network having few connections with other clusters. The network created by firms and organisations in London is similarly tightly clustered, but in this case a number of bridging connections with other sub-clusters are more noticeable involving both local and non-local universities. In the South West the network is largely polycentric in its formation, possessing a number of clusters largely anchored around local universities. Importantly, in all cases there are actors, both universities and firms that bridge connections across these clusters.

The network in the East of England resembles a hub and spoke configuration, with a dense cluster of firms and organisation connected to the University of Cambridge. However, this cluster is itself linked to range of other clusters. Interestingly, firms in these four leading regions have by far the highest proportion of ties with

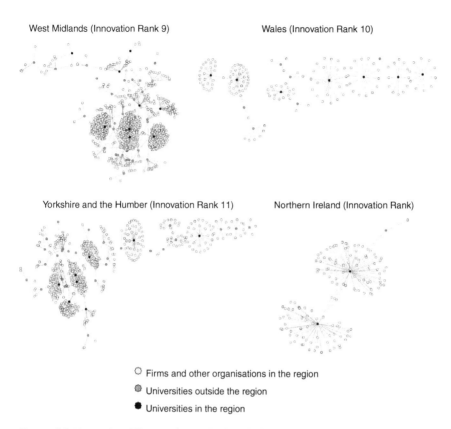

Figure 5.5 Networks of firms and organisations in lagging innovation regions.

universities outside their respective region, which indicates that they tend to be more strongly engaged within boundary spanning inter-regional networks.

As can be seen by Figure 5.4, the networks firms and organisations in regions ranked as moderate in terms of innovation tend to relatively less concentrated than those in leading innovation regions. Also, although there are a significant number of firms and organisations in both the North West and Scotland linked to universities, these linkages tend to be more with local universities than is the case for the networks in the leading innovation regions. In the case of the North West, the network is clearly highly fragmented lacking in a concentration of actors or connectivity across them. Interestingly, as shown by Figure 5.5, whilst the networks in Wales and Northern Ireland are similarly fragmented to that found in the North East, the networks for firms and organisations in the West Midlands and Yorkshire and the Humber appear to possess traits that belie their lowly innovation ranking. In general, however, firms in the moderate and lagging regions tend be more biased toward intra-regional ties, as opposed to the high proportion of inter-regional ties held by firms in leading regions, indicating more spatially closed network structures.

Table 5.2 Index of betweenness centrality of firms by region

Region	Index of Betweenness Centrality of Firms by Region	Rank
East Midlands	52.4	7
East of England	103.2	4
London	264.7	1
North East	24.2	11
North West	48.1	8
Northern Ireland	36.8	10
Scotland	43.6	9
South East	110.2	3
South West	113.0	2
Wales	18.8	12
West Midlands	68.3	5
Yorkshire and the Humber	56.4	6
Mean Average	100.0	

In order to analyse in more detail, the structure and rates of connectivity of firms in each of the regions, Table 5.2 presents an index of the mean average betweenness centrality of regional firm centrality. On average, firms in London possess the most influential positions within the network, with an average betweenness centrality that it is more than twice that of all firms in the network. With the South West, South East and the East of England ranking second, third and fourth, respectively, there appears to be a degree of correspondence with regional innovation rates, with these regions also constituting the top ranked UK regions on the European Union's Regional Innovation Index (Hollanders *et al.* 2014). Unsurprisingly, firms in Wales, the North East and Northern Ireland have the lowest rates of betweenness centrality.

In overall terms there is a positive relationship between innovation rates across regions and the betweenness centrality of firms within these regions, with the relationship generating a Spearman's correlation coefficient of 0.68 (p-value = 0.02). Similarly, there is a positive relationship between average firm level betweenness centrality across regions and regional Gross Value Added per capita. Indeed, the relationship is rather stronger in this case, with a Spearman's correlation coefficient of 0.76 (p-value = 0.004).

5.7 Regional Boundary Spanning

The analysis has so far concentrated on analysing the network as a whole. However, given the increasing interest in understanding the role of flows of knowledge across regions as a driver of regional innovation, it is instructive to focus attention specifically on the network formed solely by ties across regions. Therefore, in this section the analysis isolates these links to form an inter-regional network structure. This network covers 134 universities and 3,767 firms and organisations, with the core actors in the network shown in Figure 5.6. These

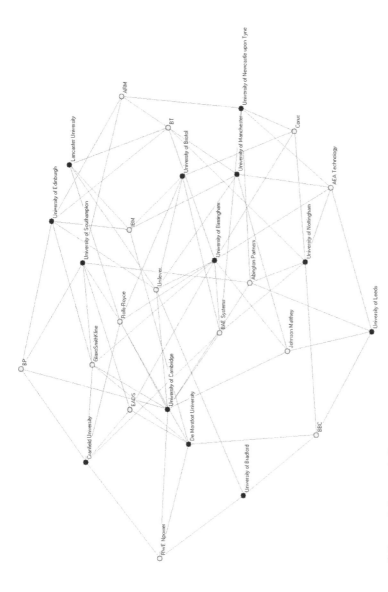

Firms and other organisations
Universities

Figure 5.6 University links with firms and other organisations – the inter-regional core sub-network.

actors can be considered to be the key boundary spanners that bridge and connect flows of knowledge across regions. As with the overall core network they consist mainly of large R&D-intensive firm, often multinationals, and research intensive universities. In particular, it is leading firms such as Rolls-Royce, BAE Systems, GlaxoSmithKline, Pfizer, Unilever, EADS and BT that occupy the most preferential and boundary spanning positions across the network. This suggests that those regions which are locations for these firms not only benefit from the innovation they generate, but also the flow of knowledge they are able to access to manage across other firms and universities.

Aggregating the betweenness centrality scores for firms based on their cross-regional links, an index of the inter-regional between centrality of firms can be constructed as shown by Table 5.3. On average, firms in London have a betweenness centrality score more than twice the average, highlighting the important boundary spanning position held by these firms. Furthermore, firms in the South West, South East and East of England are generally in significantly more influential bridging and brokering positions than firms in other regions, with the obvious exception of London. Firms in weaker regions on the other hand, in particular, the North East, Wales, and Northern Ireland, tend to be relatively isolated from these inter-regional flows of knowledge and the benefits to innovation they are likely to facilitate.

Again, there is a significant positive relationship between innovation rates across regions and the inter-regional betweenness centrality of firms within these regions, with the relationship generating a Spearman's correlation coefficient of 0.68 (p-value = 0.02), which is in line with the overall regional betweenness centrality and innovation relationship found above. However, in the case of inter-regional betweenness centrality across regions and Gross Value Added per capita, the relationship is again stronger, with a Spearman's correlation coefficient

Table 5.3 Index of inter-regional betweenness centrality of firms by region

Region	Index of Inter-Regional Betweenness Centrality of Firms by Region	Rank
East Midlands	37.1	9
East of England	95.9	4
London	211.9	1
North East	14.9	12
North West	43.2	8
Northern Ireland	29.6	10
Scotland	55.4	6
South East	103.4	3
South West	146.4	2
Wales	22.4	11
West Midlands	56.6	5
Yorkshire and the Humber	47.9	7
Total	100.0	

of 0.85 (*p*-value = 0.0004). This suggests that regional economic development may be somewhat more related to the knowledge flowing through inter-regional interactions than those bound within the spatial confines of a region.

5.8 A Network Structure Model of Regional Innovation

The preceding analysis and mapping has sought to overlay a spatial element, in the form of regions, on to the network structure formed from the knowledge-based links between universities and other actors, principally firms. Although this network structure cannot be considered to constitute a complete knowledge network it does compose a key segment, as well as being an indicative illustration of concepts such as innovation systems. The aim of the analysis and mapping is to ascertain whether or not the position of actors within this knowledge network is associated with the rate of innovation, and economic development, of the region in which network actors are spatially located. In other words, is network position related to spatial position? Although the analysis is limited to the extent that it covers only twelve regional observations at one point in time, it does provide a number of insights that allows the generation of a range of propositions relating to the role of network actor positioning and regional innovation. In particular, the analysis strongly suggests that more innovative and economically developed regions are more likely to have a higher proportion of actors holding highly central and influential positions within the knowledge network architecture, which leads the first proposition:

> Proposition 1: Knowledge network structures are an important indicator of regional innovation capacity and capability.

This proposed link between network structure and regional innovation supports the work of others (Fleming *et al.* 2007; Broekel and Hartog, 2013; Sebestyén and Varga, 2013), as well as indicating that within the network capital conceptual framework the structural tie component of such capital is likely to be as, if not more, important than the tie strength component. Of course, the underlying question stemming from this is: what causes some regions to have a higher proportion of actors with central, rather than peripheral, positions within the network? From the perspective of firms, the analysis indicates that economic and industrial structure plays a leading role. It is clear that the majority of the central positions within the network are occupied by highly R&D-intensive establishments, especially multinational concerns. Similarly, those universities at the centre of the network tend to be leading research-facing institutions with a high propensity for external knowledge-based interaction. Therefore, the existing knowledge stock of firms and other organisations in a region is likely to be an important factor impacting upon the centrality that a region as whole holds within the network:

> Proposition 2: The existing knowledge-base and economic structure of a region will be a key determinant of the centrality of the region as a whole within a knowledge network.

The analysis has shown that whilst local intra-regional interactions account for a significant proportion of links, it is the extent of the non-local inter-regional ties that appears to allow some actors to occupy more central positions than others. In general, actors with more inter-regional ties tend to be more centrally positioned. These actors often act as bridges between particular clusters within the network, and are well-positioned to manage and influence knowledge flows, and presumably to maintain high rates of innovation within their organisation. This echoes the findings of studies that have found a significant association between network structure and organisation-level rates of innovation (Whittington *et al.* 2009):

> Proposition 3: Network actors with a high propensity to engage in interactions with actors in other regions are more likely to hold central positions within a knowledge network.

> Proposition 4: Actors occupying highly central positions within a knowledge network are likely to enjoy higher rates of innovation.

From the perspective of regions and their performance, it appears to be the case that those regions with a high proportion of actors engaged in inter-regional interactions are likely to be significantly more innovation than those with a bias toward local level ties. This indicates the importance of these actors as boundary spanning and bridging agents (Cassi and Plunket, 2013), with them being at the heart of a wide spatially configured network architecture. Therefore, those regions with open and porous regional innovation systems are significantly more likely to have higher rates of innovation capability and capacity. This is an important insight to the extent that it adds weight to the argument that spatially unbounded knowledge networks and innovation systems are an increasingly important element of routes to achieving regional competitive advantage (Torré, 2008; Huggins and Thompson, 2014):

> Proposition 5: Regions with a spatially open network architecture are likely to be more innovative.

These proposed links between the knowledge-base of a region, its position within a knowledge network structure, and subsequent rates of innovation are illustrated by Figure 5.7. Furthermore, it appears that regional rates of innovation and are significantly related to overall regional economic performance. Therefore, it is important to acknowledge the cumulative and agglomerative nature of this process. In particular, as network structure influences rates of regional innovation and economic development, this is likely to make a region a more or less attractive spatial location for firms and other organisations. This ability to attract, retain and grow new organisations will itself influence the regional knowledge base and stock, which highlighted by the feedback mechanism shown in Figure 5.7:

> Proposition 6: Innovative regions will attract, retain and grow more organisations, increasing the stock of regional knowledge.

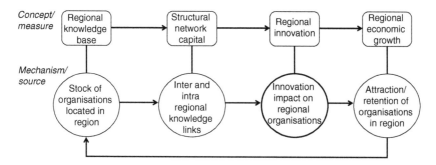

Figure 5.7 Network structure and regional innovation – a theoretical model.

5.9 Policy Implications and Conclusions

This chapter raises some important considerations for policymaking. As well as reinforcing existing messages regarding the importance regional innovation policymaking should give to network and interaction-building that goes beyond the notion of 'regional' cluster and 'regional' innovation system formulation (Ponds *et al.* 2007, 2010; Vittoria and Lavadera, 2014), the chapter suggests that regional policymakers would be well-served by having access to more intelligence as to which actors in their region occupy the most central and prominent structural position within knowledge networks. This may better facilitate the formulation of strategies that identify and utilise these actors as key network nodes in establishing more open regional innovation systems.

The results also indicate potential challenges and changes of direction for regional innovation policy in moving forward. Much regional innovation policy has principally focused on the mobilisation of entrepreneurial and start-up actors as a feature of network development policies, with the implicit assumption being that larger and more established firms can 'look after themselves' (Huggins and Thompson, 2015). Although this may be the case, it does lead to a situation whereby the role of larger and often the most knowledge-based firms are overlooked by cluster and innovation ecosystem development policies and the like. Given the role of these actors as being key bridging and boundary-spanning agents within and across networks, following the connectivity and embeddedness arguments in smart specialisation it can be argued that policymakers need to integrate them further into their smart specialisation strategies. Although it is potentially easier for policy to engage more directly with smaller concerns, given that they are likely to have both more transparent problems that require addressing and a more transparent point-of-entry for policymakers, future policy is likely be well-served by devoting adequate resources to engaging with seemingly 'regionally autonomous' larger firms.

Furthermore, the study draws attention to a range of issues relating to the role of universities in regional innovation and economic development strategies. In particular, it makes clear that many universities, especially research-leading institutions, are to a large extent geographically indiscriminate in terms of the actors with which they form networks. Also, a bias towards local ties appears to be an indicator of relatively weak regional innovation performance. Therefore, regionally policymakers should not blindly pursue the notion that regionally based knowledge transfer programmes represent a desirable, or even an effective, means for matching the demand for and supply of knowledge for innovation.

It should be noted that this study is not without its limitations, but hopefully forms the basis for further research that seeks to fill some of the gaps it leaves. Clearly, its focus only on university knowledge-based links presents a partial network structure, which should ideally be complemented by the range of firm-to-firm and university-to-university links that are likely to exist. However, it could be speculated that adding these links would have the effect of widening the gap between those firms and universities with the highest and lowest centrality. For instance, if firm-to-firm links based on joint ventures, strategic alliances and co-patenting activity were to be added, it is the larger more R&D-intensive firms that are most likely to be engaged in these activities, strengthening their centrality at the expense of those firms already occupying more peripheral positions within the network. Also, an indirect effect of adding these links would be to improve the centrality of those universities with links to these firms. A similar effect is also likely to occur if university-to-university links based on jointly funded projects, initiatives and agreements were to be added.

Finally, the nature of the data and the relatively small number of regional observations limit the capability to undertake multivariate analysis and to more empirically unpick issues relating to causality. In particular, the focus of the analysis on the more codified forms of knowledge flow necessitates an analysis that principally refers to innovation that is largely aligned to the STI mode, and it may well be that analyses that are also able to map DUI-related interactions would produce somewhat different findings. Nevertheless, as more complete data sets that go beyond the traditional reliance on co-invention, co-patenting and co-publication data emerge, richer network theories of regional innovation and development should be forthcoming.

References

Acs, Z., Audretsch, D. B. and Feldman, M. P. (1994). R&D spillovers and recipient firm size, *Review of Economics and Statistics*, 76 (2), 336–340.

Ahuja, G., Soda, G. and Zaheer, A. (2012). The genesis and dynamics of organizational networks, *Organization Science*, 23 (2), 434–448.

Andersson, M. and Karlsson, C. (2007). Knowledge in regional economic growth: the role of knowledge accessibility, *Industry and Innovation*, 14, 129–149.

Asheim, B. and Gertler M. (2005). The geography of innovation: Regional innovation systems. In T*he Oxford Handbook of Innovation*, Fagerberg J, Mowery DC, Nelson RR (eds). Oxford: Oxford University Press.

Balland P.-A. (2012). Proximity and the evolution of collaboration networks: evidence from research and development projects within the Global Navigation Satellite System (GNSS) industry, *Regional Studies*, 46, 741–756.

Bathelt, H. Malmberg, A. and Maskell, P. (2004). Clusters and knowledge: Local buzz, global pipelines and the process of knowledge creation, *Progress in Human Geography*, 28, 31–56.

Bergenholtz, C. and Waldstrøm, C. (2011). Inter-organizational network studies: A literature review, *Industry and Innovation*, 18, 539–562.

Borgatti, S. P. (2005). Centrality and network flow. *Social Networks*, 27 (1), 55–71.

Boschma, R. and Frenken, K. (2010). The spatial evolution of innovation networks. A proximity perspective. In R. Boschma and R. Martin (eds) *The Handbook of Evolutionary Economic Geography* (pp. 120–135). Cheltenham: Edward Elgar.

Boschma, R., Balland, P. A. and de Vaan, M. (2014). The formation of economic networks: a proximity approach, in Torré, A. and Wallet, F. (eds) *Regional Development and Proximity Relations*, Cheltenham: Edward Elgar.

Broekel, T. and Hartog, M. (2013). Explaining the structure of inter-organizational networks using exponential random graph models. *Industry and Innovation*, 20 (3), 277–295.

Burt, R. S. (2005). *Brokerage and Closure: An Introduction to Social Capital*. Oxford: Oxford University Press.

Capello, R. and Camilla, L. (2013). Territorial patterns of innovation and economic growth in European Regions. *Growth and Change*, 44, 195–227.

Cassi, L., and Plunket, A. (2013). Research collaboration in co-inventor networks: combining closure, bridging and proximities. *Regional Studies*, (ahead-of-print), 1–19.

Chapple, W., Lockett, A., Siegel, D. S. and Wright, M. (2005). Assessing the relative performance of UK technology transfer offices: Parametric and non-parametric evidence. *Research Policy*, 34 (3), 369–84.

Clifton, N., Pickernell, D., Keast, R. and Senior, M. (2010). Network structure, knowledge governance and firm performance: Evidence from innovation networks and SMEs in the UK, *Growth and Change*, 41 (3), 337–373.

Cohen, W. M. and Levinthal, D. A. (1990). Absorptive capacity: A new perspective on learning and innovation, *Administrative Science Quarterly*, 35, 128–152.

Coleman, J. S. (1988). Social capital in the creation of human capital, *American Journal of Sociology* 94 (Supplement), S95–S120.

Contractor, F. and Lorange, P. (2002). The growth of alliances in the knowledge-based economy, *International Business Review*, 11 (4), 485–505.

Crescenzi R., Pietrobelli C. and Rabellotti R., (2013). Innovation drivers, value chains and the geography of multinational corporations in Europe, *Journal of Economic Geography*, doi:10.1093/jeg/lbt01.

Davenport, S. (2005). Exploring the role of proximity in SME knowledge-acquisition, *Research Policy*, 34, 683–701.

D'Este, P., Guy, F. and Iammarino, S. (2013). Shaping the formation of university–industry research collaborations: What type of proximity does really matter? *Journal of Economic Geography*, 13 (4), 537–558.

Doloreux, D. and Dionne, S. (2008). Is regional innovation system development possible in peripheral regions? Some evidence from the case of La Pocatière, Canada. *Entrepreneurship and Regional Development*, 20, 259–283

Drejer, I. and Lund Vinding, A. (2007). Searching near and far: determinants of innovative firms' propensity to collaborate across geographical distance, *Industry and Innovation*, 14, 259–275.

Everett, M. and Borgatti, S. P. (2005). Ego network betweenness. *Social Networks*, 27 (1), 31–38.

Feldman, M. P. and Desrochers, P. (2003). Research universities and local economic development: Lessons from the history of the John Hopkins University. *Industry and Innovation*, 10 (1), 5–24.

Fitjar, R. D. and Rodriguez-Pose, A. (2011). When local interaction does not suffice: Sources of firm innovation in urban Norway, *Environment and Planning A*, 43, 1248–1267.

Fleming, L., King, C. and Juda, A. I. (2007). Small worlds and regional innovation, *Organization Science*, 18, 938–954.

Fritsch, M. and Slavtchev, V. (2007). Universities and innovation in space. *Industry and Innovation*, 14, 201–218.

Garnsey, E. and Heffernan, P. (2005). High-technology clustering through spin-out and attraction: The Cambridge case, *Regional Studies*, 39, 1127–1144.

Glaeser, E. L., Kallal, H. D., Scheinkman, J. A. and Shleifer, A. (1992). Growth in cities, *Journal of Political Economy*, 100 (6), 1126–1152.

Glückler, J. (2013). Knowledge, networks and space: connectivity and the problem of non-interactive learning. *Regional Studies*, 47 (6), 880–894.

Gulati, R., Sytch, M. and Tatarynowicz, A. (2012). The rise and fall of small worlds: Exploring the dynamics of social structure. *Organization Science*, 23 (2), 449–471.

Hewitt-Dundas, N. (2011). Research intensity and knowledge transfer activity in UK universities, *Research Policy*, 41 (2), 262–275.

Hewitt-Dundas, N. (2013). The role of proximity in university–business cooperation for innovation, *Journal of Technology Transfer*, 38 (2), 93–115.

Hollanders, H., Es-Sadki, N., Buligescu, B., Rivera Leon, L., Griniece, E. and Roman, L. (2014). *Regional Innovation Scoreboard* 2014, Brussels: European Commission.

Howells, J. (2005). Innovation and regional economic development: A matter of perspective? *Research Policy*, 34 (8), 1220–1234.

Howells, J., Ramlogan, R., and Cheng, S. (2012). Innovation and university collaboration: paradox and complexity within the knowledge economy, *Cambridge Journal of Economics*, 36 (3), 703–721.

Huggins, R. and Johnston, A. (2009). Knowledge networks in an uncompetitive region: SME innovation and growth. *Growth and Change*, 40 (2), 227–259.

Huggins, R. (2003). Creating a UK competitiveness index: Regional and local benchmarking. *Regional Studies*, 37 (1), 89–96.

Huggins, R. and Kitagawa, F. (2012). Regional policy and university knowledge transfer: Perspectives from devolved regions in the UK, *Regional Studies*, 46 (6), 817–832.

Huggins, R. and Thompson, P. (2013). Competitiveness and the post-regional political economy. *Local Economy*, 28 (7–8), 884–893.

Huggins, R. and Thompson, P. (2014). A Network-based view of regional growth, *Journal of Economic Geography*, 14 (3), 511–545.

Huggins, R. and Thompson, P. (2015). Entrepreneurship, innovation and regional growth: A network theory. *Small Business Economics*, 45 (1), 103–128.

Huggins, R., Johnston, A. and Steffenson, R. (2008). Universities, knowledge networks and regional policy. *Cambridge Journal of Regions, Economy and Society*, 2 (1), 321–340.

Huggins, R., Thompson, P. and Johnston, A. (2012). Network capital, social capital, and knowledge flow: How the nature of inter-organisational networks impacts on innovation, *Industry and Innovation*, 19 (3), 203–232.

Hughes, A. and Kitson, M. (2012). Pathways to impact and the strategic role of universities: New evidence on the breadth and depth of university knowledge exchange in the

UK and the factors constraining its development, *Cambridge Journal of Economics*, 36 (3), 723–750.

Knoke, D. and Kuklinski, J. (1982). *Network Analysis*. Sage, Beverley Hills, CA.

Langrish, J., Gibbons, M., Evans, W. G. and Jevons, F. R. (1972). *Wealth from Knowledge: A Study of Innovation in Industry*, London: MacMillan.

Lawton Smith, H., and Bagchi-Sen, S. (2006). University–industry interactions: The case of the UK biotech industry, *Industry and Innovation*, 13 (4), 371–392.

Lawton Smith, H., Chapman, D., Wood, P., Barnes, T. and Romeo, S. (2014). Entrepreneurial academics and regional innovation systems: The case of spin-offs from London's universities. *Environment and Planning C: Government and Policy*, 32 (2), 341–359.

Mattes, J., (2012). Dimensions of proximity and knowledge bases: Innovation between spatial and non-spatial factors. *Regional Studies*, 46 (8), 1085–1099.

Moreno, R. and Miguélez, E. (2012). A relational approach to the geography of innovation: a typology of regions. *Journal of Economic Surveys*, 26(3), 492–516.

Molina-Morales, F. X. and Expósito-Langa, M. (2012). The impact of cluster connectedness on firm innovation: R&D effort and outcomes in the textile industry, *Entrepreneurship and Regional Development*, 24 (7–8), 685–704.

Ponds, R., van Oort, F., and Frenken, K. (2007). The geographical and institutional proximity of research collaboration, *Papers in Regional Science*, 86 (3), 423–443.

Ponds, R., van Oort, F., and Frenken, K. (2010). Innovation, spillovers and university-industry collaboration: An extended knowledge production function approach, *Journal of Economic Geography*, 10 (2), 231–255.

Putnam, R. D. (2000). *Bowling Alone: The Collapse and Revival of American Community*. New York: Simon & Schuster.

Quatraro, F. (2010). Knowledge coherence, variety and economic growth: Manufacturing evidence from Italian regions, *Research Policy*, 39, 1289–1302.

Rivera, M., Soderstrom, S. and Uzzi, B. (2010). Dynamics of dyads in social networks: Assortative, relational, and proximity mechanisms. *Annual Review of Sociology*, 36, 91–115.

Roper, S., Du, J. and Love, J. H. (2008). Modelling the innovation value chain, *Research Policy*, Vol. 37, No. 6–7, pp. 961–977.

Rothwell, R., Freeman, C., Horlsey, A., Jervis, V. T. P., Robertson, A. B. and Townsend, J. (1974). SAPPHO updated – project SAPPHO Phase II, *Research Policy*, Vol. 3, No. 3, pp. 258–291.Rutten, R. and Boekema, F. (eds.) (2007). *The Learning Region: Foundations, State of the Art, Future*. Edward Elgar, Cheltenham.

Santoro, M. D. and Chakrabarti, A. K. (2002). Firm size and technology centrality in industry–university interactions, *Research Policy*, 31, 1163–1180.

Saxenian, A. (1994). *Regional Advantage: Culture and Competition in Silicon Valley and Route 128*. Cambridge, Massachusetts: Harvard University Press.

Saxenian, A. (2005). From brain drain to brain circulation: Transnational communities and regional upgrading in India and China, *Studies in Comparative International Development*, 40, 35–61.

Schartinger, D., Rammer, C., Fischer, M. M. and Fröhlich, J. (2002). Knowledge interactions between universities and industry in Austria: Sectoral patterns and determinants, *Research Policy*, 31, 303–328.

Sebestyén, T. and Varga, A. (2013). Research productivity and the quality of interregional knowledge networks. *Annals of Regional Science*, 51 (1), 155–189.

Shane, S., and Cable, D. (2002). Network ties, reputation, and the financing of new ventures. *Management Science*, 48 (3), 364–381.

Storper, M. (1995). The resurgence of regional economics, ten years later. *European Urban and Regional Studies*, 2 (2), 191–221.

Storper, M. (2000). Globalizsation and knowledge flows: An industrial geographer's perspective. In *Regions, Globalization, and the Knowledge-Based Economy*, Dunning JH (eds.). Oxford: Oxford University Press.

Ter Wal, A. L. J. and Boschma, R. (2011). Co-evolution of firms, industries and networks in space, *Regional Studies*, 45, 919–933.

Torré, A., (2008). On the role played by temporary geographical proximity in knowledge transmission, *Regional Studies*, 42 (6), 869–889.

Varga, A. and Parag, A. (2009). Academic knowledge transfers and the structure of international research networks, in: Varga, A. (ed.) *Universities, Knowledge Transfer and Regional Development: Geography, Entrepreneurship and Policy*. Edward Elgar, Cheltenham.

Vittoria, P. M. and Lavadera, G. L. (2014). Knowledge networks and dynamic capabilities as the new regional policy milieu. A social network analysis of the Campania biotechnology community in southern Italy, *Entrepreneurship and Regional Development*, 26 (7–8), 594–618.

Wellings, P. (2008). *Intellectual property and research benefits*. Lancaster: Lancaster University.

Whittington, K. B., Owen-Smith, J. and Powell, W. W. (2009). Networks, propinquity, and innovation in knowledge-intensive industries, *Administrative Science Quarterly*, 54, 90–122.

Zaheer, A. and Soda, G. (2009). Network evolution: The origins of structural holes. *Administrative Science Quarterly*, 54, 1–31.

Zaheer, A., Gözübüyük, R. and Milanov, H. (2010). It's the connections: The network perspective in interorganizational research. Academy of Management Perspectives, 24 (1), 62–77.

6 Good Growth, Bad Growth

A Wake-up Call of Smart Specialisation

Mark Thissen, Frank van Oort and Olga Ivanova

6.1 Introduction

After many years of austerity and limited or negative growth, European regional authorities dare thinking in economic growth terms again. Selectively choosing economic specialisation and diversification opportunities in line with entrepreneurial search processes are part of smart specialisation strategies. By nature or by history, some regions seem better endowed with growing or promising sectors than other regions. But even regions specialised in globally growing markets face continuous competition, and hence can become less competitive when other regions gain larger market shares in smart specialised niche markets. This chapter introduces within a conceptual framework of regional competitiveness a decomposition method of local economic growth that shows whether regions grow because of generic rising (or declining) demand for the products and services produced (demand led growth), and/or because of strengthening their competitive market positions (structural growth). Performing for better or for worse on these two dimensions of growth shows that seemingly favourable total regional growth figures may be solely attributable to demand-led growth, while structural growth is negative – meaning that the region is not competitive and loses market shares structurally ('bad growth'). On the other hand, regions may operate on generally stable or slightly declining markets, yet gain substantial market shares. Apparently these regions are very competitive and strong in structural growth ('good growth'). Exploring the scores of European regions along the two dimensions of growth, we show that demand-led and structural growth are taking place simultaneously yet independently from each other and shaping the long-run competitive advantages of regional specialisations, and hence provide crucial information on the competitive smartness of prolonging these specialisations.

Not only has this identification of different types of growth important implications for the smart specialisation way of identifying regional development opportunities, it also provides us with important policy recommendations. Policies focussing on regional conditions for competitiveness, like accessibility, labour market conditions, innovation of local firms, education, housing or agglomeration circumstances, basically impact on structural growth opportunities and are much less clear-cut on demand-led growth opportunities. Regions characterised by a large demand-led growth component therefore cannot easily better their growth positions by implementing place-based development policies (alone). Positions in international trade and investment networks are still prone to locational assets, but to a much lesser extent than localised and competitive structural growth are. In Thissen *et al.* (2016) and in this chapter it is shown that of all economic growth in European regions, about 70 percent is demand-led and 30 percent is structural growth. This varies over sectors and regions, but this average figure means that regional economic policy initiatives (place-based policies) focused on competitive locational factors seem only limited effective for stimulating economic growth. Yet these locational factors may function as necessary conditions for growth, and a lack or poor quality of them may hamper competitive development. Becoming structurally better embedded and endowed results in a stronger competitive position, but above all this needs market niche-based economic diversification that is besides place-based also network based and people (skill) based, well as place-based in nature.

Economic growth is generally equivalent to producing and selling more or better products and services. Economic growth thus defined can be due to increasing demand from other regions, or it can be due to region-internal factors raising local productivity and a region's competitive position. This chapter introduces a value added growth decomposition method based on an analysis of trade between European regions and the market shares on European regional markets. This method is implemented on the World Input-Output Data (WIOD), and is consistent with the multiregional trade data developed in the *Smartspec* FP 7 project. This growth decomposition enables us to analyse the *region and sector specific* sources of economic growth. This gives us insights in the regions that specifically outperform other regions, but also what these regions can learn from each other in terms of best practices in market behaviour and related locational assets. This, in combination with new insights regarding the concept of the firm's life cycle from a regional perspective gives, provides us with policy options to strengthen location and sector/product specific regional competitiveness, all of which are also key objectives of the smart specialisation conceptualisation.

In this chapter the economic growth performance and decomposition of several of the FP7 *Smartspec* case study regions on different geographical and product markets is analysed. This provides us with the information needed to evaluate and monitor the effectiveness and potential impact of regional policies in these regions. Moreover, our methodology allows us to evaluate regional policies in either a worldwide economic boom or recession. Exploiting the longitudinal character of the dataset used (see Thissen *et al.* 2016 for a detailed technical description), regions can be monitored for their competitive performance vis-à-vis other European regions. A careful analysis of policies implemented by competitor regions will give insights into best practice regional policies that arguably are successful on the specific region's (smartly specialised) niche markets. We show that our decomposition methodology can be implemented at the aggregate level or at the sector level, and since total trade is analyzed it can even be shown whether a European region loses competitiveness to, for instance, China or the US and in which geographical markets these gains or losses occur. In the next section we describe how this methodology connects to smart specialisation, and the place-based policy and regional competitiveness literatures. In Section 6.3 we introduce the concept of revealed competition and the methodology of growth decomposition. Using a stylized example, we show that there are winning and losing regions in terms of revealed competition in specific market niches. We link this to industry and cluster life cycle concepts in order to arrive at specific market positions evolving over time. A region should ideally have a portfolio of industries focused on emerging, growing and adapting and transforming (clusters of) industries to be resilient and competitive in the long run. The proof of the pudding is in the eating, and in Section 6.4 we illustrate the importance of our framework by analysing the growth decomposition and life-cycle positioning of sectors in a pan-European set of regions that covers the institutional and macro-economic diversity of the continent. We show that such analysis provides policymakers with useful insights that are important for regional smart specialisation and place-based strategies – and we argue that it may even function as a wake-up call. Section 6.5 discusses the implications of these conclusions for smart specialisation.

6.2 The Need for an analysis of Economic Growth in Smart Specialisation Conceptualisations

6.2.1 Smart specialisation policies and regional competitiveness

The concept of regional competitiveness is prominently present in public policy (Bristow 2005), and increasing competitiveness is an explicit policy goal by regional, national and supra-national governments (i.e. the European Commission) alike (Baldwin and Wyplosz 2009). Dedicated regional policies involve improving features such as the local accessibility, labour markets, housing markets and innovation-enhancing economic conditions under which new economic activities can prosper (Bristow 2010). A strategy of increasing competitiveness involves the ability of regional governments to learn about the effects of economic policies elsewhere, particularly through methods based on comparison or monitoring. Benchmarking and regional econometrics have become particularly popular within regional economic policy-making circles in recent years (Huggins 2010) to help measure and compare competitive regional performance in measurable and comparative settings (Melo *et al.* 2009).

Conceptually, regional benchmarking has progressed from quite simplistic forms that compare and rank different regions to more complex modes (see Huggins 2010). The main critique of such simplistic approaches highlights the distinctiveness of regional environments as limiting the utility of what is considered 'copy-and-paste' and 'one-size-fits-all' policy-making, as regional stakeholders purport to transfer perceived 'best practices' from one region to another (Huggins 2010). Concerning regional development, Malecki (2002) and Tracey and Clark (2003) have therefore drawn attention to the potential importance of global networks as sources of goods and knowledge in shaping firm competitiveness in a particular area. Spatial econometric methods and the concept of revealed competition (Thissen *et al.* 2013a) bring interregional relatedness, region-specific markets and local accessibility and production factor circumstances into the econometric and benchmark evaluation literature of regional economic performance.

6.2.2 Sources of economic growth

But it takes more than local favourable circumstances concerning production and consumption factors for a regional economy to grow. As economic growth is equivalent to producing and selling more products and services, this growth can have two distinct sources. It can be due to economic growth and demand from other regions (demand led growth), or it can be due to internal factors raising productivity (structural growth). These internal factors that increase a region's competitiveness result in a gain in the market share of this region. If we represent the total economy as a large pie, the first source of regional economic growth is due to growth of the total pie, while the second source is due to a region gaining a larger share of the pie. The first source of regional growth can hardly (or only indirectly) be influenced by the region's governments as it is due to the independent growth of markets in a region's export destinations. The second source of regional growth is due to structural factors inducing an increase in market shares, and thereby the result of an increase in a region's competitiveness. These structural factors can directly be influenced by the region itself.

Demand induced growth (or decline) is beyond a region's sphere of influence. In other words, a region may perform structurally well locally but go into recession because of a lack in demand from other regions. Vice versa, it may be the case that a region structurally underperforms but still grows due to increasing external demand. In this last case a region would underperform relative to its potential. Obviously, this leads to important implications for benchmarking and econometric analysis alike: the fact that structural growth can predominantly be affected by regional policies should be taken into account in a policy evaluation.

Although structural growth is of primal importance to evaluate regional policy, demand led growth may be the most important factor explaining regional economic growth. Thissen *et al.* (2016) actually show that for European regions, demand-led growth is at least two times more important than structural growth since it determines about 70 percent of total economic growth. Economic connections with growing markets and crucial trade hubs thus strongly affect growth opportunities. It determines the degree to which regional development is connected to growth conditions in other regions. We add to the smart specialisation and competitiveness discussions by adding to the conceptual framework of regional competitiveness a decomposition method of local economic growth that shows whether regions grow because of generic rising (or declining) demand for the products and services produced (demand led growth), and/or because of bettering competitive market share positions (structural growth). Performing for better or for worse on these two dimensions of growth shows that seemingly (un)favourable total regional growth figures may be solely attributable to demand-led growth or structural growth components outbalancing each other. Regions primarily growing due to demand-led growth while structurally losing market share and having negative structural growth rates will inevitably turn into relatively low growth economies in the long run (these regions are characterized by 'bad growth'). On the other hand, structural growth that permanently outweighs demand-led growth indicates that regions may operate on generally stable or slightly declining global markets, yet gain substantial structural markets shares to such an extent that they are actually very competitive and have strong future growth perspectives (these regions are characterized by 'good growth'). Exploring the scores of European regions along these two dimensions of growth, we want to show that demand-led and structural growth are operating simultaneously yet independently from each other shaping the long-run competitive advantages of (smart) regional specialisations. The results of the growth decomposition can subsequently be used in benchmarking or econometric analysis formulated to explain competitiveness by learning from (policies in) region, sector and market specific competitors. The detailed data of the regional trade network information of European regions is uniquely developed for the *Smartspec* FP7 project, and provides important additional information for evaluating the heterogeneous pattern of regional economic performance in Europe.

6.2.3 *Place based policies*

The additional aim of this chapter is to contribute to the recent discussion on smart specialisation and place-based development strategies in the European Commission's cohesion policy. Barca *et al.* (2012) summarise the debate on place-based versus place-neutral development in detail. Based on current economic geographical theories of innovation and the density of skills and human capital in cities, globalisation, and endogenous growth through urban learning opportunities (Glaeser 2011), spatially blind approaches argue that intervention, regardless of the context, is the best way to resolve the old dilemma of whether development should be about 'places' or about 'people' (Barca *et al.* 2012, p. 140). It is argued that agglomeration in combination with encouraging people's mobility not only allows individuals to live where they expect to be better off but also increases individual incomes, productivity, knowledge, and aggregate growth (World Bank 2009, Thissen & Van Oort 2010). From this perspective, spatially blind policies are also seen in some circles as 'people-based' policies, representing the best approach to improving people's lives (Glaeser 2008). Consequently, on this logic development intervention should be space-neutral, and factors should be encouraged to move to where they are most productive. In reality, this is primarily in large cities (Gill 2010). In contrast, the place-based approach assumes that the interactions between institutions and geography are critical for development, and many of the clues for development policy lie in these interactions. To understand the likely impacts of a policy, the interactions between institutions and geography, therefore, requires explicit consideration of the specifics of the local and wider regional context (Barca *et al.* 2012, p. 140). In the context of this chapter, the finding in Thissen *et al.* (2016) of relatively limited impact of regional economic policies because of dominant demand-led growth questions such place-based development strategy. On the other hand, it is also important to realise that the fact that adequate place-based policies can structurally make a difference in the competitiveness of local niche markets related to the entrepreneurial search process in smart specialisation strategies. Hence, our interpretation of growth analysis is a useful and much-needed addition to the place-based and smart specialisation discussion.

6.3 Revealed Competition and Growth

6.3.1 Revealed competition

While competitiveness is abundantly used in the policy oriented literature, much less attention is given to the measurement of actual competition and its relation to economic growth. The most traditional approach to the measurement of competitiveness is the measurement of revealed comparative advantage. However, revealed comparative advantage only tells us what a region is economically relatively good in, without taking spatial markets into account. It also does not deal with actual competition. In Thissen *et al.* (2013a) a revealed competition measure is therefore introduced that addresses this shortcoming by looking at geographically and sectoral market overlap in detailed niche markets. When we use this new measure for revealed competition dynamically over time it gives us the possibility to decompose regional economic growth in the two distinct components. While, as already mentioned, economic growth is in general equivalent to producing and selling more products and services, we distinguish the component that is due to an increase in demand from other regions from the component that is due to the regions internal factors raising regional productivity.

The traditional measures for revealed comparative advantage (RCA) commonly used in the trade literature are all variants of the Balassa (1965) Index. The Balassa index is based on the shares of different product categories in the total exports of a country in relation to the shares of a group of reference countries. A Balassa index value which is larger than one implies that these product categories are overrepresented in a country's exports. This overrepresentation is interpreted as the specialisation of this country and the production of these product categories is apparently something this country is relatively 'good' in. Competition between two regions is commonly measured by comparing the export structure of two regions in a specific market using Finger and Kreinin's (1979) export similarity index. Analogous to the Balassa index it measures to what degree two regions have the same comparative advantage in a specific regional market.

The principle of revealed competition (Thissen *et al.* 2013a) between regions concerns the overlap in their industry's sales markets. The competition that industries from a region A receive from a region B depends therefore on both the overlap they have on sales in markets C and the respective importance of these markets for region A. The overlap of industries from two regions on a sales market is measured by the market share of the competitors from region B on this market.

The importance of the different sales in market C is measured by the share in total sales from region A that is sold on this market C. Accordingly, region A receives strong competition from region B if region B has a large market share on the markets which are important for region A. The total competition between the regions A and B is determined by adding up the overlap on market C weighted with the importance of this market C for region A. Notice that the revealed competition between A and B is not symmetric, and that symmetry was a major drawback of the RCA and the export similarity measure.

6.3.2 *Value added regional growth decomposition*

The growth decomposition introduced in this chapter places the concept of revealed competition in a dynamic context by analysing the developments in a region's sales markets. This growth decomposition is most easily explained by representing the total economy as a large pie divided into equal pieces representing equal regional economies. When the total economy grows the pie becomes larger. As a consequence, all 12 equal shares become larger in absolute terms. This represents our first source of economic growth which is due to an increase in the overall demand for products from all regions. We define this source of regional economic growth as demand-led growth. The second source of regional economic growth in our example is represented by one of the regions taking a larger share of the pie. This second source of regional growth is due to structural factors (regional characteristics) inducing an increase in market shares, and this represents an increase in a region's competitiveness resulting in the growth of the region. These structural factors can be influenced by the region's policymakers.

We can define this regional growth decomposition more formally as follows. In equation (1) we therefore define the market share $M_{i,j,t}$ in products p of (producing) region i in (market) region j during time period t.

$$M_{p,i,j,t} = \frac{H_{p,i,j,t}}{D_{p,j,t}} \tag{1}$$

where $H_{p,i,j,t}$ is the trade from region i to region j and $D_{p,j,t} = \sum_i H_{p,i,j,t}$ is the demand or size of the market in region j. The two different growth components can now be defined using the definition of the market share.

The demand led growth $G_{p,i,t}^{dem}$ measured in value added is equal to

$$G_{p,i,t}^{dem} = \sum_{s,j} M_{p,i,j,t-1} \left(V_{s,i,t} T_{s,p,i,t} D_{p,j,t} - V_{s,i,t-1} T_{s,p,i,t-1} D_{p,j,t-1} \right) \tag{2}$$

and the structural growth $G_{p,i,t}^{struc,va}$ in value added is therefore defined as

$$G_{p,i,t}^{struc} = \sum_{s,j} \left(M_{p,i,j,t} - M_{p,i,j,t-1} \right) V_{s,i,t} T_{s,p,i,t} D_{p,j,t} \tag{3}$$

Where $V_{s,i,t}$ can be directly taken from a regional use table and is the value added used per unit production of sector s in region i, and $T_{s,p,i,t}$ can be directly taken from a regional supply table and is the technology parameter that gives the share of products p produced per unit production of sector s in region i. Notice that the overall growth rate in value added also equals the sum of both the demand-led and the structural growth.

It is important to calculate the structural and demand led growth in value added terms and not in total production, since the growth of the total production value may be the result of only an increase in the price or number of intermediate goods and thereby production costs. As a consequence, the growth in the total production value may not be representative for the actual growth of regional GDP. A complicating factor is that our analysis of sales markets is based on trade in products while data on value added is only available at the industry level. It is not straightforward to attribute growth in product markets to value added growth since industries make different products and the same products can be made by different industries. We therefore had to combine data on value added by industry from the use table with data on the production of goods by industry from the supply table in order to translate the growth in the value of production into the growth in value added.[1]

6.3.3 A stylized example

We illustrate the difference between structural and demand induced growth by use of a stylized example based on hypothetical fictional data. This example of a decomposition of regional growth is shown in Table 6.1. In this table we see that the region of Vienna experienced a growth rate of 3% over a certain period of time. It seems therefore that the region of Vienna performed well and no policy intervention is needed. A more detailed look at the decomposition of the growth shows however that the region actually had a structurally negative growth. It underperformed relative to its potential and a change in policy may be required.

The main part of the growth of Vienna is decomposed on the first line of Table 6.1 into growth due to an overall change in demand (growth of the pie) and growth due to a gain in market share (a larger share of the pie). We see that the growth of Vienna was mainly due to an increase in demand (6%) although there was also a recession in some of the demanding regions resulting in a decline in demand (2%) and an overall total net increase in demand (4%). In the last two columns of the first row of Table 6.1 we see however that Vienna lost a substantial part of its market share (2%) on markets where losses occurred and gained only little (1%) in the other markets. Thus, although the region is growing with 3% it is actually losing ground to other regions.

In the last rows of Table 6.1 the growth is further decomposed over different regional markets. In the first column we see those regions that induced growth in Vienna due to an increase in their overall demand. In the second column we see all those regions that induced a decline in Vienna because they were faced with a recession themselves. Although the growth of a region due to the demand from other regions is an important determinant of economic growth we are more interested in the last two columns with a decomposition of the structural growth (decline) of Vienna. We observe in our example that Vienna gains market share

Table 6.1 An example of structural and demand-led growth in a region

	Growth *of* GDP in a region (Vienna, 3%)							
Type of growth	Growth (Demand induced)		Decline (Demand induced)		Structural growth (market share gain)		Structural decline (market share loss)	
Total (3%)	(6%)		(−2%)		(1%)		(−2%)	
Regional decomposition of growth	China	(1.0%)	Athens	(−0.5%)	Graz	(0.2%)	China	(−1.0%)
	US	(0.5%)	Seville	(−0.3%)	Liège	(0.1%)	Munich	(−0.4%)
	Munich	(0.4%)	Palermo	(−0.1%)	Alsace	(0.1%)	Budapest	(−0.2%)
	...	(...)	...	(...)	...	(...)	...	(...)

from the neighbouring Austrian region of Graz and regions in France and Belgium. However, it loses more of its market share to China, Munich and Budapest.

The third column of Table 6.1 gives a detailed ranking of regions that perform worse than the region of Vienna. Vienna improved its competitive position vis-a-vis these regions. The fourth and last column of Table 6.1 gives the regions that outperformed the Vienna region. They all performed better than Vienna and got a larger part of the economic pie at the cost of Vienna.

The hypothetical Austrian regional example of a decomposition analyses presented here is much more than simply a vis-a-vis comparison of regions. Competition of firms between regions takes place on many markets and all these markets have to be taken into account simultaneously (Thissen *et al.* 2013a). In our example, Vienna may gain in competitiveness from China in Paris while losing from China in Munich. It is therefore crucial that the decomposition is performed on trade flows on a low aggregation level. The demand induced growth should also be determined on a low level of aggregation since trade is highly dependent on distance and countries are therefore often simply too high an aggregation level to be meaningful for many types of insights. The example also showed that a comparison of growth rates of regions that are susceptible to different demand-induced shocks is of limited value to evaluate regional economic policy. Standard regional econometric growth analysis which is often used in policy evaluation can only be applied under the assumption of comparable demand-induced growth. Whether spatial econometrics can capture the decomposition effect is still to be analysed and more information on the decomposition of regional growth is therefore needed (for a first exercise of a geographically weighted regression approach see Thissen *et al.* 2016).

6.3.4 Competition: Gaining and failing regions

We can derive several insights from this decomposition by classifying all European regions in a dynamic Boston diagram such as presented in Figure 6.1. In this way we will be able to monitor the actual performance of regional industries and derive policy conclusions based on their positioning in terms of market dynamics. In a traditional Boston diagram, the axis represents the market share

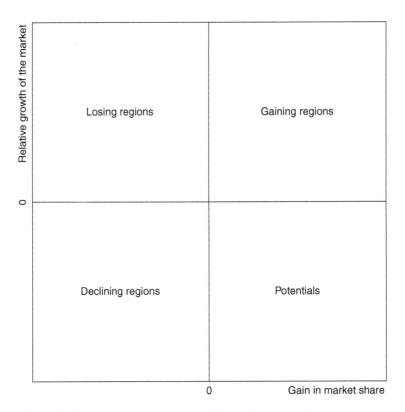

Figure 6.1 A dynamic Boston diagram of the performance of European regions.

and the size of the market. In our dynamic Boston diagram, we look at differences. On the horizontal axis we therefore have the gain or loss in market shares (structural growth) and on the vertical axis we have the growth of the market relative to the median growth of the market (demand led growth).

   In the top right corner of the diagram we position 'gaining regions': the top regions whose firms grow both because of economic growth in the markets they are active in (external factors) and who also gain a larger market share on these markets due to structural factors in the regions (intrinsic factors). The firms in these regions are the driving forces of economic growth in Europe. We also positioned 'potentials' in the bottom right corner of the Boston diagram. These potentials are firms that are winning market share on their sales markets, but they are active in the markets that are not growing. The firms in these regions may therefore gain market share due to good structural policies but they are currently active in declining markets or have an unfavourable regional location. The entrepreneurial systems in these regions perform well, but their growth lags behind because of external factors. In the top left corner, we positioned 'losing regions'. The firms in these regions lose market share and therefore underperform to their expectations, but they still have a positive growth rate due to external factors.

These firm's clearly fall into the danger zone of regional economic development since they could do much better. Policymakers in a region with many sectors in this 'losers' segment are in danger of getting the wrong signals because they are not aware of economic problems due to persistent economic growth. However, other regions outperform these regions structurally and if the competing firms from other regions keep increasing their market share they will eventually push the other firm's out off the market. Finally, we have the 'declining regions' in the bottom left corner of the Boston diagram. The firms in these regions lose market share and they sell their products on relatively shrinking markets. Regions with many declining firms are clearly having the largest economic problems.

6.3.5 Firm, industry and cluster life cycles

Our classification of winning and losing regions in the dynamic version of the Boston diagram can be related to Porter's (1980) concept of the life cycle of an industry. However, although Porter's theory is centred on the firm's development within the industry, our concept is centred on the firm's performance on spatially differentiated markets. According to Porter, the industry is central in the environment of the firm and determines its necessary strategy for survival and development in a competitive setting. This concept is commonly extended with Abernathy and Utterback's (1978) model of dynamics in process and product innovations. It should be noted that Porter's concept of the industry is not exactly the same as our concept that is more related to the data and the national accounts. The concept of the industry or cluster life cycle is depicted in Figure 6.2.

The industry lifecycle concept starts with the introduction phase where firms start with new product or process innovations. This is the dynamic phase with not

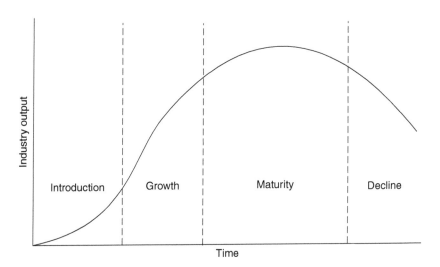

Figure 6.2 Phases of the Industry life cycle.

Source: Adapted from Porter (1980, p. 156).

only new firms, but also exits from firms with competing inventions that are not consistent with customer preferences and therefore not demanded on the market. In the subsequent growth phase there is a shift from the introduction of new products towards process innovations where cost reductions lead to fast growth in the surviving firms. During the maturity phase the complete market gets satisfied and there exists a stable distribution of firms with market leaders and followers, or another oligopolistic or monopolistic distribution. In the last phase of decline the firms face increased competition of newly introduced products that are significantly different but are replacing the existing products (or functions) produced by the firms in decline. We could see these newly introduced products as a new industry starting a new industry lifecycle.

The industry concept used in this chapter incorporates a broader group of products. Porter's 'new' industries would therefore be incorporated in our broader industry concept. We therefore additionally use the market positions of firms in the quadrants determined by the industry and cluster life cycle concept. In this way, we are able to frame our interpretation of Porter's industry life cycle in co-evolution with our classification of region-sector combinations in the Boston diagram (compare Braunjerhelm & Feldman 2006, Brenner 2004, and Fornahl *et al.* 2010). The market positioning of firms within the life cycle is depicted in Figure 6.3. In the evolution of market positions shown, the new and potentially successful start-ups will be classified as a potential. Typically, these firms gain market share because they have successfully introduced a new product and gain market share in the sales markets they are active in. These sales markets will commonly be randomly chosen and therefore they will often only profit from the growth of the market to a limited extent. Incidentally some of the start-ups may be classified as gainers because they may have started in a fast growing region.[2] These start-ups generally need capital and investment and there may be a role for local government to help them in expanding to new markets.

The most successful firms in the growth and mature phase of the life cycle are typical gainers. They will be active in most markets and therefore at the least have an average in the demand-led growth component. They will also gain in market share (when they are in the growing phase) or keep their market share (when they are mature). These firms need little government intervention since they are flourishing.

The group of Losing firms lose market share but they are active in growing markets. They are therefore characterised by growth but in the precarious situation that competitors are pushing them out of the market. These firms are threatened by the competition due to a competitive disadvantage. Depending on the type of problem these firms should either focus on product innovations if they are in Porter's declining phase, or they should focus on process innovations when they are still in Porter's maturity phase. If they are still in Porter's maturity phase they are probably producing at too high costs and therefore they should concentrate on process innovation and regional factors to increase their competitive advantage. In this last case there may be a role for the regional government in improving these regional characteristics to give their firm's a competitive edge.

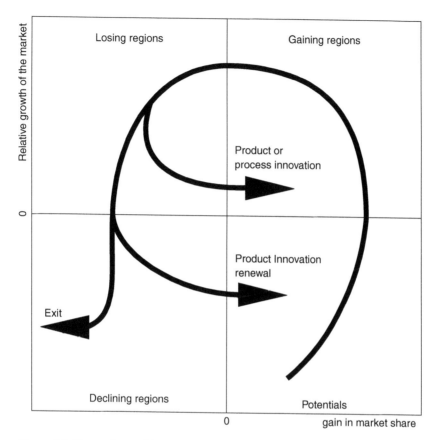

Figure 6.3 The market positions of firms in the industry life cycle.

The final category is the Decliners. Firms in this category are facing declining market share and are only active in not growing markets. They may look for 'new' markets but this will not solve all of their problems since their competitors are out-performing them. However, these firms are moving in a direction towards an exit from the market and therefore there is a strong urge for action. It seems that firms in this category have to reinvent themselves and focus on product innovation to strengthen their position in the market.

The process of market positions of firms within cluster and industry life cycles are sectors and region specific, and has always functioned in capitalist markets (Fornahl *et al.* 2010). But the last decades we witness that the time it takes to move from the potential to gaining and eventually losing stages of development are speeded up by technological advancement. New products and processes generally have ever shorter life expectancies, and hence firms in (smart special-ised) regional clusters and industries constantly have to think about adaptation, renewal and the transforming of their products and processes in order to remain competitive. This may be at odds with cluster policy strategies and instruments that may actually function for longer periods of time. Flexibility is also needed in policy making and the running time of policy instruments. A region should ideally have a portfolio of industries and clusters, and a set of policy settings focused on emerging, growing, adapting and transforming the local clusters and industries so as to be resilient and competitive in the long run.

6.4 Structural and Demand-led Regional Growth in Europe

6.4.1 Empirical analysis

In this section we move from the stylized example of Vienna to the analysis of growth decomposition and life-cycle market positioning of a heterogeneous set of regions that are focused on in the FP7 *Smartspec* project. Empirical testing of these concepts that are arguably important for smart specialisation strategies requires a large amount of data on regional and sectoral specialisations and linkages. The unique, consistent and complete database of the PBL Netherlands Environmental Assessment Agency with detailed regional trade between 249 European Nuts2 regions and the trade of these regions with the rest of the world (Thissen *et al.* 2013a, b and c) in a regional supply and use framework contains all the information to make a detailed decomposition of European regional growth from 2000 to 2010. We can decompose the growth at the sector or aggregate level, for every year during this period or for the total period of 11 years.

Table 6.2 shows the average absolute growth decomposition in these 249 EU NUTS2-regions. The growth decomposition is determined for total production and for 14 typical economic sectors covering the total economy. It is calculated by taking the absolute demand-led and structural GDP growth divided by the GDP in 2000.

Table 6.2 Decomposition of sectoral GDP growth in percentages (2000–2010)

	Structural growth	(In percentage of total growth)	Demand led growth	(In percentage of total growth)
Total production	13%	(27%)	36%	(73%)
Agricultural sector	26%	(62%)	16%	(38%)
Food sector	54%	(69%)	24%	(31%)
Materials sector	43%	(54%)	36%	(46%)
High-technology sector	39%	(57%)	30%	(43%)
Chemical sector	40%	(56%)	31%	(44%)
Energy sector	37%	(36%)	65%	(64%)
Financial services sector	22%	(31%)	50%	(69%)
Business services sector	20%	(28%)	51%	(72%)
Mining sector	41%	(42%)	57%	(58%)
Manufacturing sector	29%	(53%)	26%	(47%)
Electricity sector	40%	(57%)	30%	(43%)
Construction sector	16%	(26%)	45%	(74%)
Private services sector	12%	(26%)	33%	(74%)
Public services sector	8%	(15%)	47%	(85%)

As in Thissen *et al.* (2016), demand-led growth is about three times larger than structural growth in European regions (73% to 27%). The highest growth rates have been in the Energy and mining sectors, although this is partly caused by the high price increase in these sectors. The financial and business services have grown at almost the same high growth rate, while among the industrial sectors the highest growth rates were in the high-tech, materials and chemical sectors. Among these fast growing sectors materials, high technology, and the chemical sectors have been the most competitive with a relative high share of structural growth. In other words, these sectors where characterised by a high share of gains and losses in regional market shares. The low growth agricultural and food sector is also characterised by strong competition. The growth in services sector activities are mainly driven by demand led growth and seem less competitive in European regions. These average growth figures may, however, be very different for sectors in individual regions since they are active in geographically different markets.

In the following sections we will therefore break down these average growth figures over the individual European NUTS2 regions.[3] This will enable us to evaluate regional and sector specific performance over the first decade of this century. It will not only show us promising region-sector combinations, but also those that are in need of change via either policy intervention or a change in firms' policies in the region. Subsequently we will turn to the perspective of regions that intend to stimulate specific sectors in their region by pursuing some form of industrial policy.

6.4.2 Regional performance

We analyse the performance of sectors in European regions over the period 2000–2010 using the concept of the regional firm's market position in life cycles within the framework of the dynamic Boston diagram. We start with the growth of total production in the region and subsequently turn to the growth of two different dynamic sectors (see Table 6.2): the chemical industry that is relatively mature, and the high-tech industry that is between growth and maturity. We specifically focus on regions that have participated in the FP7 *SmartSpec* project and that can be linked to a European NUTS2 region. In the discussion in this chapter we only limit ourselves to (several of) these cases, but the results for all 246 regions will be made available via the PBL Netherlands Environmental Assessment Agency website (www.pbl.nl).

In Figure 6.4 we present the Boston diagram showing the overall regional performance for total production in Europe. The figure shows that regions are distributed over all quadrants of the Boston diagram and can therefore be classified in all of our four different categories. There is however a slight bias towards positive gains in market shares (the horizontal axis). This can only be due to a difference in size between losing and gaining regions. A more careful inspection of the results showed that this indeed is the case. In general, smaller regions more often gained market share while larger regions more often lost market share. This is an indication for convergence between the regions over the time period 2000–2010.

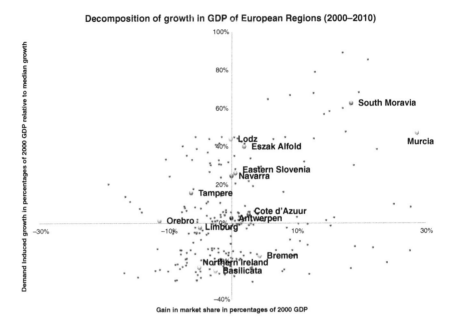

Figure 6.4 Regional performance in Europe (total production).

* FP7 Smartspec case-study regions (living labs).

We see this difference in the size of regions also clearly with regions like South Moravia (Brno, Czech Republic) and Eszak Alfold (Debrecen, Hungary) positioned as gaining regions. Larger regions such as Antwerp in Flanders and Limburg in The Netherlands perform less favourably. They are both losing market share in their respective specialisations, although Antwerp is still active in growing markets while Limburg is predominantly active in declining markets. The large 'losing region' of Őrebrő/Linköping (Sweden) clearly underperformed with losing a large share of the markets on which its firms are active, which was 'disguised' by the slight growth of the market. According to the European Commission (2015), two types of lagging regions currently seem to stand out in Europe: low income regions that are concentrated in Central and Eastern European (CEE) countries, and low growth regions that are in the South of the EU (Greece, Southern Italy, Portugal and Southern Spain). Although both types of regions face structural difficulties in terms of their resilience to the economic shock(s) witnessed in the recent past, the Southern regions seem to be better endowed with more developed industries and opportunities for diversification than many of the CEE regions. In many of the CEE regions, the diversifying conditions for human and physical capital appear to be lacking outside the capital regions due to their past political, social and economic developments. CEE countries are also in more need of reforms in labour markets, education, structural policies, and governance and institutional issues than the Southern regions, as argued by Dogaru *et al.*, in their chapter in this book. Yet, smart specialization as a development concept suggests that there are place-based opportunities for all regions in the EU (Foray 2015). Remarkably, our analysis in Figure 6.2 shows that CEE (low income) regions perform very well in terms of both demand-led growth and competitiveness; see for example, the positions of the regions of Debrecen and Brno.

In order to derive policy lessons from this analysis we have to analyse the sector and region's situation at a lower aggregation level. To derive good policies, we should not look at the general winners but at specifically those regions that won market share as a consequence their own region's industries. We therefore present in Figure 6.5 the dynamic Boston diagram for the chemical industry only. Again, in the case of the chemical industry we observe the strong growth in smaller (CEE) regions such as South Moravia and Lodz. Of interest here, however, are the differences in three regions with a relatively large chemical sector: the Dutch Limburg region, the Flemish Antwerp region and the German Bremen region. Clearly, firms from Antwerp are outperforming the firms from the other two regions while all the firms from the three regions are selling their products in regions that are relatively not growing fast. The access to a nearby port cannot be the main distinguishing factor since Bremen is losing market share while Antwerp is gaining market share. Other forces seem to be at work that makes the difference in the competitiveness of firms from the three regions.

Figure 6.6 focuses in a similar fashion on the high-tech industry. As was already concluded from Table 6.2, the dynamics in the high-tech industries illustrated by

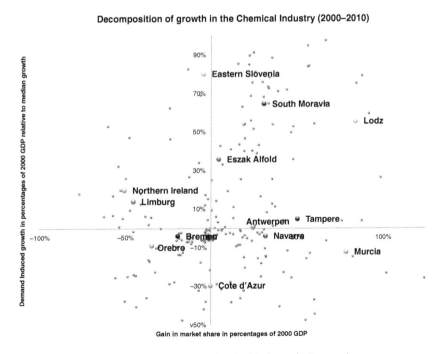

Figure 6.5 Regional performance in the chemical industry in Europe.*

horizontal scale between Figures 6.5 and 6.6 is comparable. The main difference is the performance of the sectors in the respective regions which are located at a different position in both Figures. In Figure 6.6, in particular, the position of the Őrebrö/Linköping region in Sweden is striking. This region can clearly be classified as a losing region. Its growth in the high-tech sector is driven by its strong position in the past (with firms like Saab Aerospace, Siemens, Ericsson and Toyota Industries) and therefore is mainly determined by strong growth in the markets where it sells its products. However, this growth is accompanied by a loss in competitiveness resulting in a loss in market share vis-à-vis firms from other regions. The long run prospects of this sector are therefore limited unless changes are made by the industry. This provides an important 'wake-up call' for a region profiling itself as high-tech region based on the large firms and clusters that are present. The region is currently switching to more open innovation and smart specialisations in sustainable systems, security, advanced materials and simulation & visualisation (Östergötland 2014). However, time will tell whether this refocus is timely and sufficient for this particular region to regain its competitive market power. Arguably, the joint public and private local smart specialisation strategy is partly responsible for current and future performance of 34% structural growth potentials. Much of the high-tech industry appears self-organising though in the region. Obviously, spatial-economic conditions like accessibility, employment matching and education and systems of innovation help in this process, but

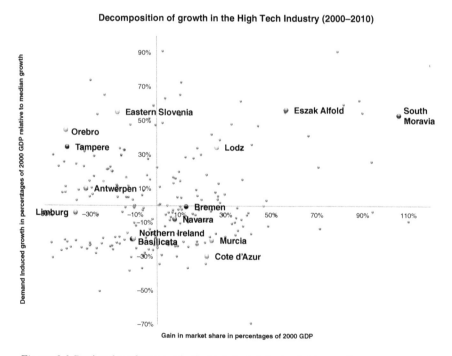

Decomposition of growth in the High Tech Industry (2000–2010)

Figure 6.6 Regional performance in the high-tech industry in Europe.*

this was also the case before smart specialisation strategies. Smart specialisation stresses the need for entrepreneurial search processes, alongside processes of diversification, scaling up and governance renewal.

6.4.3 Industrial policy in the region

Regional policy involves policy choices regarding the selection of industries, activities, and projects, between the different industries, sectors, firms and networks which are active in the regional economy. These choices will not only involve direct support or subsidies to firms or networks of firms, but also choices between thematic demands such as a better accessibility, the sharing of research lab facilities, the promotion of campus or regional innovation systems, and policy choices and priorities which do not facilitate all industries equally. Every region therefore wants to evaluate the relative performance of the different sectors within the region, and in Figure 6.7 we present as an example the performance of the different sectors of Antwerp (Flanders, Belgium) in the dynamic Boston diagram.

The business services sector in Antwerp outperforms the other services sectors because it sells its products in regional markets that grow more than elsewhere in Europe. On the other hand, this is clearly not the case for the financial services, and this is probably due to the economic crisis that badly hit the financial

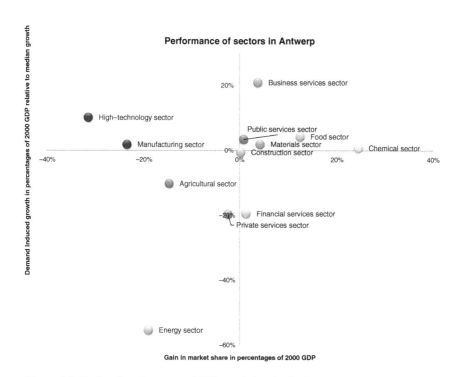

Figure 6.7 Regional performance of different industries in Antwerp.

sector in the UK and the Benelux countries during the time period of our analysis. The chemical sector in Antwerp, on the other hand, gains market shares in many markets, but is not active in the strongest growing regions. The high-tech, manu-facturing and energy sectors underperform and are declining sectors losing market share. However, the high-tech sector is still active in strong growing markets while the energy sector is mainly active in markets that declined. Similarly, the diagrams for competing regions like Rotterdam and Hamburg (for the chemical industry, business services and distribution) may provide Antwerp policymak-ers with information on better or worse comparative practices. However, when analysing the prospects of different industries in a region we should not only look at the performance of the firms in the region but also at the absolute change in demand for the products these industries are selling. Otherwise we may end up supporting excellent industries selling products that are not demanded for in the market, resulting in a small or even a negative economic growth rate. We there-fore present the growth potential of different industries in our example region of Antwerp in Figure 6.8. This figure has the same horizontal axis representing the gain in market share, but a different vertical axis than Figure 6.7: the vertical axis here represents the total growth in value added due to the increase in demand from the different regions where the firms are active. Thus, on the vertical axis we have the growth in all of the sales markets in which firms from a region are active.

When comparing Figure 6.8 with Figure 6.7 we observe that although the energy sector is not performing well, it is active in slight growing markets. The High-tech sector has a stronger growing market. Restructuring in order to increase the compet-itiveness may therefore be more profitable in the high tech sector than in the energy sector. Alternatively, the other manufacturing sector is even faced with a declin-ing demand for its products. Although improving its competitiveness will help the sector, its growth potential is limited. The markets for services are growing most prominently and especially the demand for business services is growing faster than any other type of services. The services sector is the largest part of the economy and the high growth rates suggest that this will stay this way in the future. At the same time, the chemical industry is currently the strongest and amongst the most competi-tive sectors in the Antwerp region. In figure 6.8 it is shown that it is also faced with a relative strong and diversified growth in demand for chemical products.

6.5 Discussion

In this chapter we have introduced a framework to analyze regional economic competitiveness in the form of a growth decomposition of value added earned on different product markets. Our analysis has shown that about 30 percent of regional economic growth can be structurally characterised as related to the local competitive performance of firms and regional-economic circumstances. On the one hand this limits the possibilities of regional policy makers because to a large extent (75%) regional economic development is demand-driven and beyond their control. On the other hand, all (smartly) specialised regions in Europe face this structural disadvantage in their respective niche markets, and thus the on average

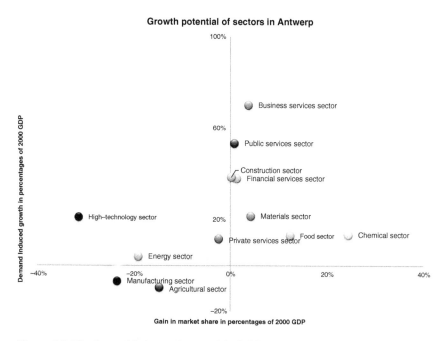

Figure 6.8 The demand-led growth potential of different industries in Antwerp.

25% structural entrepreneurial and spatial-economic conditions can make regions win the game from competing systems elsewhere. A careful analysis of policies implemented by competitor regions will also give insights into best-practice regional policies that arguably can be successful in one's own region. Performing for better or for worse on these two dimensions of growth shows that region can have competitive 'good growth' (related to structurally gaining market shares) and 'bad growth' (with declining market shares). By exploring the many European regions along the two dimensions of growth for a representative set of European regions we show that demand-led and structural growth are simultaneously, yet independently from each other, shaping the long-run competitive advantages of regional specialisations, and hence provide crucial information on the competitive smartness of these specialisations.

Showing that the life cycles of industries, sectors and clusters can be plotted within the alternative outcomes of our growth decomposition, leads to important insights. Eastern-European regions, although lagging in income, may have better demand-led and competitive growth cards to play than Southern-European regions that are lagging in growth altogether recently. Traditionally powerful Western-European regions, like the Linköping/Örebrö region of Sweden, which specialised in high-tech manufacturing, may face a loss in their competitive and demand-led growth power despite the generic growth in the sector. Such an outcome may function as a 'wake-up call' for regions which are experiencing sustained economic growth, while also becoming less competitive in their niche market specialisations as other regions catch-up and outperform them. This is, or should be, of genuine concern to the smart specialisation agenda – a policy-driven conceptualisation that by its nature puts a central emphasis on unique entrepreneurial search processes that eventually evolve in diversifying yet sustainable growth trajectories. Likewise, using our methodology we are able to identify large growth potentials for the chemical sector in Antwerp, Belgium, a sector that generally declines relative to the services sectors, but one which also is in niche markets showing particularly strong growth potentials. Given their positioning in the dynamic market structure, Antwerp has managed in recent years to become smartly specialised in exactly such niche markets.

The growth decomposition presented here suggests that with regard to spatial and economic policy, any 'one-size-fits-all' policy settings are unlikely to be successful. Although there are general economic processes at work, these operate in specific geographical and product markets that therefore require location-specific policies. We find that regional economic development differs strongly among sectors and regions with a strong geographical component in the location of growth. Growth does not only take place in size-based classes of the largest conurbations or regions, but also in regions that have specific niche market characteristics or are embedded in typical niche-market networks. This supports European place-based development strategies, where becoming structurally and competitively better embedded and endowed involves market niche-based economic diversification processes that integrate skills and networks.

Notes

1   Supply and use tables are a part of the system of national accounts. The regional supply tables show the detailed production of goods and services by the region's industries and the additional supply of these products and services by imports from other regions. The regional use tables show the use of goods and services by the region's industries and different final demand categories, and the compensation for the production factors (i.e. the value added). An informative discussion of supply and use tables in a system of national accounts can be found in Eurostat (2008).

2   Please note that a start-up has no market share to start with thus if the start-up would be unsuccessful and lose market share it would be immediately bankrupt. This is what will often happen to start-ups, but these will immediately disappear from our classification.

3   As we work with growth figures the results are very sensitive to regions with small sector values. In particular, the relocation of multinationals to or from smaller regions distorts the figures substantially. We therefore excluded from the analysis NUTS2 regions that had growth rates larger than 400 percent and sectoral value added below 50 million Euros. We also excluded any region with a growth rate larger than 500 percent. In these occasions the strange results were due to either an administrative change of the region, or to relocation or a merger of a very large firm.

References

Abernathy, W. J. & J. M. Utterback (1978). Patterns of Industrial Innovation, Technology Review, 80.

Balassa, B. (1965), 'Trade liberalization and "revealed" comparative advantage', *The Manchester School of Economic and Social Studies*, 33: 92–123.

Baldwin, R. & C. Wyplosz (2009), *The Economics of European integration*, London: McGraw-Hill.

Barca, F. (2009), 'An agenda for a reformed cohesion policy: a place-based approach to meeting European Union challenges and expectations'. Report for the European Commission, Brussels.

Barca, F., P. McCann & A. Rodriguez-Pose (2012), The case for regional development intervention: place-based versus place-neutral approaches. *Journal of Regional Science* 52: 134–152.

Braunerhjelm, P. & M. A. Feldman (2006), *Cluster genesis. Technology-based industrial development*. Oxford: Oxford University Press.

Brenner, T. (2004), *Local industrial clusters. Existence, emergence and evolution*. London: Routledge.

Bristow, G. (2005), 'Everyone's a "winner": problematising the discourse of regional competitiveness'. *Journal of Economic Geography*, 5: 285–304.

Bristow, G. (2010), 'Resilient regions: re-"place"ing regional competitiveness'. *Cambridge Journal of Regions, Economy and Society* 3: 153–167.

Finger & Kreinin (1979), 'A measure of export similarity and its possible uses'. The Economic Journal 78: 905–912.

Foray, D. (2015), Smart Specialization: Opportunities and Challenges Regional Innovation Policy, Routledge, London.

Fornahl, D., S. Henn & M. P. Menzel (2010), *Emerging clusters: theoretical, empirical and political perspectives on the initial stage of cluster evolution*. Cheltenham: Edward Elgar.

Gill, I. (2010), 'Regional development policies: place-based or people-centred?' Paris: OECD Regional Development Policy Division.

Glaeser, E. L. (2008), *Cities, agglomeration and spatial equilibrium*. Oxford: Oxford University Press.

Glaeser, E. L. (2011), *Triumph of the city*. London: MacMillan.

Huggins, R. (2010), 'Regional competitive intelligence: benchmarking and policy-making'. *Regional Studies* 44: 639–658.

Malecki, E. J. (2002), 'Hard and soft networks for urban competitiveness'. *Urban Studies* 39: 929–945.

Melo, P. de, Graham, D. & Noland, R., 2009, 'A Meta-Analysis of Estimates of Urban Agglomeration Economies', Regional Science and Urban Economics, 39 (3), 332–342.

Östergötland (2014), 'Smart Specialization Strategy'. Linkopping, Sweden.

Porter, M. (1980), Competitive Strategy: Techniques for Analyzing Industries and Competitors, The Free Press.

Thissen, M. & F. van Oort (2010). 'European place-based development policy and sustainable economic agglomeration'. *Tijdschrift voor Economische en Sociale Geografie* 101: 473–480.

Thissen, M., F. van Oort, D. Diodato & A. Ruijs (2013), *Regional competitiveness and smart specialization in Europe. Place-based development in international economic networks*. Cheltenham: Edward Elgar.

Thissen, M., D. Diodato & F. van Oort (2013b), 'Trade between European Nuts2 regions in 2000'. Working paper, The Hague: The PBL Netherlands Environmental assessment Agency.

Thissen, M., D. Diodato & F. van Oort (2013c), 'Trade between European Nuts2 regions from 2000 to 2010; An update of trade data for 2000'. Working paper, The Hague: The PBL Netherlands Environmental assessment Agency.

Thissen, M. F., T. de Graaff & F. van Oort (2016), Competitive network positions in trade and structural economic growth: A geographically weighted regression analysis for European regions, *Papers in Regional Science*, forthcoming, doi:10.1111/pirs.12224.

Tracey, P. & G. Clark (2003), 'Alliances, networks and competitive strategy: rethinking clusters of innovation'. *Growth and Change* 34: 1–16.

World Bank (2009), *World Development Report: Reshaping economic geography.* Washington, DC: World Bank.

7 New Measures of Regional Competitiveness in a Globalizing World

Bart Los, Maureen Lankhuizen and Mark Thissen

7.1 Introduction

Improvements in information and communication technologies have allowed companies to relocate parts of their production process to countries with more favorable comparative advantages, as a consequence of which gross exports require the imports of intermediate inputs and gross export values are no longer indicative of the welfare consequences of a country's exports. This 'second global unbundling' (Baldwin, 2006) has similar implications for the measures of competitiveness of regions defined at subnational level. Dudenhöffer (2005), for example, found that only 33% of the value of a high-end Porsche produced in a Leipzig (Sachsen) factory was actually added in Germany as a whole, after the firm decided to offshore important parts of the production process to the Bratislava region in the Slovak Republic. Before such offshoring was possible, each Porsche sold to e.g. a Bavarian or Austrian customer could be seen as a sign of competitiveness of Sachsen's car manufacturing industry. After the second unbundling, such a regional gross export value indicates much less about Sachsen's competitiveness in car manufacturing, because Sachsen's own contribution is low. In this chapter, we use a newly developed database to provide the first assessments of the competitiveness of regions that address this problem. Such information is essential for the proper design of smart specialization strategies for these regions, since these should take into account the fact that regions and countries have become much more interdependent than they used to be.

Timmer *et al.* (2013) argue that the new organization of production processes calls for a novel set of indicators of national competitiveness, taking value chains as the unit of analysis. Such a chain contains all of the value-adding activities that are needed to produce a final manufacturing product. In the case of cars assembled in Sachsen, these do not only include the assembly activities, but also the production of parts and components in Sachsen, other German regions and elsewhere in the world and the supply of all kinds of services that facilitate the design, manufacturing, marketing and sales. Using data from the, at the time, very recent World Input-Output Database and simple matrix algebra dating back to Leontief (1936), Timmer *et al.* (2013) could identify internationally fragmented value chains. To stress the international dimension, they borrowed the term 'Global Value Chains' (GVCs) from authors like Gereffi (1999), Kaplinsky (2000), Humphrey and

Schmitz (2002) and Sturgeon *et al.* (2008), who mainly studied the causes and consequences of the international fragmentation of production from a case study perspective. Timmer *et al.* quantify the value added generated by a country in a GVC (or a set of GVCs), label this GVC Income and consider changes in GVC Income as an indicator of changes in national competitiveness.

This chapter develops measures of competitiveness for EU regions at NUTS2-level, along the same lines as Timmer *et al.* (2013) did for countries. Within countries, transportation costs and transaction costs (due to, for example, exchange rate risks and legal and cultural differences) will be relatively low, leading to situations in which small differences in comparative advantage across regions can lead to the relocation of stages of production from one region to another one. Hence, the main research question addressed in this chapter is: 'To what extent did regions in the EU maintain or improve their GVC Income?' Participating in Global Value Chains and upgrading to higher value added activities within these has become an essential aspect of regional development. Our analysis quantifies the success of European regions in doing so, and emphasizes the heterogeneity of regions within countries in being successful in this respect. We will not only focus on GVC Income at the aggregate level, but also pay attention to (changes in) its composition. The analysis will be based on global input-output tables based on the World Input-Output Database (see Dietzenbacher *et al.* 2013b and Timmer *et al.* 2015) for which the EU-part is disaggregated into regions at the NUTS2-level, using data and techniques described in Thissen *et al.* (2013). The period of analysis is 2000–2010. In a number of analyses, we will split this period into a sub-period before the global financial crisis (2000–2007) and a sub-period afterwards (2007–2010).

7.2 Competitiveness and the Concept of Global Value Chain Income

For a long time, gross exports were a good indicator of what could be called the 'revealed competitiveness' of regions or countries.[1] If the products of a country sold well on international markets, the country was considered to be competitive with respect to these products. High transportation costs or high costs of coordinating the various stages of production led to a situation in which firms minimized costs by locating important subsets of these stages at geographically close sites. Hence, the value of an exported product was generally a good reflection of the value added in the exporting country.[2] This situation has changed quite dramatically in recent times. The internet revolution has led to substantial reductions in the costs of communication and coordination. Not only have e-mail and video-conferencing offered new ways of communication, but also databases on inventories etc. can be maintained and consulted instantaneously form virtually anywhere in the world. Next to this, some large countries have opened up to trade and foreign direct investment. As a consequence of these developments, firms are much more able to benefit from differences in comparative advantages between countries (and regions) than before.

Table 7.1 A stylized global value chain

Country	A →	B →	C →	D
Domestic value added	10	10	10	
Export value		10	20	30

Source: *Los and Timmer (2015)*.

Table 7.1 shows that in a world in which internationally fragmented production processes are prominent, gross exports do not give a good impression of the competitiveness of countries (or regions) anymore. Table 7.1 is based on the supposition that the production process of a particular final product (say a car) requires three stages of production, carried out in countries A, B and C. A Global Value Chain (GVC) is identified by the industry and country in which the last stage of production takes place (in this case, the car manufacturing industry in country C). This country is called the country-of-completion. The gross exports of the car manufacturing industry in C amount to 30 units (euros, for example). This value is not a good reflection of C's competitiveness in the production of cars, since its own activities generate only €10 of value added. If activities worth €29 would have taken place in A and B, C might also have exported €30, but it would have benefitted from a considerably lower GDP contribution of these exports.

The GVC approach advocated by Timmer *et al.* (2013) traces the contributions of every country that participates in the production process. It builds upon the simple accounting identity that the value of the final product that is consumed (either domestically or abroad) equals the sum of the value added generated in each activity required to produce the final product. In the case of Figure 7.1, the value of the final product exported by C to D consumed by D (€30) is found to be composed of value added in A, B and C (€10 each). In our view, changes in the value added shares of a country in a value chain can be seen as a more accurate indication of changes in its competitiveness in this chain. Furthermore, we think that competitiveness indicators in a world with geographically fragmented production processes should not remain limited to value added contributions to final products that are exported. If increasingly more components going into Porsches are produced in the Slovak Republic rather than in Germany (the country-of-completion), this should affect Germany's competitiveness in producing cars, irrespective of whether the Porsches are mainly exported or sold in Germany itself.

Since the world consists of many countries and even more regions (defined as geographical entities at subnational level), each of which produce several types of final products, the world production structure can be seen as a huge network of GVCs. Generally speaking, industries in these regions contribute to multiple value chains. The Slovakian car manufacturing industry not only engages in activities required to produce Porsches in Sachsen, but also supplies its intermediate products to the value chains of e.g. Czech cars, and possibly also to GVCs of final products other than cars. Timmer *et al.* (2013) suggested to use the label 'GVC Income' for the value added generated by a country in the production of all

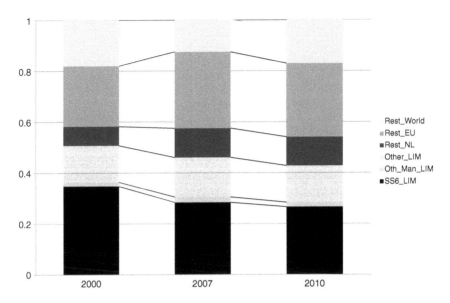

Figure 7.1 GVC Income shares in value chain for Limburg's electrical and transport
equipment.

Source: Authors' computations.
Notes: LIM: Limburg; NL: The Netherlands; Rest_World: all non-EU countries; SS6: Electrical and
transport equipment industry; Oth_Man: Other manufacturing.

final manufactured products completed anywhere in the world. The reason for not
including the production of final services and other non-manufactured products
relates to the low international or interregional 'contestability' of these products.
Many final services cannot but be produced very close to the consumer of the
service. Furthermore, they generally require few intermediate inputs. Hence, the
production processes of such products are characterized by very low degrees of
fragmentation, as a consequence of which the concept of GVC Income is much
less appropriate. It should be noted, though, that many activities in services are
part of GVCs, since the supply of financial services and business services are
indispensable in the production of final manufactured products.[3]

Changes in the GVC Income of a region can be attributed to two broadly defined
sources. First, the region can increase its GVC Income in one or multiple GVCs, by
upgrading its activities. It can, for example, engage in higher-value added activities
than before, or start participating in GVCs it had not contributed to before. These
are examples of increased regional competitiveness due to the types of upgrading
in GVCs as popularized by Humphrey and Schmitz (2002). The second source of
changes in regional GVC Income relates to differences in the rate of growth of the
output of GVCs. The GVCs with fast-growing regions-of-completion tend to grow
more rapidly than other GVCs, in particular when the product considered has a
favorable demand elasticity with respect to income. Regions participating heavily
in such GVCs will see their GVC Income grow relatively fast, other things equal.[4]

This chapter presents results of the first attempt to quantify the competitiveness of regions in the EU, using the GVC Income yardstick. The next section is devoted to a brief discussion of the data that have been constructed to arrive at these quantifications.

7.3 Global Input-Output Tables with Regional Detail

Timmer *et al.* (2013) computed their GVC Income levels by country on the basis of global input-output tables produced in the World Input-Output Database (WIOD) project (see Dietzenbacher *et al.* 2013b for technical details, and Timmer *et al.* 2015 for an accessible introduction). A *national* input-output table for a given year contains information about the value of transactions in that year between any pair of industries in the country considered, as well as information about the value of transactions in that year between any industry and any final demand category (e.g. household consumption and gross fixed capital formation). As such, it gives a quantitative representation of the national production structure and its links with users of the final products that it delivers. A *global* input-output table provides similar insights, but in the context of the global production structure and its links with users of final products. As such, it not only shows the value of sales by the French chemicals industry to French agriculture, but also the value of sales by the French chemicals industry to Spanish agriculture. Exports of final products are included as well. Global input-output tables also report the value added as generated in each of the industries in each of the countries. These also play a pivotal role in computing GVC Income, as we will show below.

The construction of WIOD's global input-output tables basically required three types of data: national accounts data, national supply and use tables and bilateral trade data. Dealing with inconsistencies between these data (most often due to differences in measurement concepts and differences in product and industry classifications) provided the main challenges. The first release of WIOD contained global input-output tables with 40 countries (the 28 current EU member countries except Croatia, and twelve economically important countries on other continents, such as the US, Brazil, India, China and Japan) and one composite 'country' labeled the 'Rest of the World'. Each country contains 35 industries and the data were available for 1995–2011.

Measuring GVC Income for EU regions requires extended global input-output tables. Interregional input-output tables for the EU would not suffice, since China might well add value to intermediate products it imports from an EU region. Hence, we used WIOD's global input-output tables as the starting point, and split EU countries into NUTS2 regions.[5] In order to treat each of these 200+ regions as pseudo-countries in the global input-output table, a number of additional sources of data had to be employed. These include regional economic accounts, regional supply and use tables (or, depending on availability, input-output tables) and transportation data to estimate trade among EU-regions and between EU-regions and non-EU countries. Regional supply and use tables were only used if they are based on survey data, and had not been obtained via updating methods based on national production structures. This implies that this kind of data could only be used for a limited number of countries, i.e. Spain, Italy and Finland.[6] If these data were unavailable, coefficients derived from national supply and use tables were imputed. This is clearly a weaker aspect of the data, but it should be borne in mind that differences between regions regarding specialization patterns (by means of the regional economic accounts data) and openness to trade (by means of the transportation data, see Thissen *et al.* 2013) could be incorporated.[7]

The database used for the GVC Income analyses in this chapter contains global input-output tables for 2000–2010. We will focus on changes in regional competitiveness in the pre-crisis period, 2000–2007 and in the immediate aftermath of the crisis, 2007–2010. The industry classification is less detailed than the classification used in the conventional WIOD tables, as a consequence of the rather aggregated nature of regional economic accounts. Each regional economy has been split into 14 industries (agriculture; mining and energy supply; five manufacturing industries; construction; and six services industries). The number of regions varies across countries. Eight EU-countries (Bulgaria, Cyprus, Estonia, Latvia, Lithuania, Luxemburg, Malta and Romania) have been included as a single country, either because of the small size of the country or because of data limitations. At the other end of the spectrum, we have the United Kingdom and Germany, which have been represented by 37 and 41 regions, respectively.

7.4 Regional Competitiveness in the EU: Results

With the data as described in the previous section at hand, relatively simple input-output computations (dating back to Leontief, 1936) can be used to compute the GVC Income of regions in a GVC, or a set of GVCs. We denote the number of regions/countries by M and the number of industries per country/region by N. For a given year, the ($MN \times MN$) matrix $\mathbf{Z}$ contains the values of the intermediate inputs sold by each of the MN industries in the rows to each of the MN industries in the columns.[8] These include transactions among firms within an industry. Let us denote the MN-vector with gross output levels (the values of all sales for each industry) by $\mathbf{x}$. The double-entry book-keeping identity ensures that all expenses by an industry (including payments for production factors, i.e. value added) add up to the corresponding value in $\mathbf{x}$. The ($MN \times MN$) matrix $\mathbf{A}$ contains the input coefficients, which are defined as the cents of each of the MN industry outputs required as intermediate inputs per euro of gross output in the industry corresponding to the column of $\mathbf{A}$. It is computed as $\mathbf{A} = \mathbf{Z}\hat{\mathbf{x}}^{-1}$. $\mathbf{A}$ thus gives information on, for instance, the Alsatian electrical equipment requirements to produce a car in Baden-Württemberg. The production of Alsatian electrical equipment in turn requires production of Alsatian financial intermediation services. Following Leontief's logic, the gross output levels of all MN industries required to produce one unit of final demand of a specific product is given by the elements in the column of the 'Leontief inverse' ($\mathbf{L} \equiv (\mathbf{I} - \mathbf{A})^{-1}$), associated with the final product considered.[9] The value added contributions associated with unit final demand levels can then be expressed as the $(MN \times MN)$ matrix $\mathbf{V} = \mathbf{\hat{w}L}$, in which $\mathbf{w}$ contains the MN value added over gross output ratios. Finally, actual final demand levels are not equal to unity. If we denote levels of final demand (aggregated over the regions and countries in which it is exerted) by the MN-vector $\mathbf{f}$, we can write $\mathbf{gvci} = \mathbf{V\hat{f}u}$, in which u stands for an MN-vector with ones in cells related to manufacturing industries and zeros elsewhere. The MN-vector $\mathbf{gvci}$ gives the GVC Income of all industries. Elements of this vector can be added to arrive at the GVC Income of an entire region.

7.4.1 Illustrations for the Dutch region Limburg

An illustration of the results of the above-described computations regarding changes in competitiveness in a particular GVC is presented in Figure 7.1. This graph shows the shares of six (groups) of industries in all income associated with the production of final output by the electrical and transport equipment in the Dutch region Limburg.

The GVC Income share of this industry in Limburg has steadily decreased, from about 35% in 2000 to less than 27% in 2010. The shares of other industries in Limburg have been relatively stable, which implies that the Limburg's GVCI share in this GVC has decreased from 51% to almost 43%.[10] Part of Limburg's loss in GVC share was picked up by industries in the Rest of The Netherlands, but most of the fruits of fragmentation were reaped by other European countries. In the years after the crisis, the share of the non-EU countries grew, at the expense of the EU. Both in 2000 and in 2010, nearly 20% of the value of final products of the Limburgian electrical and transport equipment industry was contributed outside the EU, indicating the truly global character of this value chain.

The results depicted in Figure 7.1 do not indicate that the region of Limburg in general and its electrical and transport equipment industry in particular have become less competitive in the production of final products delivered by electrical and transport equipment industries around the world. It might be that the increased opportunities to benefit from differences in comparative advantages across regions and countries have led to more pronounced specialization patterns within these GVCs. Limburg might, for example, have seen its 'pure manufacturing' activities relocated elsewhere, for example because these could be performed cheaper in other regions or countries. This should not be considered as a loss of competitiveness if it would have contributed more R&D, design or marketing activities to GVCs with a different region-of-completion than it did before. Figure 7.2 shows how Limburgian industries fared in all GVCs for electrical and transport equipment together. The Rest of The Netherlands has been included in the graph to give a first illustration of the heterogeneity of changes in regional competitiveness across regions within a country.

If GVCI shares would have remained stable between 2000 and 2007, the bars in the left-hand side panel of Figure 7.2 would have reached 100. The right-hand side panel of the figure refers to the period 2000–2010. The results show that

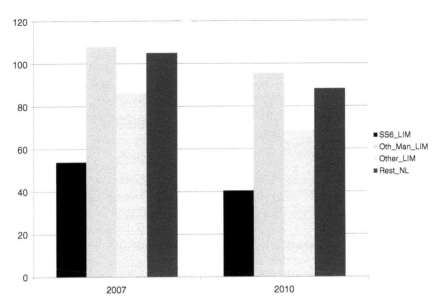

Figure 7.2 Change in GVC Income shares in all value chains for electrical and transport equipment (2000 = 100), Limburg and The Netherlands.

Source: Authors' computations.
Notes: LIM: Limburg; NL: The Netherlands; Rest_World: all non-EU countries; SS6: Electrical and transport equipment industry; Oth_Man: Other manufacturing.

Limburg has lost in terms of competitiveness in these GVCs. The GVCI share of the Limburgian electrical and transport equipment industry fell by about 46% between 2000 and 2007, and continued to fall afterwards, to only slightly more than 40% of its 2000 value in 2010. The losses in competitiveness did not remain confined to this industry. The share of non-manufacturing industries (mainly providing business ser-vices) fell by about 14% over 2000–2007 and by roughly another 18% over 2007–2010. Figure 7.2 also shows that the trend in losing competitiveness in GVCs for electrical and transport equipment as found for Limburg is not resembled by tenden-cies for the Dutch economy in general. The rest of the Dutch economy (the aggre-gation of all Dutch regions apart from Limburg) even gained some GVC Income share in the period 2000–2007, and only started to falter when the crisis hit. Still, the Rest of The Netherlands lost 12% of its competitiveness over 2000–2010, but this reduction amounted to as much as 43% for Limburg. Apparently, opportunities for geographical fragmentation of production processes in the electrical and transport equipment industry have hurt Limburg more than the national Dutch economy.

The analysis so far focused on the competitiveness of Limburg in a single GVC (for electrical and transport equipment completed in the region itself) or a small subset of GVCs (for electrical and transport equipment completed any-where in the world). Our main regional competitiveness indicator, however, is the trend in the share of regional GVC Income in global GVC Income (i.e., all value added generated to produce worldwide final demand for manufactured products). Figure 7.3 presents the results for 2000–2007 and 2000–2010.

The decreases in competitiveness of the electrical and transport equipment manufacturing industry in Limburg are almost identical to those reported in Figure 7.2. This is not surprising, since this industry performs the vast majority of its activities for GVCs producing final electrical and transportation equipment. Even if this industry would have gained in competitiveness in other GVCs, the effects of this would have been dwarfed by its competitiveness losses in GVCs to which it caters most of its activities.

Figure 7.3 also shows that the declining performance of the electrical and transport equipment industry in Limburg is not representative of the Limburgian economy in general. The other manufacturing industries considered together actually managed to increase their GVC Income share between 2000 and 2007. This share grew by 3% in this period. Right after the crisis, it lost more than these gains. Other industries in Limburg lost competitiveness during the entire period, but at a much slower pace than the electrical and transport equipment industry. Actually, the share in Limburgian GVC Income generated in the electrical and transport equipment industry dropped from 20% in 2000 to just above 10% in 2010.

The changes for the Rest of The Netherlands resemble those reported for the EU27 as a whole by Timmer *et al.* (2013, p. 634). In the pre-crisis period, Dutch competitiveness remained about stable, despite the increasing role of China and

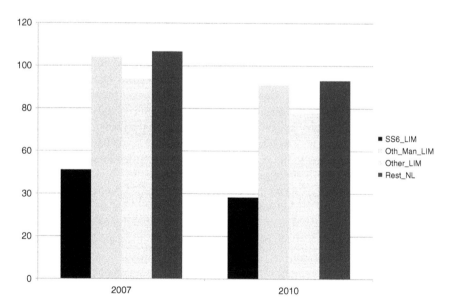

Figure 7.3 Change in GVC Income in all value chains for manufactured products (2000 = 100), Limburg and The Netherlands.

Source: Authors' computations.

Notes: LIM: Limburg; NL: The Netherlands; Rest_World: all non-EU countries; SS6: Electrical and transport equipment industry; Oth_Man: Other manufacturing.

some other emerging economies. In 2000, The Netherlands as a whole had a GVC Income share of 1.26%, which slightly increased to 1.33% in 2007. Only when the crisis hit, the EU27 started to lose competitiveness. As Figure 7.3 shows, this also happened to the Rest of The Netherlands. The GVC Income share of The Netherlands as a whole dropped to 1.15% in 2010, which implies a decrease of approximately 8% in the 2000–2010 period. The aggregate regional economy of Limburg lost as much as 25% of its GVC Income share in the same period.

When interpreting results like those in Figures 7.1–7.3, it is important to realize that all global input–output tables that have currently been constructed (including ours) attribute value added to the territory where it is generated, and not to the territory where the income is enjoyed. For the part of value added that is earned as labour income, this is a relatively minor issue. The vast majority of workers live in the region where they work. Things might be different regarding the part of value added called gross operating surplus (the compensation for capital defined in its broadest sense, including intellectual property). Frequently, profits are repatriated to the corporate headquarters, which are often located in other regions or in other countries (in the case of FDI). Shareholders, the 'ultimate investors' who receive parts of the profits, might reside in even other countries. Issues like these imply that Limburg might have remained more competitive in terms of income generation by its inhabitants, by developing activities elsewhere. As long as activities on regional soil are considered, it did considerably worse than the Rest of The Netherlands.

7.4.2 Within-country heterogeneity in regional competitiveness trends

The illustration for the case of the Limburg region shows that trends in competitiveness can vary considerably, both across industries within regions and across regions within countries. In this subsection, we will analyze the latter type of heterogeneity a bit more systematically, for three countries: The Netherlands, Italy and Spain.

Figure 7.4 depicts the changes in competitiveness of the twelve Dutch NUTS2 regions between 2000 and 2007 (horizontal axis) and 2000 and 2010 (vertical axis), as measured by changes in the region's share in worldwide Global Value Chain Income. The light-coloured dot refers to the performance of The Netherlands as a whole. Its position below the 45 degrees line shows that The Netherlands became less competitive in the period after the crisis. This holds for all Dutch regions, apart from Groningen, which is represented by the diamond in the upper right corner. This region is known to be an outlier in many regional analyses, due to the extraction of natural gas.[11]

Seven out of the remaining eleven regions already lost competitiveness before the crisis. Limburg performed worst in this respect (it lost 11% of its 2000-GVC Income share), but also Friesland (–5%), Gelderland (–3%), Utrecht (–3%) and Noord Brabant (–2%) became less competitive. The regions that became clearly more competitive in this period were Zuid Holland (+14%), Zeeland (+22%) and Flevoland (+29%). Flevoland is the newest of the Dutch provinces and was reclaimed from the sea after World War II. Its largest city (Almere) is the fastest growing city of The Netherlands and is favorably located in the vicinity of Amsterdam. The

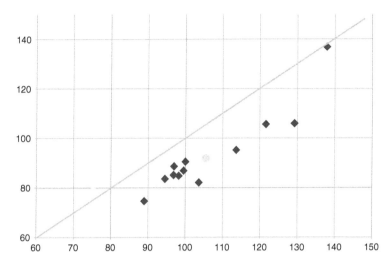

Figure 7.4 Heterogeneity in regional competitiveness trends, The Netherlands.

Source: Authors' computations.

Notes: The index on the horizontal axis indicates the growth in a region's GVC Income share between 2000 and 2007 (2000 = 100). The index on the vertical axis indicates the growth in a region's GVC Income share between 2000 and 2010 (2000 = 100). The diamonds represent regions, the dot indicates the position of the national economy.

province as a whole is benefiting from improvements in its infrastructure. These features might explain the good competitiveness performance of this region.

The crisis and its aftermath did not imply a good deal of change regarding the trends in competitiveness, with one main exception. The Northern region of Drenthe had a higher GVC Income share in 2007 than in 2000, but its 2010 share was 18% lower than in 2000. With that score, only Limburg lost more over 2000–2010.

Figure 7.5 presents a similar representation of regional heterogeneity regarding changes in competitiveness within a country, but this time for Italy. Unlike in The Netherlands, two regions are located above the 45 degrees line, which indicates that these regions were more competitive after the crisis than before. Molise (a small mountainous region in Central Italy) managed to extend its competitiveness gains from 2000–2007 further in 2007–2010, while the Northern region of Bolzano (close to Austria) reverted its 9% loss in GVC share in the early period into a 5% gain for the entire period considered. The national Italian economy was almost as competitive in 2007 as it was in 2000, but lost about 20% of its GVC Income share in and immediately after the crisis. The regions that lost most in the entire 2000–2010 period were Marche (–65%), Emilia-Romagna (–59%), Lombardia (the industrial heart of Italy, –29%) and Basilicata (–24%). Apart from Molise (+16%) and Bolzano (+5%), Sardegna (+10%) and Valle d'Aosta (another small region, +3%) were the only regions to become more competitive in 2000–2010.

The trends for Spanish regions are summarized in Figure 7.6. The Spanish economy saw its GVC Income share grow by 2.5% from 2000 until the advent of

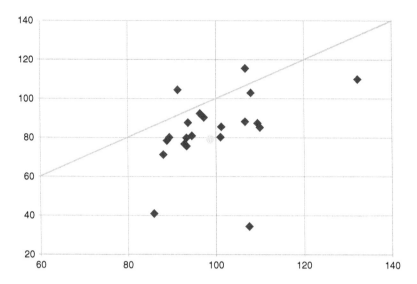

Figure 7.5 Heterogeneity in regional competitiveness trends, Italy.

Source: Authors' computations.
Notes: The index on the horizontal axis indicates the growth in a region's GVC Income share between 2000 and 2007 (2000 = 100). The index on the vertical axis indicates the growth in a region's GVC Income share between 2000 and 2010 (2000 = 100). The diamonds represent regions, the dot indicates the position of the national economy.

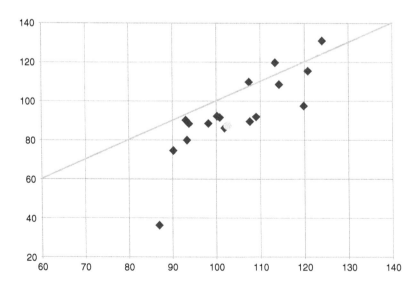

Figure 7.6 Heterogeneity in regional competitiveness trends, Spain.

Source: Authors computations.
Notes: Basque Country: 2001 = 100. In addition, see the notes to Figure 7.4.

the crisis, but lost 13% over the entire 2000–2010 period (as compared to 8% for the Netherlands and 21% for Italy). The regions that lost most in terms of competitiveness from 2000 to 2010 were Valencia (–64%), Aragon (–25%) and Asturias (–20%). Next to these 'failures', five regions can be considered as 'miracles', in the sense that these became more competitive in this time span. These were the island regions Illes Balears (+31%) and Canarias (+20%), Murcia (+15%), Galicia (+10%) and the capital region Madrid (+9%).

Figures 7.4–7.6 show that regions within countries are often very heterogeneous with regard to changes in their competitiveness when measured by means of changes in their GVC Income shares. In all three countries considered, a number of regions lost competitiveness, while others became more competitive. Before turning to some statistics that might account for such differences, it might be interesting to compare a number of countries with respect to this type of heterogeneity.

Table 7.2 presents this type of results. In the column labeled '2000–2007', we document the unweighted population standard deviation for the observations projected on the horizontal axis in Figures 7.4–7.6. The larger this standard deviation, the more heterogeneous the regional competitiveness changes within the country are considered have been in the period that preceded the crisis. In the column labeled '2000–2010', similar standard deviations are presented, but this time they are based on the observations projected on the vertical axis in Figures 7.4–7.6. We add results for three big countries (France, Germany and the United Kingdom) which are not covered by Figures 7.4–7.6.

The standard deviations in the table show that regional heterogeneity with regard to changes in competitiveness in the pre-crisis period was smallest in France and the UK. In both countries, the vast majority of regions lost significant proportions of their GVC Income shares. The largest heterogeneity is found for Germany. Examination of region-level results (not reported here) shows that this large heterogeneity is mainly due to the strong performance of regions in the Eastern part of the country. These regions continued to become more integrated after German reunification, as a consequence of which their shares in GVC Incomes grew. The results for 2000–2010 indicate that the negative effects of the crisis for those countries that were hit hardest (Italy and Spain) were not evenly

Table 7.2 Within-Country heterogeneity in regional competitiveness trends

	2000–2007	*2000–2010*
France	4.7	6.9
Germany	15.7	12.8
Italy	10.5	18.6
The Netherlands	14.7	15.8
Spain	11.0	20.4
United Kingdom	7.8	11.2

Source: Authors' computations.
Notes: Numbers present unweighted population standard deviations for regional GVC Income shares compared to their 2000 levels (2000 = 100).

spread over the regions in these countries. For both countries, the reported standard deviations almost doubled from 2007 to 2010, whereas the increases in dispersion were much less marked in The Netherlands, France and the United Kingdom. In Germany, the heterogeneity in competitiveness growth was even smaller for 2000–2010 than for 2000–2007.

7.4.3 Within-country heterogeneity in specialization patterns

As discussed in Section 7.2 of this chapter, changes in regional GVC Income shares can be caused by two broad categories of changes. First, the region concerned can upgrade its activities within (some of) the GVCs it is active in already. Alternatively, it might lose ground in such chains, for example because trade barriers with a country offering an attractive mix of factor prices make companies decide to relocate part of the production process that originally took place in the region considered. Secondly, regions might have specialized in GVCs that grow relatively fast (or slow). Regions that perform activities for GVCs with China as the country-of-completion generally see their GVC Income grow faster than regions that mainly cater to GVCs with more stagnant countries as the country-of-completion. The output growth rates of GVCs do not only vary according to the country in which the final stage of production takes place, but also differ across the types of products these deliver. In a world in which living standards (at least if measured in terms of material well-being) continue to increase, the production of luxury products tends to grow faster than the production of products that mainly fulfil basic needs. In this subsection, we will present some results on the heterogeneity of regions within countries with respect to the product-specific GVCs in which they generate their GVC Income.

   To depict this type of heterogeneity, we follow Timmer *et al.* (2013) in using a modified Revealed Comparative Advantage (RCA) indicator. Balassa (1965) introduced this indicator as the value share of gross exports of a product in all gross exports by a country, divided by the average share computed for the full set of countries considered. If this ratio for a product exceeded one, Balassa considered the country under consideration to be specialized in exporting this product. In line with the contents of the chapter so far, we will not consider the shares of exported products in the total export bundle, but will consider the share of a region's GVC Income that is generated in producing for GVCs producing a specific product group. The relatively high level of industry aggregation in the global input–output tables dictates our choice to consider five broadly defined GVCs: those producing food, beverages and tobacco; those producing textiles and leather products; those which have fuels and chemicals as their final output; those producing electrical and transportation equipment (see the illustration regarding the Dutch province of Limburg in subsection 7.4.1); and the GVCs producing other manufactured final products. We do not distinguish between countries-of-completion. We compare a region's share of GVC Income due to a product-specific set of GVCs to the corresponding share in the national economy to which the region under consideration belongs.

   We will present results for regions in the three countries that we also studied in the previous subsection, i.e. The Netherlands, Italy and Spain. For each of these countries, we focus on two regions. Figure 7.7 presents results for Limburg and Zuid Holland, two regions in The Netherlands. As Figure 7.7a shows, in 2000 Limburg was quite specialized in creating value added in GVCs producing electrical and transport equipment. The GVC Income-RCA had a value of 1.43. Limburg contributed much less to GVCs for fuels and chemicals than Dutch national economy did, which is reflected in an GVC Income-RCA of 0.41. The shares of GVC Income generated in the remaining three types of GVCs were more or less in line with the Dutch average, as indicated by GVC Income-RCAs relatively close to one. Figure 7.7b shows a similar diagram for Zuid Holland, one of the more successful Dutch regions in the sense that it lost less than 5% of its GVC Income share over the period 2000–2010. In comparison to Limburg, Zuid Holland had a very different specialization pattern in 2000. It was highly specialized in activities contributing to fuel and chemicals GVCs (GVC Income-RCA: 1.48), and had an otherwise not very prominent specialization pattern.

Figure 7.7 also shows that the specialization pattern of Zuid Holland remained relatively stable over the decade. Its specialization in activities in GVCs for fuels and chemicals weakened a bit (the GVC Income-RCA decreased from 1.48 to 1.32) and the de-specialization in 2000 regarding GVCs for electrical and transport equipment almost disappeared (0.87 in 2000, 0.96 in 2010). The changes in specialization patterns in Limburg were much more marked. Its specialization in contributing to electrical and transport equipment weakened substantially (the indicator decreased from 1.43 to 1.17) and it became specialized in catering to

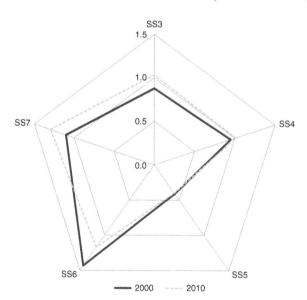

Figure 7.7a Heterogeneity in Dutch regional GVC specialization, Limburg.

Source: Authors' computations.
Notes: SS3: GVCs of food, beverages and tobacco; SS4: GVCs of textiles and leather products; SS5: GVCs of fuels and chemicals; SS6: GVCs of electrical and transport equipment; SS7: GVCs of other manufacturing; The reported values represent Revealed Comparative Advantages in contributing value added to a particular type of GVCs, as compared to the national average.

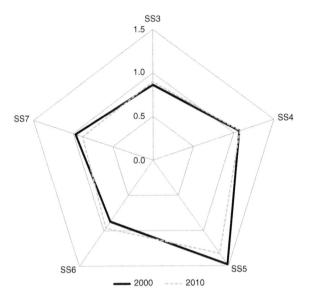

Figure 7.7b Heterogeneity in Dutch regional GVC specialization, Zuid Holland.

Source: Authors' computations.

Notes: SS3: GVCs of food, beverages and tobacco; SS4: GVCs of textiles and leather products; SS5: GVCs of fuels and chemicals; SS6: GVCs of electrical and transport equipment; SS7: GVCs of other manufacturing; The reported values represent Revealed Comparative Advantages in contributing value added to a particular type of GVCs, as compared to the national average.

GVCs of other manufacturing instead (the GVC Income-RCA grew from 1.10 to 1.30. Moreover, its negative specialization in adding value to food and beverages GVCs turned into a slightly positive specialization (0.88 to 1.03). Apparently, Limburg's loss of competitiveness as reflected in its diminishing GVC Income shares were accompanied by shifts between activities contributing to different value chains. In Zuid Holland, which managed to stay competitive before and after the crisis, specialization patterns have also remained much more stable.

Figures 7.8 and 7.9 present results for pairs of regions in Italy and Spain, respectively.

Lombardia, which is one of the regions that lost a large proportion (29%) of its GVC Income share between 2000 and 2010, was slightly specialized in contributing to fuel and chemicals GVCs, but became negatively specialized into these activities during the decade analyzed here (Figure 7.8a). Simultaneously, it strengthened its already strong specialization in textiles and leather products. For the Southern Italian region Basilicata, which also lost a large fraction (24%) of its GVC Income share, we do not find this type of increased specialization (Figure 7.8b). As opposed to Lombardia, it became considerably less specialized over time: its strong specialization in activities contributing to food-related GVCs and other manufacturing GVCs vanished and its strong de-specialization in adding value in the remaining three types of GVCs became considerably less prominent.

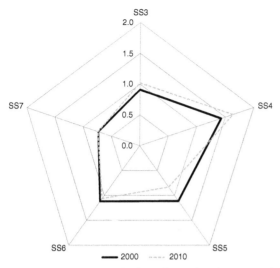

Figure 7.8a Heterogeneity in Italian regional GVC specialization, Lombardia.

Source: Authors' computations.
Notes: SS3: GVCs of food, beverages and tobacco; SS4: GVCs of textiles and leather products; SS5: GVCs of fuels and chemicals; SS6: GVCs of electrical and transport equipment; SS7: GVCs of other manufacturing; The reported values represent Revealed Comparative Advantages in contributing value added to a particular type of GVCs, as compared to the national average.

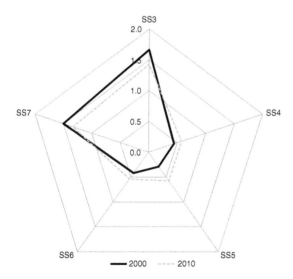

Figure 7.8b Heterogeneity in Italian regional GVC specialization, Basilicata.

Source: Authors' computations.
Notes: SS3: GVCs of food, beverages and tobacco; SS4: GVCs of textiles and leather products; SS5: GVCs of fuels and chemicals; SS6: GVCs of electrical and transport equipment; SS7: GVCs of other manufacturing; The reported values represent Revealed Comparative Advantages in contributing value added to a particular type of GVCs, as compared to the national average.

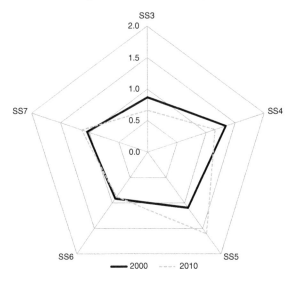

Figure 7.9a Heterogeneity in Spanish regional GVC specialization, Valencia.

Source: Authors' computations.

Notes: SS3: GVCs of food, beverages and tobacco; SS4: GVCs of textiles and leather products; SS5: GVCs of fuels and chemicals; SS6: GVCs of electrical and transport equipment; SS7: GVCs of other manufacturing; The reported values represent Revealed Comparative Advantages in contributing value added to a particular type of GVCs, as compared to the national average.

The two panels in Figure 7.9 also show that the dynamics of regional specialization in a world increasingly characterized by international and interregional fragmentation of production processes can be very different within a country. As discussed in the previous section, Valencia lost a large part of its competitiveness (its GVC Income share dropped by 64%). Figure 7.9a reveals that its specialization patterns also changed rather drastically. It became less specialized (in comparison to the Spanish national economy) in activities related to GVCs of textiles and leather products and de-specialized much further in food-related GVCs. These changes were accompanied by a strong increase in specialization in GVCs related to energy and chemicals. The decrease in Navarra's competitiveness was similar to that of Spain as a whole (losses in GVC Income share of about 13% over 2000–2010). In this period, its specialization pattern remained almost unchanged. Navarra continued to generate relatively much value added in GVCs of electrical and transport equipment. The slight initial specialization in GVC activity related to other manufactures disappeared, while it started to generate shares of GVC Income in food and beverages chains much more in line with the national average. The negative specialization in textiles and leather products GVCs remained virtually unchanged.

7.5 Conclusions

Increased opportunities for firms to split production processes of final products into stages that can be located in distant countries have led to new views on

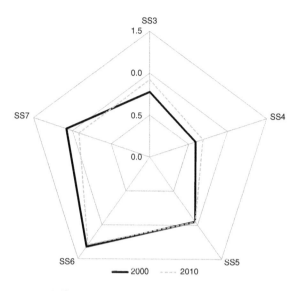

Figure 7.9b Heterogeneity in Spanish regional GVC specialization, Navarra.

Source: Authors' computations.

Notes: SS3: GVCs of food, beverages and tobacco; SS4: GVCs of textiles and leather products; SS5: GVCs of fuels and chemicals; SS6: GVCs of electrical and transport equipment; SS7: GVCs of other manufacturing; The reported values represent Revealed Comparative Advantages in contributing value added to a particular type of GVCs, as compared to the national average.

international trade (see, e.g., Johnson and Noguera, 2012, and Koopman *et al.* 2014). Purchasing high-quality imports of intermediate products can be crucial for the competitiveness of firms selling final products on domestic and foreign markets. This calls for new types of trade policies. Attracting FDI to promote domestic economic activity can yield disappointing results if investment policies and trade policies are not well-aligned.

Many issues like these also play a role at subnational level. Hence, it is of utmost importance that regional policy-makers can modify their smart specialization strategies to benefit as much as possible from the opportunities provided by the emergence of global value chains, while minimizing the downsides. Hence, accurate insights into the properties of networks of GVCs and the positions of countries in these networks are needed. In this chapter, we provided some first analyses based on a novel dataset that consists of global input-output tables with regional detail at NUTS2 level for EU countries. We focused on changes in shares in worldwide GVC Income as a measure of changes in regional competitiveness. Probably the most important conclusion of our illustrative examples (mainly for regions in The Netherlands, Italy and Spain) is that changes in competitiveness have been very heterogeneous across regions that are part of the same country. We observed such marked heterogeneity both for the period 2000–2007 (before the crisis hit) and for the period 2007–2010 (the crisis and its immediate aftermath). We also found that the specialization patterns of regions (and changes in those patterns) were very heterogeneous across regions within a country. In order to quantify such specialization patterns, we adopted a revealed comparative advantage indicator that focuses on the type of GVC a region contributes its activities to, rather than on the type of products it exports.

We feel that much more can be done with this rich database. Adding more variables, for example related to employment of persons of different skill levels and occupational status, would allow for evaluations of tendencies regarding employment in GVCs and the design of employment policies that take the 'chained' nature of economic activities into account. But even without such additional data, much more can be done. One could, for example, focus on the extent to which pairs of regions (or regions and non-EU countries such as China) are connected with each other through GVCs, and how such strengths of linkages change over time, and under what conditions. Such results provide important inputs to policymakers. These inputs are complementary to the existing types of policy-relevant insights regarding regional competitiveness and specialization.

Notes

1 The adjective 'revealed' should convey the message that the underlying determinants of competitiveness could not be studied by focusing on export performance. More detailed studies focusing on factor prices, productivity of factors, institutional quality, innovation performance etc. have always been needed to give policy-makers handles for competitiveness-enhancing policies.

2 The major exception was the value added associated with producing natural resources (e.g., the mining of iron ore required for the production of steel needed to produce a car) of which the availability is not evenly spread over the world.

3 Timmer *et al.* (2013) report that more than 40% of all EU-27 persons employed in GVCs in 2008 were active in services industries.

4 Opinions on whether these differential demand growth effects should be part of regional competitiveness measures vary. Some authors argue that successfully 'picking winners' by specializing in growing markets is an element of increasing competitiveness, whereas others see it as the beneficial effects of exogenous changes (see, for example the arguments contained in Chapter 6 of this book, and also those discussed in detail in Thissen *et al.* 2013).

5 As far as we know, this is the first project aimed at geographically disaggregating an entire trade bloc in global input-output tables. In a similar fashion, Dietzenbacher *et al.* (2013a) focused on Brazilian regions, Inomata and Meng (2013) on regions in China, Japan and South Korea, and Cherubini and Los (2016) on Italian macro-regions.

6 For the United Kingdom, data on production structures for entities much larger than NUTS2 regions could be used (tables for England and Northern Ireland, Wales, and Scotland).

7 For details regarding the database construction, see Thissen *et al.* (2016).

8 Following conventions in the input-output literature, we denote matrices by bold capital symbols, (column) vectors by bold lowercases and scalars by lowercases in italics. Primes indicate transposition and hats stand for diagonal matrices (see Miller and Blair, 2009).

9 I stands for the $(MN \times MN)$ identity matrix.

10 The contribution of other manufacturing industries in Limburg might seem low at first hand. This result is partly driven by the high level of industry aggregation. Some of

the components are supplied by other firms in the electrical and transport equipment industry.

11 This is an example of a situation as discussed above: our data show that the natural gas is drilled in the Groningen region, but we do not have information about the regions to which the non-labor income associated with this activity is transferred.

References

Balassa, B. (1965), 'Trade Liberalisation and 'Revealed' Comparative Advantage', *The Manchester School*, 33, 99–132.

Baldwin, R. E. (2006), 'Globalisation: The Great Unbundling(s)', In: *Globalisation Challenges for Europe*, Helsinki, Office of the Prime Minister of Finland.

Cherubini, L. and B. Los (2016), 'Regional Employment Patterns in a Globalizing World: A Tale of Four Italies', In: 'Global Value Chains: New Evidence and Implications', R. Cappariello (ed.), Bank of Italy Workshops and Conferences series, no. 21.

Dietzenbacher, E., J. J. M. Guilhoto and D. Imori (2013a), 'The Role of Brazilian Regions in the Global Value Chain', FEA-USP Working Paper 2013–15, University of Sao Paulo.

Dietzenbacher, E., B. Los, R. Stehrer, M. P. Timmer and G. J. de Vries (2013b), 'The Construction of World Input–Output Tables in the WIOD Project', *Economic Systems Research*, 25, 71–98.

Dudenhöffer, F. (2005), 'Wie Viel Deutschland Steckt im Porsche?', *ifo Schnelldienst*, 58, 3–5.

Gereffi, G. (1999), 'International Trade and Industrial Upgrading in the Apparel Commodity Chain', *Journal of International Economics*, 48, 37–70.

Humphrey, J. and H. Schmitz (2002), 'How Does Insertion in Global Value Chains Affect Upgrading in Industrial Clusters?', *Regional Studies*, 36, 1017–1027.

Inomata, S. and B. Meng (2013), 'Compilation and Use of the 2005 Transnational Interregional Input–Output Tables for China, Japan, and Korea', Institute of Developing Economies, Japan External Trade Organization, Chiba.

Johnson, R. and G. Noguera (2012), 'Accounting for Intermediates: Production Sharing and Trade in Value Added', *Journal of International Economics*, 86, 224–236.

Kaplinsky, R. (2000), 'Globalisation and Unequalisation: What Can Be Learned from Value Chain Analysis?', *Journal of Development Studies*, 37, 117–146.

Koopman, R., Z. Wang and S.-J. Wei (2014), 'Tracing Value-Added and Double Counting in Gross Exports', *American Economic Review*, 104, 459–494.

Leontief, W. (1936), 'Quantitative Input and Output Relations in the Economic Systems of the United States', *Review of Economics and Statistics*, 18, 105–125.

Los, B. and M. P. Timmer (2015), 'Appendix – Analysis of Global Production Networks: Approaches, Concepts and Data', in: J. Amador and F. di Mauro (eds.), *The Age of Global Value Chains: Maps and Policy Issues*, eBook, London: CEPR Press, 201–208.

Los, B., M. P. Timmer and G. J. de Vries (2015), 'How Global are Global Value Chains? A New Approach to Measure International Fragmentation', *Journal of Regional Science*, 55, 66–92.

Miller, R. E. and P. D. Blair (2009), *Input–Output Analysis; Foundations and Extensions* (2nd ed.), Cambridge: Cambridge University Press.

Sturgeon, T., J. van Biesebroeck and G. Gereffi (2008), 'Value Chains, Networks and Clusters: Reframing the Global Automotive Industry', *Journal of Economic Geography*, 8, 297–321.

Thissen, M., F. van Oort, D. Diodato and A. Ruijs (2013), *Regional Competitiveness and Smart Specialization in Europe*, Cheltenham: Edward Elgar.

Thissen, M., M. Lankhuizen and B. Los (2016), 'Construction of a Time Series of Fine-Grained detailed Nuts2 Regional Input–Output Tables for the EU embedded in a Global System of Country Tables', mimeo, PBL Netherlands Environmental Assessment Agency, The Hague.

Timmer, M. P., B. Los, R. Stehrer and G. J. de Vries (2013), 'Fragmentation, Incomes and Jobs: An Analysis of European Competitiveness', *Economic Policy*, 28, 613–661.

Timmer, M. P., E. Dietzenbacher, B. Los, R. Stehrer and G. J. de Vries (2015), 'An Illustrated User Guide to the World Input–Output Database: The Case of Global Automotive Production', *Review of International Economics*, 23, 575–605.

8 The Co-Evolution of Regional Innovation Domains and Institutional Arrangements

Smart Specialisation Through Quadruple Helix Relations?

Paul Vallance

8.1 Introduction

The development of a regional smart specialisation strategy has been interprcted as requiring the participation of a diverse range of actors in an entrepreneurial discovery process. According to the European Commission *Guide to Research and Innovation Strategies for Smart Specialisation (RIS 3)* these should include conventional innovation actors such as private sector enterprises and investors, public authorities and their agencies, and public research and educational/training organisations, but also wider representatives of regional civil society with a stake in local development processes (Foray *et al*. 2012). This position draws on the concept of the quadruple helix – which adds civil society, the community or the public to the triple helix of government, industry, and universities – and the more open and user-centred innovation processes that this is suggested to underpin (see Arnkil *et al*. 2010). It also makes a related link between smart specialisation and broader forms of innovation that are oriented towards social goals or challenges (for a critical discussion of this see Richardson *et al*. 2014). A subsequent paper by Carayannis and Rakhmatullin (2014) has reaffirmed this association between the quadruple helix model and smart specialisation by viewing it in its context of the EU Europe 2020 'smart, sustainable and inclusive growth' agenda. Others have suggested that quadruple helix models of innovation that include the wider community could be particularly important for peripheral or less favoured regions with a thinner institutional ecology of firms and research organisations (Kolehmainen *et al*. 2015) and this can provide an alternative to the pursuit of high-technology based growth as part of their smart specialisation strategies (Nordberg, 2015).

The quadruple helix is, however, (like smart specialisation itself) still at a stage of becoming more widely established as an academic concept. Therefore, despite the appealing nature of the confluence between these contemporary ideas (smart specialisation, quadruple helix, social innovation), there is a need for more reflection on the ways in which they are actually articulated with one another in innovation policy and practice. This chapter will approach this task by considering quadruple helix relationships as a particular institutional arrangement that may form in a region around a specific innovation domain. The importance of institutional and governance contexts (including previous innovation strategies) in shaping smart specialisation approaches in different regions has been noted in previous work (e.g. Morgan, 2013; McCann and Ortega-Argilés, 2014). However, this chapter is equally interested in how smart specialisation, as a process of identifying and developing regional innovation priorities, can itself be a dynamic through which institutional arrangements change. This can therefore contribute to the wider, but still relatively neglected, question in economic geography of how institutions co-evolve with the emergence of new paths in national or regional economies (see Strambach, 2010). By viewing this in relation to smart specialisation it also adds to the growing number of studies that highlight the role of regional policy in this process of path creation (e.g. Dawley, 2014; Coenen *et al.* 2015).

These themes will be explored through two case studies of the institutional development of smart specialisation domains in the regions of Northern Ireland in the UK and Tampere in Finland (Vallance and Kempton, 2015; Vallance and Goddard, 2015). The specific strategic priorities focused on in both regions – respectively connected health/stratified medicine and smart city – although referring to very different innovation domains, do have in common technological development and application with a strong social as well as economic dimension. Related to this, in both cases there is also a prospective role for societal users, whether patients or city residents, in the innovation process. This suggests the relevance of the quadruple helix framework, but the analysis will show that the actual applicability of this concept to these empirical cases needs to be qualified in reference to the ongoing emergence of an innovation system in which these societal actors can be integrated. The priority areas of connected health/stratified medicine and smart city are not unique to the regions of Northern Ireland or Tampere, but fields that are developing on at least a European scale. Indeed, in both cases the region is part of a growing cross-border partnership or transnational network around the area in question. However, the particular form they are taking as innovation domains in these regions is strongly shaped by specific institutional factors that will be outlined as part of the analysis below. These factors include multi-level governance systems, inherited policy and economic development paths, and the mix of different organisational actors in the innovation ecology and their patterns of systemic interaction.

The chapter has four further sections. A literature review positions the quadruple helix concept in an innovation system framework. The middle two sections are the regional case studies. These are based on key actor interviews (16 in Northern Ireland and 12 in Tampere) carried out during 2014 and 2015, supplemented with analysis of policy documents and other secondary sources. The concluding section discusses the parallels between the two cases and the implications for our understanding of institutional processes underpinning smart specialisation.

8.2 Conceptual Framework: Quadruple Helix Arrangements as Emerging Innovation Systems

The quadruple helix is an extension of the triple helix concept introduced by Henry Etzkowitz and Loet Leydesdorff. This concept broadly represents an innovation system framework formed of university, industry, and government relations (Leydesdorff and Etzkowitz, 1996). Like other approaches in this evolutionary systems tradition, therefore, it is based on the understanding of innovation as a non-linear dynamic arising from the interaction of different organisations (Etzkowitz and Leydesdorff, 2000). By designating that this interaction takes place between actors from three institutional spheres this framework allows for a more complex set of connections than models based on dyadic relations (e.g. bi-lateral university–industry links), and hence scope for variety that can prevent the system in question from becoming locked into a single technology trajectory (Leydesdorff, 2000; Viale and Pozzali, 2010). An important element of the triple helix concept that follows from this is a concern with institutional transformation via co-evolutionary processes of network formation and adaptation between (as well as within) each of the three helices (Etzkowitz *et al.* 2000). A key example of this is the emergence of an entrepreneurial model of the university through the growth of the academic sphere's interface with business and the development of linkages through intermediary organisations such as industry-focused research centres or technology transfer offices (Etzkowitz *et al.* 2000; Etzkowitz, 2003). This process, seen as first occurring in select U.S. universities (e.g. Stanford, MIT) during the twentieth century, is central to a normative account of transition to the knowledge-based economy that has informed the adoption of the triple helix concept as a paradigm for national or regional development as well as an analytical framework for understanding innovation processes (Etzkowitz, 2008).

The quadruple helix concept has also been positioned in relation to normative discourses around the changing nature and role of knowledge production in contemporary economies and societies. For instance, Arnkil *et al.* argue that:

> Quadruple Helix (QH), with its emphasis on broad cooperation in innovation, represents a shift towards systemic, open and user-centric innovation policy. An era of linear, top-down, expert driven development, production and services is giving way to different forms and levels of coproduction with consumers, customers and citizens. This also sets a challenge for public authorities and the production of public services.
>
> (Arnkil *et al.* 2010; executive summary)

This leads them to place the role of the user in innovation at the heart of their definition of the quadruple helix – i.e. as the fourth helix in cooperation with firms, universities, and public authorities. However, while this emphasis on users may not have been an explicit focus in the arguably more science and technology focused triple helix framework, it is recognised in the concept of interactive learning processes in the original national innovation systems concept, referring particularly to user-producer (firm) relationships (Lundvall, 1992). Subsequently, a focus on users – whether firms, communities, or individual customers – has become a central concern in innovation studies (e.g. Franke and Shah, 2003; Von Hippel, 2005; Grabher *et al.* 2008). Therefore, defining the quadruple helix in terms of being 'user-oriented' alone is not a strong enough basis on which to differentiate it as a new model: instead it is necessary to specify the role of civil society organisations, community groups or individual citizens as users, and address the distinctive challenges to more traditional understandings of innovation processes that this entails. The inclusion of these actors also reinforces the prospect that innovation in the quadruple helix can be towards broadly social goals; compared to the economic goals that are still the focus if, for instance, the users in question were taken to be members of the public as consumers helping firms to create new products.

Work by Carayannis and Campbell (2009; 2012), which represents the highest profile attempt to formulate a quadruple helix model in the academic literature, does specify that the fourth helix refers to what they call 'media-based and culture-based public' and 'civil society'. These categories particularly reflect their aim of promoting a connection between principles of democracy and knowledge or innovation processes (Carayannis and Campbell, 2012). Here the quadruple helix concept is positioned as part of a wider proposed framework describing a '21st century fractal innovation ecosystem', which includes an assortment of linked concepts put forward by the authors: for instance, mode 3 knowledge production (which combines the dynamics of mode 1 and mode 2 knowledge outlined by Gibbons *et al.* (1994)); academic firm (a private sector analogue of the entrepreneurial university); and even the Quintuple Helix (extending the model further to include the natural environment) (Carayannis and Campbell, 2009; 2012; Nordberg, 2015). This proliferation of new theoretical constructs, many of them an iteration on existing ideas, however seems speculative and not strongly grounded in either conceptual reasoning or empirical evidence. As Leydesdorff (2012) argues, the analytical validity of the quadruple helix concept should not in itself be assumed, but needs to be verified through research studies of different types (e.g. see Marcovich and Shinn, 2011). Indeed, in an earlier discussion, anticipating the quadruple helix development, Leydesdorff and Etzkowitz (2003) argue that civil society should not be separated out as a fourth institutional actor, but its presence should be seen as a precondition for innovation to occur through the triple helix configuration.

The position taken in this chapter is that the quadruple helix concept, like the triple helix before it, should be approached as a potentially useful variant on wider innovation system theories. By viewing it in this context, certain well established principles, common to different territorial (national and regional) or non-territorial (technological or sectoral) innovation system concepts, can be drawn on to help substantiate the quadruple helix framework. As summarised by Edquist (1997), these characteristics include a holistic view of innovation (i.e. not just narrowly R&D) and its underlying context-specific conditions (including institutional factors), a historical (and evolutionary) perspective on the development of innovations, and an emphasis on the interdependency of organisations in a non-linear innovation process. Crucially here, the innovation system approach also underpins the conceptualisation of 'system failures' as a theoretical rationale for innovation policies (see Lundvall and Borrás, 1997; Metcalfe, 2005; Laranja *et al.* 2008). This is of analytical value because it focuses on the network, institutional and capability failures that can prevent a functioning innovation system from emerging (Smith, 2000). Metcalfe *et al.* argue that innovation *systems* should not be seen as pre-given entities, but as only forming when various elements of what they call the innovation *ecology* of a territory become 'connected and focused upon the solution of particular innovation problems' (Metcalfe *et al.* 2012, p. 22). This view of innovation systems, therefore, directs us that the interrelationships between the different institutional spheres of the triple helix, and even more so with the non-traditional innovation actors introduced by the quadruple helix, should not be assumed to exist in advance. Instead they emerge and evolve over time around the development of particular problems or domains.

For Metcalfe (2005; Metcalfe *et al.* 2012) this emergence of an innovation system occurs through a process of self-organisation driven largely by market competition. In the case studies that follow, however, the more deliberate role of innovation policy in the regions (encompassing their smart specialisation strategies) will be emphasised. For both of these examples the sections below will describe the co-evolution of the innovation domain in question and related institutional arrangements in the region. The quadruple helix concept in itself does not prescribe the spatial scale at which it should be applied,[1] but the focus of these case studies is on the given regions (including their extra-regional governance settings and network linkages). This allows the features of embedded capabilities, technological relatedness, and external connections that are identified by McCann and Ortega-Argilés (2015) as central to smart specialisation in this territorial context to be reflected. Barriers that remain to the full emergence of innovation systems around these domains, and particularly to the formation of quadruple helix relations, will also be highlighted in the case studies.

8.3 Northern Ireland: Connected Health and Stratified Medicine

Innovation policy in Northern Ireland began developing during the early 2000s, following the establishment in 1998 of the current Northern Ireland Assembly as a devolved administration within the UK. This was driven by an understanding that the prevailing industrial policy focus on providing grants and subsidies to individual firms in the region would need to be supplanted by measures that could increase collective innovation capabilities and systematic network connections (Best, 2000; Cooke *et al.* 2002). From the first innovation strategy, however, there was a recognition that, because of its small size, Northern Ireland would have to prioritise capacity building in certain areas of science and technology (DETINI, 2004). This informed the establishment in 2007 of a Science Industry Council for the region called Matrix, which has produced a series of reports aimed at identifying future market opportunities for Northern Ireland in key areas through an analysis of existing technical capabilities and horizon-scanning foresight activities covering periods of 2, 5 and 10 years. The broad areas covered by these reports are life and health sciences, information and communication technologies, agri-food, advanced materials, advanced engineering, and sustainable energy. As an organisation providing advice to government Matrix has become influential in Northern Ireland, and despite most of its Horizon reports not having been updated since they were first written in 2008, the market opportunities they identify form the core priorities in the smart specialisation framework for the region and the recent innovation strategy from which this is derived (DETINI, 2014a; 2014b). These foresight exercises have therefore been the de facto form that the entrepreneurial discovery process has taken in the region. In this respect, the Matrix vehicle has the attribute of bringing together a sub-panel for each report that has a wide participation from across different sectors (including smaller companies).

The first Life and Health Sciences Horizon report gave a clear focus on two areas as market opportunities for Northern Ireland: home-based care and personalised medicine (Matrix, 2008). The former of these, home-based care, has come to be referred to by the slightly wider term of connected health, which is defined as:

> a model for healthcare delivery that uses technology to provide healthcare remotely. … Connected Health encompasses programs in telehealth, remote care (such as home care) and disease and lifestyle management, often leverages existing technologies such as connected devices using existing cellular networks and is associated with efforts to improve chronic care.
>
> (Matrix, 2015, p. 18)

The latter of these opportunities, personalised medicine, at 'its most basic … refers to the use of information about a person's genetic makeup to tailor strategies for the detection, treatment, or prevention of disease' (Matrix, 2008, p.6). It is linked to the fields of stratified and precision medicine, and their development in Northern Ireland can be seen here as broadly overlapping. Life and Health Sciences was the first of the Matrix areas for which an updated Horizon report was produced in 2015. This takes a more holistic view of the life and health sciences sector in Northern Ireland, but still features connected health and precision medicine (with clinical trials, health data analytics, and diagnostics) as key strengths of the region that can enable the development of treatments or interventions in a number of areas (e.g. oncology, cardiology, diabetes, etc.) (Matrix, 2015).

The selection of these two areas as strategic priorities was based on a number of existing health and life science capabilities distributed across the academic, private, and public sectors in the region. Northern Irish expertise in connected health can be traced back to the invention of the portable defibrillator by Frank Pantridge, a clinical academic at Queen's University Belfast (QUB), during the 1960s. This laid a foundation for further academic research into this and other areas related to mobile healthcare, which is now mainly concentrated in the other university in the region, the University of Ulster (UU), and specifically its Nanotechnology and Integrated BioEngineering Centre (NIBEC) founded in 1990 (then as the Northern Ireland BioEngineering Centre) by a former colleague of Pantridge (John Anderson). NIBEC has also been the source of several spin-out firms, including two important medical device companies (Intelesens and HeartSine). In reference to stratified medicine, as the more research-intensive university of the two in the region overall and home of its medical school, QUB has significant life and health science capabilities of relevance, particularly in cancer and cell biology. As part of the UK higher education system, the presence of a medical school ensures that the university has very close institutional relationships with local National Health Service (NHS) hospital trusts around both clinical training and research (Goddard and Vallance, 2013). The University of Ulster, however, also has a biomedical research capability, and has recently (2013) established the Northern Ireland Centre for Stratified Medicine in Derry (the second largest city in the region). This centre is attached to the Clinical Translational Research and Innovation Centre (C-TRIC), a partnership between Derry City Council, UU, and the local health and social care (HSC) trust. Because UU does not have a medical school itself, this partnership has allowed the Centre for Stratified Medicine to have the access to patients that is essential for their research. Away from academic research, Northern Ireland does have some existing life and health science industry to match this smart specialisation priority. This is, however, mainly comprised of three relatively large, indigenous companies that have been active for at least thirty years; Norbrook Laboratories (veterinary pharmaceuticals), Almac (services to the pharmaceutical and biotechnology industries), and Randox Laboratories (clinical diagnostics). Smaller innovative life and health science related companies are, by contrast, not currently as well represented in the region.

As mentioned earlier, the Matrix exercises have been influential in guiding the innovation strategy priorities of the Department of Enterprise, Trade and Investment (DETI) in the Northern Ireland Executive, and the economic development agency (Invest NI) that is its main delivery vehicle. The clear signalling of these two areas in the first life and health sciences report has, therefore, fed into them becoming a target of government promotion and investment in the region. For example, Invest NI has provided core funding for the establishment of the Connected Health Innovation Centre (CHIC). This is one of three Competence Centres that have been operating in Northern Ireland since 2013 (with two more in the process of being set-up) that support business-led research projects involving collaboration between at least three companies at a 'pre-competitive' stage before commercialisation.[2] CHIC is hosted by NIBEC in UU, and runs on a subscription model with (at the time of the research) around thirty member companies. As well as managing the centre and its operations, NIBEC supports the companies by guiding them in developing project ideas (through for instance issuing calls for interest in certain areas), and then provides researchers (employed with the Invest NI funding) to carry out the research. In this way, the CHIC model (similar to the other Competence Centres) can be understood as an attempt to leverage the academic expertise and organisational capacity in the University to increase the wider innovation capabilities of the region, and particularly the relatively small companies that comprise most of its membership. The model developed does include a mechanism for the companies to commercialise intellectual property generated by the projects, but more often the benefits for them relate to exploratory opportunities for learning, testing ideas, and (given the collaborative nature of the projects) networking with other companies. CHIC can also potentially be a vehicle for bringing companies closer to the HSC service in Northern Ireland, building on the existing relationships that NIBEC has with this sector.

Government support for connected health in Northern Ireland has equally come from the department responsible for health and social services (DHSSPS). As part of a landmark review of Northern Ireland's HSC sector in 2011 (*Transforming Your Care*) the potential value of more extensive use of connected health technologies was advocated, particularly in reference to the goal of allowing more patients to be treated in their own homes (Compton *et al.* 2011). In the same year DHSSPS and DETI/Invest NI signed a memorandum of understanding (MoU) to 'develop Health, Social Care, and Economic opportunities in Connected Health for Northern Ireland, through better coordination of public assets and funding' (Invest NI/DHSSPS, 2011, p. 2). Although not including binding commitments, this formalised agreement is still a useful expression of intended future collaboration in Northern Ireland where political and administrative divisions often make joined-up policy between government departments challenging. This MoU was followed-up with the formation of a project group to advise government on steps to maximise the potential economic and employment benefits from the adoption of connected health in the HSC sector.[3] The momentum generated by the MoU also enabled plans to establish a Northern Ireland Connected Health Ecosystem as a permanent organisation to be realised in 2012. This Ecosystem runs regular meetings in the region that provide networking opportunities for its various members from the HSC sector, universities and colleges, and private companies of different types with an interest in this area. In parallel with this, a larger European Connected Health Alliance began to develop that now links members of this Northern Irish community with a growing number of other ecosystems representing various locations (and markets) in the rest of the UK, the Republic of Ireland, continental Europe, and now also North America and (through an affiliated organisation) China.

In relation to the strategic priority in stratified/precision medicine, Invest NI has also made some significant investments in developing the scientific capability of the region. These include funding for the UU Centre for Stratified Medicine mentioned above, but also for research activities in Queen's University Belfast – most notably a joint R&D and staff secondment initiative with local company Almac around cancer drug discovery. An opportunity for further institutional development in this area arose with the announcement in 2014 of a new UK Catapult Centre in Precision Medicine. Catapult Centres are technology and innovation centres in a number (currently ten) of strategic areas that have been established by the UK government's innovation agency to carry out business-focused research and development. None of the previous Catapult Centres has, however, had a presence in Northern Ireland. During the period covered by this research, Northern Ireland was in the process of bidding to host all or part of this Precision Medicine Catapult. This bid had support from the government and Invest NI, and drew together the different actors with research or commercial assets related to this field in the region. The result of this competition is that the Catapult Centre will be across multiple locations in the UK, with the main base in Cambridge and six regional hubs including Belfast. Being part of a wider network, therefore, means that the level of associated resource received by Northern Ireland will be relatively limited, and direct involvement in the centre seems likely to be restricted to Queen's University and parts of the health service based in Belfast. However, interviewees identified benefits for Northern Ireland of the Catapult related to the status it conveys as a UK centre of excellence in this field, and the future opportunities it presents to build new relationships with the rest of the UK.

The new institutional arrangements outlined above have undoubtedly contributed to the formation of more systematic relationships across university, HSC, and private sector actors around these strategic innovation domains in Northern Ireland. There are, however, also barriers within this system that will have to be overcome if these relationships are to be extended or deepened in the future. The least developed part of this institutional configuration currently is the private sector, particularly beyond the three larger companies mentioned above. In the case of stratified/precision medicine this is perhaps unsurprising given the still mainly exploratory nature of this scientific field. The commercial applications of connected health are arguably also still emerging, but the political commitment to this in DHSSPS in Northern Ireland (which has already implemented large programmes in health telemonitoring) means that there is potentially a significant market within the region. However, the interviews indicated that local companies have thus far found it difficult to sell their connected health products to the health service. This some suggested could be related to the procurement rules the NHS operates under, but others cited the lack of clinical engagement by companies – particularly early on in the product development process and by those entering this new field from a technology rather than health background. The adoption of connected health technologies in the HSC sector itself, however, also represents a change to instituted ways of working in large public sector organisations that will take time and require the clinical benefits of, for instance, telemonitoring to be more comprehensively demonstrated. This is despite the sector in Northern Ireland having distinctive institutional features that should facilitate this process, including already integrated health and social care NHS trusts, and being the first part of the UK to introduce an effective electronic care record system for easy access to patient data by clinicians. Beyond the public sector, the widespread use of connected health technologies for home-based care will also need the participation of the health workers delivering this care in Northern Ireland, many of whom are employed by independent companies. As this is currently a role which involves only limited use of technology, the upskilling of these staff in the appropriate techniques and procedures to, for instance, effectively and ethically handle patient data will also require a considerable programme of training the workforce. The conceptual implications of these systemic barriers will be discussed following the second case featured in this chapter.

8.4 Tampere: Smart City

Finland has for the past three decades had a very strong innovation-focused economic development policy (Schienstock, 2004). The main expression of this at the sub-national level has been the Centre of Expertise (OSKE) programme, which ran across three phases from 1994 to 2013. Tampere, as the largest city in Finland outside the Helsinki metropolitan area, was centrally involved in this programme from the start. Following a cluster-based logic, the OSKE programme encouraged participating localities to specialise in certain sectors or technologies. For Tampere, this entailed a sustained prioritisation of areas related to information and communication technologies (ICT), as well as mechanical engineering and automation, health technologies, and digital media. Reflecting national policy (see Ali-Yrkkö and Hermans, 2004), the ICT theme was to a large degree founded on the role of Nokia Corporation, which has one of its main research and development centres in Tampere, as an anchor firm. While this strategy was clearly beneficial for a period, Nokia's recent dramatic loss of global market share in its core mobile phone business has exposed the flaws of overdependence on this single actor. The Nokia Research Centre in Tampere has remained open (unlike branches in other Finnish localities), but following 2011 has decreased significantly in size. This structural development in the economy contributed to an evolution of innovation policy thinking in the region, which has moved from the focus on sectoral and technological specialisation of the OSKE programme towards support of innovation platforms or ecosystems that can support cross-cutting development opportunities. Elements of this new 'platform' thinking were reflected at a national level in the Innovative Cities (INKA) programme, which began operating in 2014 as a replacement for the OSKE programme. As the name suggests, the move to the INKA programme involved a scaling back to focus on the largest cities in Finland outside of the core Helsinki region. It was organised around: 'Demand-driven, solution-centred and multisectoral themes that combine several competence areas [which] were selected for the programme from among proposals submitted by the urban regions'.[4] Policymakers from Tampere were influential in shaping this approach, and it became the only city to be the lead participant for two themes identified through a local consultation process: smart cities and renewing industry.

These INKA programme themes also became the basis for the priority fields in the region's smart specialisation strategy (embedded in a broader 2014 Regional Strategy).[5] The organisation responsible for this strategy (as part of the local implementation of EU Structural Fund programmes) is the Regional Council, a statutory joint municipal authority covering the 22 municipalities in the Tampere region (Pirkanmaa). For the INKA programme, however, the main responsibility has been given directly to the largest single municipality, the City of Tampere (that alone accounts for almost half the population of the wider region). The programme itself has been managed through the economic development agency (TREDEA) for the City of Tampere and seven surrounding municipalities that together form a core city-region within Pirkanmaa.

In practice the Regional Council and City of Tampere are closely connected through functional links and inter-personal networks, but this shift in governance is significant for the smart city theme that is the focus here. The role of the City of Tampere as the most important actor in articulating a vision for this theme in the region is reflected in the emphasis being as much on how innovation in this domain can help improve the delivery of public services for local citizens as it has been on how it can create new market opportunities for companies. Three smart city sub-themes have been adopted – intelligent traffic systems, resource-efficient city, and smart buildings and spaces – that aim to link new technological capabilities to urban development functions that are the responsibility of local government in Finland. Central to the smart city strategy in Tampere, therefore, is the mobilisation of the considerable resources that the urban municipalities have to support innovation in these areas; for instance, through use of public procurement (existing examples include initiatives in commissioning new electric buses and street lighting) and making municipal data openly available to companies and other actors such as university researchers or student teams.[6] The City plans to run demonstrator pilots in real-life environments, which will function as platforms to trial new forms of public service delivery as well as for companies to test new applications. Notably this approach is being deployed in a declining suburb with high levels of social exclusion in the city (Tesoma) with the aim of encouraging residents to actively participate in its regeneration.

Shortly after the completion of our research in Tampere, and following a general election in Finland, a new government programme was announced that included a substantial reduction in the budget of the national technology and innovation funding agency Tekes. One consequence of this was that the INKA programme will be discontinued in 2016, and not as planned run until 2020. This removes a potential income stream for smart city related activities in Tampere, but does not necessarily mean that these activities will not proceed. While the INKA programme has been important in Tampere in terms of the renewal of innovation priorities and related institutions (for instance feeding into the smart specialisation strategy), it still required that projects it supported would be match funded from local sources. It seems likely, therefore, that the City of Tampere will still be able to take forward its smart city strategy through the abovementioned mobilisation of its own resources in this direction. The City was also already drawing on other projects as tools to help implement this strategy and will continue to do so in the future. Most notably is an ongoing national programme (the Six City Strategy – Open and Smart Services) involving the six largest municipalities in Finland, which meets the current requirement for a proportion of EDRF funding to be used on sustainable urban development. This programme, which was in many ways synergistic with the planned INKA smart city activities, has three priority axes: open innovation platforms, open data and interfaces, and open (citizen) participation.

While the development of smart city as an innovation priority in Tampere has been driven particularly from within local government, other institutional actors in the region have the potential to play an important role. This includes the two universities in the city – the University of Tampere (UTA) and Tampere University of Technology (TUT) – that have been central to the innovation-focused economy that has emerged since the decline of the region's traditional manufacturing industries (Kostiainen and Sotarauta, 2003). The research strengths of TUT in particular, which has an inherent connection with industry from its profile in applied engineering and computing fields, are closely aligned with development priorities in the region. In the private sector, the receding importance of Nokia to the local economy has freed up resources, especially human capital, to be deployed in other enterprises. A government supported national scheme (Nokia Bridge) starting in 2011 helped former Nokia employees to form new technology start-ups utilising their considerable experience. The innovation platform programmes operated in Tampere by the New Factory organisation (including the Demola programme discussed below) also have a common concern with helping to foster a more entrepreneurial culture amongst students, recent graduates, and experienced workers. By creating opportunities for new applications of the ICT capabilities in the region, the smart city domain can be seen as one possible route for the economy to branch into a new but related path.[7] The smart city sub-theme that is currently the leading candidate to emerge as a new industrial path in the region is that which relates to intelligent transport systems (ITS). This is in part due to the existence of a number of companies already active in this sector. A formal network vehicle, ITS Factory, has been formed to help engender collaborative projects involving these companies, local higher education/research institutions, and in some cases also the City of Tampere. Both universities have strengths in transport related research, but the UTA has been particularly active in this ITS Factory through a team led by a former Nokia expert in mobile ecosystem creation.

The Regional Council and City of Tampere have also sought to develop this smart (and sustainable) city theme by making it a focus of a nascent crossborder partnership with the Swedish region of Scania (and its two university cities of Malmo and Lund), which aims to capitalise on potentially complementary strategic interests and institutional structures between these two Nordic localities (also see Trippl *et al.* 2015). It is hoped that this partnership will grow into a sustained collaborative relationship involving multiple institutional actors from both regions, but in its initial form it has been taken forward by the respective Regional Councils under their mutual membership of the EU Vanguard Initiative for New Growth through Smart Specialisation. Another important mechanism at this early stage has been the Demola network, which supports multidisciplinary student teams from different higher education institutions to work together on small innovation projects around a case or problem provided by a third-party private or public sector organisation. Demola began operating in Tampere (in 2008) instigated by individuals from Nokia and the Hermia technology park as a way of encouraging more open innovation processes within the region, and its success helped to stimulate the abovementioned adoption of the platform approach in policy. Subsequently Demola (as a separate organisation attached to New Factory) has started operating through affiliates in around eight other locations throughout Europe including Scania (South Sweden), and part of its value for Tampere is now seen to be its use as a tool for building stronger international connections with other regions. This existing link with Scania, therefore, was utilised in 2014 through the running of a Smart City Accelerator across the two regions, which involved numerous Demola projects working with local city municipalities and companies relating to the priority themes of smart mobility, citizen participation, and smart city ecosystem (focusing on open data). Hence, this joint platform has proved to be an effective vehicle for generating activity in this smart and sustainable city area, and even if none of the ideas or solutions presented by the student teams is implemented in a real world environment, it has still given the partner organisations a valuable opportunity to explore where future collaboration could take place in, for instance, areas like public procurement or use of traffic data.

As with the Northern Ireland case described above, however, there are still institutional barriers to the formation of a fully functioning innovation system relating to this domain in Tampere. The most immediate of these, given its role in mobilising this smart city agenda, is the challenge of embedding appropriate practices (e.g. smart procurement) throughout the City of Tampere organisation that is oriented to core service delivery rather than innovation. Interviewees acknowledged that currently there is strong vision from a small number of people in leadership roles within this and related agencies (e.g. TREDEA), but it is acknowledged that the goal of encouraging the majority of its employees, habituated to more traditional ways of providing municipal services, to adjust to this vision will require a process of gradual institutional change. Similarly, while there is a high-level commitment to using smart city related initiatives to engage citizens more directly as participants in innovation processes, this is still seen as a novel approach that needs to overcome the tendency for many residents to think of themselves as just passive recipients of public services. In relation to the economic development, the further growth of an area like smart traffic into a significant industry for Tampere is contingent on the ability of local companies to scale-up their products or services so they can be exported to other markets with different urban infrastructure systems. This, interviewees foresaw, will require these companies to work with the larger multinational companies who are likely to emerge as global leaders in fields like electric cars over the next decade (echoing the earlier process through which the telecommunications industry underwent internationalisation).

8.5 Conclusion

By outlining the development of specific innovation domains that have become strategic priorities in the two regions, the case studies above illustrate the reciprocal relationship between smart specialisation and local institutional, governance and economic contexts. In both instances the basis for these domains are inherited research and technological capabilities in the region that relate to strengths built up over time in research organisations and firms (e.g. health technologies in Northern Ireland's universities, the Nokia-anchored ICT cluster in Tampere). The identification of these domains as opportunities for path development or branching by policymakers in the region also occurred through governance mechanisms – Matrix in Northern Ireland and the INKA programme consultation in Tampere – that already existed separately to the European Commission's requirement to produce a smart specialisation strategy. At the same time the case studies have shown that the signalling of these domains as priorities has facilitated the further development of new or modified institutional relationships within the regions as part of a co-evolutionary dynamic. In Northern Ireland this has mainly taken the form of government departments and agencies (relating to both health and the economy) being prompted into investing in new vehicles such as CHIC, the Northern Ireland Connected Health Ecosystem, and Centre for Stratified Medicine. In Tampere it has taken the form of local actors, principally the City of Tampere municipality but also universities, firms and innovation intermediaries (e.g. Demola), mobilising their assets around the implementation of smart city applications in the region.

In the theoretical framework being explored here, these new institutional arrangements mainly represent a strengthening of connections between organisational actors in the triple helix (government, industry, universities). As discussed earlier, the existence of an innovation system should not be assumed from the presence of these actors in a regional innovation ecology alone, but from the selective formation of systematic connections between them around specific problems (Metcalfe *et al.* 2012). If the institutional developments noted above indicate that this formation of innovation systems around the strategic domains focused on has been proceeding within the two regions, the case studies equally highlight institutional barriers to this process occurring more fully, and in doing so help demonstrate the value of a system failure perspective to understanding smart specialisation dynamics (see Vallance, 2016). The main barriers identified in both regions include those that relate to the economic challenges of successfully leveraging the local knowledge domains into commercial enterprises with global market potential, but also to the organisational and cultural challenges of adapting to working with new technologies in the public sector (see Hughes *et al.* 2011).

Together the case studies also support the argument that the emerging innovation systems have yet to take the form of a quadruple (rather than triple) helix arrangement in which societal users are centrally integrated. This is despite both regions exhibiting aspirations to move in this direction. In Tampere especially, there is a strong commitment to engage local citizens and use urban areas as 'living laboratories' as part of the municipality-led smart city agenda. In Northern Ireland there is also a growing recognition of the potential of broader forms of social innovation that encompass developments in areas such as connected health (Warnock, 2014). Actors in the domains covered in both regions also rely on the use of data generated by, for instance, public transport passengers or recipients of healthcare treatments. Currently, however, these non-professional users themselves seem to have a relatively limited role in actually shaping innovations in the two cases, and their access to be able to do this is mediated by public sector organisations (e.g. local authorities or the health service). This may, therefore, approximate the version of the quadruple helix that Arnkil *et al.* (2010) call the 'public-sector-centred living lab model', but this does not necessarily equate to a system in which users or citizens are actively involved in co-development processes. It also means the system will be especially susceptible to the challenges of public sector innovation mentioned above. These issues, therefore, need to be taken into account when deciding on the appropriateness of the quadruple helix as a framework for analysing smart specialisation processes.

Notes

1   Indeed, in the extended framework proposed by Carayannis and Campbell (2009), the multi-level (global and local) nature of innovation processes is emphasised.
2   The other four operating or planned Competence Centres are also in areas that align with the Matrix technology areas (sustainable energy, advanced engineering, agri-food, and cloud computing).
3   A direct recommendation of this group, currently in the process of being implemented, is the creation of a physical facility (the HILS Hub) that will aim to help coordinate joint projects between HSC, academic, and private sector health and life science actors in the region.
4   See http://www.oecd.org/effective-public-investment-toolkit/finland.pdf. Accessed 13 September 2016.
5   As well as smart city and renewing industry, another priority area in the region included in the RIS3 is the emerging scientific field of regenerative medicine. For an account of the development of area in Tampere see Sotarauta and Mustikkamäki (2015).
6   The development of this municipality-led smart city approach has overlapped, and been informed, by a slightly earlier (starting in 2010) City of Tampere programme (Eco2 – Eco-efficient Tampere 2020) to promote more sustainable energy use across its different urban planning and service functions, particularly relating to the building environment (construction) and transport.
7   The related nature of the region's ICT capabilities to smart city applications are, for instance, reflected in one of the two Competence Clusters that Tampere was coordinating city for in the third iteration of the OSKE programme (2007–2013) being Ubiquitous Computing, which was concerned with the implications of these technologies being embedded in evermore distributed environments.

References

Ali-Yrkkö, J. and Hermans, R., 2004, 'Nokia: a giant in the Finnish innovation system', in Schienstock, G. (ed.), *Embracing the Knowledge Economy: The Dynamic Transformation of the Finnish Innovation System*, Edward Elgar: Cheltenham, pp. 106–127.

Arnkil, R., Järvensivu, A., Koski, P. and Piirainen, T., 2010, 'Exploring quadruple helix: outlining user-oriented innovation models. Final report on Quadruple Helix Research for the CLIQ project', *Työraportteja 85/2010 Working Papers.*

Best, M., 2000, *The Capabilities and Innovation Perspective: The Way Ahead in Northern Ireland*, Northern Ireland Economic Council: Belfast.

Carayannis, E. G. and Campbell, D. F. J., 2009, '"Mode 3" and 'Quadruple Helix': toward a 21st century fractal innovation ecosystem', *International Journal of Technology Management*, 46.3–4, 201–234.

Carayannis, E. G. and Campbell, D. F. J., 2012, *Mode 3 Knowledge Production in Quadruple Helix Innovation Systems*, Springer: New York.

Carayannis, E. G. and Rakhmatullin, R., 2014, 'The quadruple/quintuple innovation helixes and smart specialisation strategies for sustainable and inclusive growth in Europe and beyond', *Journal of Knowledge Economy*, 5.2, 212–239.

Coenen, L., Moodysson, J. and Martin, H., 2015, 'Path renewal in old industrial regions: possibilities and limitations for regional innovation policy', *Regional Studies*, 49.5, 850–865.

Compton, J., Ham, C., Heenan, D., Rutter, I., Simpson, P. and Ennis, M., 2011, *Transforming Your Care: A Review of Health and Social Care in Northern Ireland*, DHSSPS: Belfast.

Cooke, P., Roper, S. and Wylie, P., 2002, *Developing a Regional Innovation Strategy for Northern Ireland*, Northern Ireland Economic Council: Belfast.

Dawley, S., 2014, 'Creating new paths? Offshore wind, policy activism, and peripheral region development', *Economic Geography*, 90.1, 91–112.

DETINI, 2004, *The Regional Innovation Strategy for Northern Ireland: Action Plan September 2004 to August 2006*, DETI: Belfast.

DETINI, 2014a, *Northern Ireland Framework for Smart Specialisation 2014*, DETI: Belfast.

DETINI, 2014b, *Innovation Strategy for Northern Ireland – 2014–2025: Innovate NI*, DETI: Belfast.

Edquist, C., 1997, 'Systems of innovation approaches – their emergence and characteristics', in Edquist, C. (ed.), *Systems of Innovation: Technologies, Institutions and Organizations*, Pinter: London, pp. 1–35.

Etzkowitz, H., 2003, 'Research groups as 'quasi-firms': the invention of the entrepreneurial university', *Research Policy*, 32.1, 109–121.

Etzkowitz, H., 2008, *The Triple Helix: University–Industry–Government Innovation in Action*, Routledge: Abingdon.

Etzkowitz, H. and Leydesdorff, L., 2000, 'The dynamics of innovation: from national systems and mode 2 to a triple helix of university-industry-government relations', *Research Policy*, 29.2, 109–123.

Etzkowitz, H., Webster, A., Gebhardt, C. and Terra, B.R.C., 2000, 'The future of the university and the university of the future: evolution of ivory tower to entrepreneurial paradigm', *Research Policy*, 29.2, 313–330.

Foray, D., Goddard, J., Beldarrain, X. G., Landabaso, M., McCann, P., Morgan, K., Nauwelaers, C. and Ortega-Argilés, R., 2012, *Guide to Research and Innovation Strategies for Smart Specialisation (RIS 3)*, European Commission: Brussels.

Franke, N. and Shah, S., 2003, 'How communities support innovative activities: an exploration of assistance and sharing among end-users', *Research Policy*, 32.1, 157–178.

Gibbons, M., Limoges, C., Nowotny, H., Schwartzman, S., Scott, P. and Trow, M., 1994, *The New Production of Knowledge: The Dynamics of Science and Research in Contemporary Societies*, Sage, London.

Goddard, J. and Vallance, P., 2013, *The University and the City*, Routledge: London.

Grabher, G., Ibert, O. and Flohr, S., 2008, 'The neglected king: the customer in the new knowledge ecology of innovation', *Economic Geography*, 84.3, 253–280.

Hughes, A., Moore, K. and Kataria, M., 2011, *Innovation in Public Sector Organisations: A Pilot Survey for Measuring Innovation Across the Public Sector*, NESTA: London.

Invest NI/DHSSPS, 2011, *Connected Health and Prosperity Memorandum of Understanding Between the Department of Health, Social Services, and Public Safety, and Invest Northern Ireland (Sponsored by the Department of Enterprise, Trade and Investment)*, Invest NI/DHSSPS: Belfast.

Kolehmainen, J., Irvine, J., Stewart, L., Karacsonyi, Z., Szabó, T., Alarinta, J. and Norberg, A., 2015, 'Quadruple Helix, Innovation and the Knowledge-Based Development: Lessons from Remote, Rural and Less-Favoured Regions', *Journal of the Knowledge Economy*, DOI: 10.1007/s13132-015-0289-9.

Kostiainen, J. and Sotarauta, M., 2003, 'Great Leap or Long March to Knowledge Economy: Institutions, Actors and Resources in the Development of Tampere, Finland', *European Planning Studies*, 11.4, 415–438.

Laranja, M., Uyarra, E. and Flanagan, K., 2008 'Policies for science, technology and innovation: translating rationales into regional policies in a multi-level setting', *Research Policy*, 37.5, 823–835.

Leydesdorff, L., 2000, 'The triple helix: an evolutionary model of innovations', *Research Policy*, 29. 2, 243–255.

Leydesdorff, L., 2012, 'The triple helix, quadruple helix, …, and an *n*-tuple of helices: explanatory models for analyzing the knowledge-based economy?', *Journal of Knowledge Economy*, 3. 1, 25–35.

Leydesdorff, L. and Etzkowitz, H., 1996, 'Emergence of a Triple Helix of university–industry–government relations', *Science and Public Policy*, 23.5, 279–286.

Leydesdorff, L. and Etzkowitz, H., 2003, 'Can 'the public' be considered as a fourth helix in university–industry–government relations? Report on the Fourth Triple Helix Conference, 2002', *Science and Public Policy*, 30.1, 55–61.

Lundvall, B.-Å. (ed.), 1992, *National Systems of Innovation: Towards a Theory of Innovation and Interactive Learning*, Pinter: London.

Lundvall, B.-Å. and Borrás, S., 1997, *The Globalising Learning Economy: Implications for Innovation Policy*, European Commission: Brussels.

Marcovich, A. and Shinn, T., 2011, 'From the triple helix to a quadruple helix? The case of Dip-Pen Nanolithography', *Minerva*, 49.2, 175–190.

Matrix, 2008, *Life & Health Sciences Horizon Panel Report: Prosperity and Health Delivered by Science*, DETI: Belfast.

Matrix, 2015, *Life & Health Sciences Northern Ireland: Capability Assessment & Foresight Report*, DETI: Belfast.

Metcalfe, J. S., 2005, 'Systems failure and the case for innovation policy', in Llerena, P. and Matt, M. (eds.), *Innovation Policy in a Knowledge-Based Economy: Theory and Practice*, Springer: Berlin Heidelberg, pp. 47–74.

Metcalfe, J. S., Gagliardi, D., De Liso, N. and Ramlogan, R., 2012, 'Innovation systems and innovation ecologies: innovation policy and restless capitalism', *Working Paper No. 3/2012*, Openloc.

McCann, P. and Ortega-Argilés, R., 2014, 'Smart specialisation in European regions: issues of strategy, institutions and implementation', *European Journal of Innovation Management*, 17.4, 409–427.

McCann, P. and Ortega-Argilés, R., 2015, 'Smart specialization, regional growth, and applications to European Union Cohesion policy', *Regional Studies*, 49.8, 1291–1302.

Morgan, K., 2013, 'The regional state in the era of Smart Specialisation', *Ekonomiaz*, 83.2, 103–126.

Nordberg, K., 2015, 'Enabling Regional growth in Peripheral Non-University Regions – the Impact of a Quadruple Helix Intermediate Organisation', *Journal of the Knowledge Economy*, 6.2, 334–356.

Richardson, R., Healy, A. and Morgan, K., 2014, 'Embracing social innovation', *Smart Specialisation for Regional Innovation WP3 Reflection Paper*.

Schienstock, G. (ed.), 2004, *Embracing the Knowledge Economy: The Dynamic Transformation of the Finnish Innovation System*, Edward Elgar: Cheltenham, UK.

Smith. K., 2000, 'Innovation as a systemic phenomenon: rethinking the role of policy', *Enterprise & Innovation Management Studies*, 1.1, 73–102.

Sotarauta, M. and Mustikkamäki, N., 2015, 'Institutional entrepreneurship, power, and knowledge in innovation systems: institutionalization of regenerative medicine in Tampere, Finland', *Environment and Planning C: Government and Policy*, 33.2, 342–357.

Strambach, S., 2010, 'Path dependence and path plasticity: the co-evolution of institutions and innovation – the German customized business software industry', in Boschma, R. and Martin, R. (eds.), *The Handbook of Evolutionary Economic Geography*, Edward Elgar: Cheltenham, pp. 406–431.

Trippl, M., Miörner, J. and Zukauskaite, E., 2015, 'Scania', *FP7 Smart Specialisation for Regional Innovation WP5 Regional Living Laboratories Reports*.

Vallance, P., 2016, 'Institutional barriers in smart specialisation: a system failure perspective', *Smart Specialisation for Regional Innovation WP1 Research Paper*.

Vallance, P. and Goddard, J., 2015, Pirkanmaa (Tampere), *FP7 Smart Specialisation for Regional Innovation WP5 Regional Living Laboratories Reports*.

Vallance, P. and Kempton, L., 2015, 'Northern Ireland', *FP7 Smart Specialisation for Regional Innovation WP5 Regional Living Laboratories Reports*.

Viale, R., and Pozzali, A., 2010, 'Complex Adaptive Systems and the Evolutionary Triple Helix', *Critical Sociology*, 33.4, 575–594.

Von Hippel, E., 2005, *Democratizing Innovation*, MIT Press: Cambridge, MA.

Warnock, R., 2014, *Harnessing the Power of Social Innovation to Drive the Northern Ireland Economy*, DETI: Belfast.

9 Smart Specialisation and Local Economic Development in Eastern Europe

Teodora Dogaru, Frank van Oort and Nicola Cortinovis

9.1 Introduction

Since its inception, the European Union (EU) has aimed at consolidating the economies of its Member States to guarantee a competitive place on the global trade map. The expansion of the European free trade area has been considered beneficial, and at present, the EU consists of 28 members. However, the more states have entered the Union, the more complex the socio-economic framework has become: economic and social disparities among regions have become larger, thereby possibly affecting the Union's efficiency. Two types of lagging regions currently stand out (EC 2015): low income regions that are concentrated in Central and Eastern European (CEE) countries, and low growth regions that are in the South of the EU (Greece, Southern Italy, Portugal and Southern Spain). Although both types of regions face structural and employment-related difficulties in resilience because of the economic shocks experienced in the recent past, the Southern regions seem to be better endowed with more developed industries and opportunities for diversification than CEE regions. In the CEE regions, diversifying conditions for human and physical capital are lacking outside capital regions due to past political, social and economic development. CEE countries are also in greater need of institutional reforms regarding labour market, as well as educational, environmental, structural and governance systems and policies than are Southern regions (EC 2015). However, smart specialisation as a development concept suggests place-based opportunities for all regions in the EU (Foray 2015). In this chapter, we concur with the view that opportunities might indeed be present in capital and second-tier city regions in CEE countries, but we also argue that much more focused policy effort and directed investments are needed for such opportunities to materialize in CEE regions than elsewhere in Europe. Yet, even if such necessary reform conditions are satisfied, diversification and innovation processes are not guaranteed as these are largely globally self-organizing in economic and knowledge networks.

Despite the warning and questioning nature of this chapter, we aim at identifying economic development opportunities for CEE-regions and the implications for investments and smart specialisation strategies. Both capital regions and second-tier city regions can competitively capture economic market niches related to value-chain positions and specific knowledge networks. Such niches cannot be identified easily with regional econometric or place-based case-study research alone. Instead, economic trade, FDI and knowledge network-based research affecting place-based developments are also needed. Nonetheless, functional and economic network relationships between (CEE) transitional and leading regions turn out to be much more complex than the standard empirical spatial economic modelling frameworks are able to capture (Thissen *et al.* 2013; 2016). Therefore, in line with the contributions by Thissen *et al.* (Chapter 6) and Los *et al.* (Chapter 7), we emphasize the role of incorporating network effects within empirical smart specialisation research to link the global with the local and facilitate complementarities within regional settings, particularly in CEE regions. We stress the urgency of the need for the research and policy agenda to draw upon economic development opportunities for regions in CEE-countries based on the principle of *interplay* between people, place and network-based policies.

9.2 Regional Heterogeneity and Smart Specialisations of EU Regions

The European Union started with an agreement of six of the most powerful economies at the time. As the Common Market grew, the newly added countries entered a space in which they were far behind their elders despite having achieved an acceptable level of economic development. In that regard, different European policies, legal settings and financial instruments have been created to balance the disparities among countries and regions. The EU Cohesion Policy comprises various policy agendas (Bachtler *et al.* 2013). Its latest economic efficiency and competitiveness front is marked by the Smart Specialisation concept (Foray 2015), a system of theories and instruments that challenges policymakers to reassess development priorities for long-term growth on the basis of local characteristics. Every resource is to be weighed in cost-benefit terms and every policy action is to be better tailored to the local place characteristics (McCann 2015, Thissen *et al.* 2013). Due to the economic heterogeneity that characterizes the countries of the economic and political alliance, competition has taken on new dimensions and features. Industrial sectors no longer prevail in regard to bringing wealth to cities and regions, and instead the new information society has meant that service sectors bring in new dimensions to the business arena. Innovation increasingly relates to intangible assets such as software, human capital and financial services (Dettori *et al.* 2012) while manufacturing industries face an acute scarcity of physical resources, which leads to the need for innovation in recycling processes and environmental programmes.

Increasingly, empirical research suggests that regional economic growth and resilience patterns differ between the 'old' Europe and the mainly Central and Eastern European (CEE) countries of the 'new' Europe (Marrocu *et al.* 2013). The causes of these disparities lie in the various degrees and opportunities for specialisation and diversification among regions (Cortinovis and Van Oort 2015), variations in knowledge and innovation endowments among regions

(Moreno *et al*. 2005, Breschi & Lissoni 2009, Hoekman *et al*. 2009, Guastella & van Oort 2015) and heterogeneity between regions in terms of their levels of institutional embedding and international connectivity (Frenken & Hoekman 2006). The fact is that Western Europe (the 'old' Europe) leads in the service markets and responds easier to new economic demands due to its higher quality physical and human capital, knowledge institutions, higher degrees of global connectivity and access to business and knowledge networks. 'New' European countries and regions are not yet able to build in these path-dependent structures. In the early stages of economic transition from 1989 onwards, the elimination of European customs' barriers between East and West led to a disadvantage for the CEE newcomers in terms of the out-migration of knowledge workers. Subsequently, in the recent past, so-called 'people-based' policies focused on education and vocational training of the local labour force in CEE-countries, have been complemented with place-based policies to help to create jobs and the regional institutional embedding of those with a higher education (Barca *et al*. 2012). However, despite considerable investment in so-called Objective-1 regional development regions, doubts still remain as to the effectiveness of such EU investment schemes (Gripaios *et al*. 2008, Rodriguez-Pose & Garcilazo 2013). These doubts involve the legacy of economic specialisation and institutions of the past. CEE-countries (Poland, Czech Republic, Slovakia, Romania, Bulgaria, Hungary, Estonia, Latvia, Lithuania) previously played a major role when it came to physical resources (e.g., wood, steel or basic metals, salt, agricultural products) and were characterized by high degrees of specialisation in various heavy industries (Muller *et al*. 2005). Country level investments, particularly geared toward capital cities and regions, and limited foreign direct investment (FDI) characterized these places in the pre-EU era, capitalizing upon cheap labour, existing infrastructure, low costs of property ownership and access to new markets, whereas local economies benefited from employment and capital injections. In this context, multiple national industries became obsolete following the privatizations that began after 1989. One of the main reasons consisted of the inability of local enterprises to upgrade their knowledge or endowments at the same pace set by the competition. Despite knowledge externalities among firms, local economies were unable to catch up. Moreover, international business network access, which has been focused on the capital regions in particular, appears to have had only a moderate beneficial effect for national business growth (Dogaru *et al*. 2015).

This chapter focuses on one of the key concepts of smart specialisation, namely the recognition and fostering of entrepreneurial opportunities and market niches in smartly chosen regional specialisations. Generally, the idea of new cluster and product life cycle creation is embedded in the recent literature of evolutionary economic geography – most prominently in the concept of related variety (Foray 2015), i.e., regions diversifying into industries that are related to those in which they already show strength while, creating new local niche market opportunities followed by the creation of employment and productivity growth in later stages. As we will argue in this chapter, recent empirical research on the process of economic structural development shows that the practice has been hampered in CEE regions for several reasons. CEE regions and cities may not be able to profit from endogenous local diversification opportunities as they start from lower-level and lower-quality economic structures (EC 2015). Furthermore, they do not profit optimally from exogenously induced trade- or FDI-network sources of renewal and growth because they are not (yet) well embedded in the most knowledge-intensive ones.

These observations bear important policy implications, suggesting that (endogenously fuelled) diversification and (exogenously fuelled) foreign investment alone are not sufficient to reap the benefits of urban and regional growth externalities. To be effective, policies must consider the context and features, such as knowledge and technological endowments, of any (targeted) region. As agglomeration economies operate differently in different areas, a one-size-fits-all call for diversification and/or (smart) specialisation alone is unlikely to be effective everywhere. This confirms the beliefs that smart specialisation and diversification strategies may have positive implications for growth in *all* European regions, yet differently in each of them. As Foray (2015, p. 65–66) formulates:

> The smart specialisation strategy seeks to avoid hindering relative positions between followers and leaders with the less advanced regions being locked into the development of applications and incremental innovations. Of course, smart specialisation does not have magical properties to transform laggard into global leaders. However, at the very least, a smart specialisation strategy transforms less advanced regions to good followers [...] or even leaders, not in inventing the generic technology but in co-inventing applications. [...] Smart specialisation is definitely not only for the best regions but just the opposite. It is a unique stairway to excellence for less developed and transition regions.

It is this staircase argument that we criticize in this chapter as recent empirical evidence collected for the Smartspec FP7-project shows that this staircase may be considerably steeper than suggested and may be missing essential steps from the outset.

9.3 Smart Specialisation, Entrepreneurial Discovery and Related Variety

The conceptualization of smart specialisation leans heavily on that of related variety. Foray (2015) introduces related variety in his initiatory book on page 28–29 in light of the entrepreneurial discovery process that firms, knowledge institutes, consumers and governance mechanisms are constantly seeking in regions. The literature has shown the significant role played by specialised local clusters in regional growth (Asheim *et al*. 2006). Clusters are concentrations of firms specialised in a certain sectoral activity. By co-locating, firms in clusters benefit from increased interaction in economic networks benefiting from matching, sharing and learning externalities (agglomeration economies). Rosenthal and Stange (2004) summarise the literature that looks at urbanisation economies as advantages brought by cities to all firms and consumers equally. This literature has found relatively consistent evidence: doubling the population of a city increases productivity by 3–8%. In analytical terms, the earliest works (before the 1990s) measured agglomeration density through population and its relation to productivity. Subsequent studies extended their focus to sectors and network effects in employment growth (Glaeser *et al.* 1992), introducing increasing returns operating in a dynamic rather than static context. In the literature, sector-specific localisation economies are generally counterbalanced against general urbanisation economies, enhanced by economic diversity instead of specialisation. Diversity advantages may be related to endogenous growth potentials but also to diversifying FDI and input–output relations, human capital externalities and knowledge spillovers. In particular, Jane Jacobs (1969) initiated the idea that variety in regional industry or the technological base may positively affect economic growth, although in empirical studies, the relation between agglomeration and growth is ambiguous and equivocal with regard to whether urban or local specialisation or diversity is more advantageous (Melo *et al.* 2009).

One possible way out of this seemingly locked-in debate was introduced by applying the concepts of related and unrelated variety in the empirical modelling of growth across European regions (Van Oort *et al.* 2015, Cortinovis *et al.* 2016). The importance of cultural and cognitive proximity fuelling the transmission of ideas and knowledge between firms is increasingly acknowledged by economic geographers as well as institutional and evolutionary economists. Frenken *et al.* (2007) argue that companies from related branches of industry have overlapping knowledge bases. This overlap facilitates intercompany communication: shared knowledge, frames of reference and applied technology make it easier for them to understand one another. The partial feature of this overlap means that there is room for mutual learning. A key in this discussion stands in the concept of proximity – clarifying that not all knowledge is equal. More 'proximate' knowledge, from a cognitive rather than geographical perspective, is important as it can move and be recombined more easily across the economy. On the contrary, in a highly specialised economy, knowledge will not be naturally recombined as firms have access to the same pool of technical expertise, which might even lead to a situation of cognitive lock-in. Alternatively, when the cognitive distance between two sectors in a diversified economy is substantial, it is also unlikely that knowledge and ideas will be exchanged as actors in the two sectors do not 'speak the same language' (Breschi *et al.* 2003).

The presence of a high volume of related economic activities in a region thus facilitates the generation of new combinations of existing technologies, products and production processes, or rather 'entrepreneurial opportunities' in the smart specialisation vocabulary. Nevertheless, the diversity of activities also spreads risk and a region is therefore not dependent only on a handful of sectoral branches. A recent study of long-term diversification in various regions of Sweden by Neffke *et al.* (2011) provides empirical proof of the entrepreneurial opportunity conceptualisation. This study shows that it is easiest for regions to attract new branches of industry that are related to existing ones. Conversely, companies in certain branches of industry are more likely to leave a region if no related activity is present. Consequently, branches of industry related to those already existing in a region fit the region's industrial profile better than those for which this is not the case. Identifying such branches of industry is therefore vital for a region's economic policy as it is important to determine which branches of industry are related.

In line with the two functions of diversification, sectoral diversity is divided by Frenken *et al.* (2007) into related and unrelated variety to discriminate between sectors in which proximity allows knowledge to move from one sector to another (related variety) and sectors in which ideas and skills are unlikely to spill over (unrelated variety). Each of the two sides of variety has its advantages. Related variety allows firms and organisations to access knowledge from complementary sectors and recombines it into new products or processes. As the level of knowledge-relatedness influences the opportunities for firms to innovate (Breschi *et al.* 2003), high levels of related variety are likely to have a positive effect on employment as new goods and products will come into production. However, an economy with highly unrelated sectors will benefit from this diversification, especially by being better protected against sectoral shocks (resilience). At least in the short run, a high level of unrelated variety is therefore likely to be associated with lower unemployment growth. From this theoretical result, the conceptualisation by Frenken *et al.* (2007) has been applied in a number of cases, especially in regional analyses of European countries. In most applications, the results match the hypotheses, especially in terms of related variety, thus confirming that employment growth increases with high relatedness across sectors. However, until recently, cross-regional and pan-European analyses of the hypotheses on related and unrelated variety have been scarce.

Nonetheless, in the Smartspec FP7-project, the effects of different types of agglomeration economies in relation to regional economic growth in European NUTS2-regions were investigated by Van Oort *et al.* (2015) using a cross-sectional approach, whereas Cortinovis and van Oort (2015) use a spatial panel estimation approach. Particularly important within the smart specialisation discussion is the question of whether the endowment of technological and knowledge resources in an economy influences the functioning of agglomeration economies, as suggested by prior research (Hartog *et al.* 2012). In Cortinovis and Van Oort (2015), the impact of variety and specialisation is therefore studied in technological regimes defined according to the levels of technological progress and knowledge intensity of each region using a study by Wintjes and Hollanders (2011). In this study, different indicators of employment, human resources, technology, activity rates and the overall economic situation are used to divide EU regions into seven types of knowledge economies (Figure 9.1). High-technological regional profiles are present in Southern Germany, London and the surrounding area, Paris, Toulouse, Scandinavian urban regions and Eastern European capital regions.

Following this approach, regions are ranked according to their capacities in terms of knowledge accessibility, knowledge absorption and knowledge diffusion.

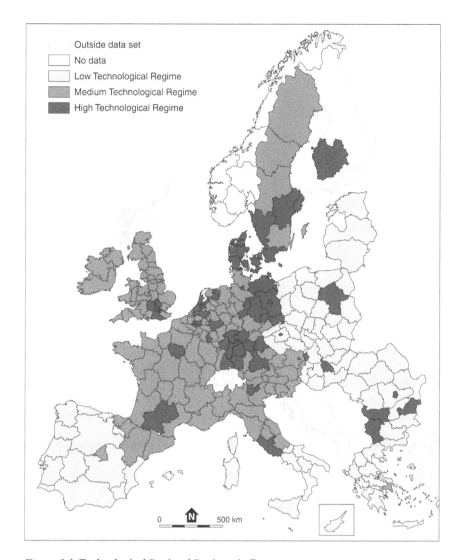

Figure 9.1 Technological Regional Regimes in Europe.

Building on this fact, regions are assigned into three technological regimes ('High technological regime', 'Medium technological regime' and 'Low technological regime'), as shown in Table 9.1.[1]

From both studies (Cortinovis and Van Oort 2015, Van Oort *et al.* 2015), outcomes add important insights to the growing European diversification, specialisation and economic growth debates of smart specialisation – for both academia and policy. Diversity, and especially related variety, in most models does indeed have a positive effect on growth, but predominantly when the technological and knowledge

Table 9.1 Technological regimes and types of regions

Technological Regimes	Type of Region	Features
High technological regime	Metropolitan knowledge-intensive services regions	High absorption capacity
	Public knowledge centres	High accessibility
	High-tech regions	High diffusion, accessibility and absorption capacity
Medium technological regime	Knowledge-absorbing regions Skilled technology regions	Average performance in diffusion, accessibility and absorption capacity
Low technological regime	Traditional Southern regions	Below average in diffusion, accessibility and absorption capacity
	Skilled industrial Eastern EU regions	Below average in diffusion and absorption capacity

Source: *Elaboration from Wintjes and Hollanders 2011, by Cortinovis and Van Oort 2015.*

endowment of the region is high (as identified in figure 9.1 and table 9.1). In other words, agglomeration economies have differential effects across regions in distinct regimes, but distinctly sort themselves into knowledge-intensive regions. The reason may be obvious: externalities associated with knowledge flows 'pay off' only in economies with a high stock of knowledge and technology.

This conclusion bears important policy implications for smart specialisation, suggesting that diversification alone is not sufficient to reap the benefits of so-called Jacobean externalities. Investment in human capital, technological upgrading and R&D are preconditions for related and unrelated variety that have beneficial effects on an economy. Apart from the capital regions, these preconditions are absent from most CEE regions. This means that CEE regions are unlikely to profit at all from place-based related and unrelated diversification opportunities, questioning the universal applicability of one of the basic ingredients of smart specialisation strategies.

9.4 Institutional Quality, Economic Diversification and Smart Specialisation

From the literature we know that there is a strong connection between the unequal levels of institutional quality in regions, technological progress and opportunities for regional economic excellence (Rodriguez-Pose 2013). In CEE regions, negative interpretations of these aspects explicitly reinforce each other. There is a common understanding of institutions, culture and social capital influencing entrepreneurship and economic growth in Europe (Akcomak & ter Weel 2009, Gedaljlovic *et al.* 2013), and recently there is increasing evidence for variations and impact on regional levels in the European Union (Arbia *et al.* 2010, Beugelsdijk & van Schaik 2005, Charron *et al.* 2014). Recently, it has been argued that little attention has been given in the literature to the intermediate function of economic diversification processes regarding the impact of institutions on economic performance. Building on Hall and Soskice (2013) on varieties of capital argumentation, Boschma and Capone (2015) show that the link between institutions and sectoral composition of regions is the first of a set in smart specialisation decompositions, the second being the relation between sectors and types of innovations and entrepreneurial opportunities. Although these arguments attempt to explain the complementary relations between institutions and innovative structural change, the intermediate process of sectoral diversification in the original varieties of the capitalism framework is taken for granted.

In addition, the effects of different hard (formal) and soft (informal) institutional arrangements on the behaviour of agents vis-à-vis obstacles and opportunities for diversification have received limited attention in recent studies. Developing the approach set out by Boschma and Capone (2015) on national EU scales, Cortinovis *et al.* (2016) explore the interplay between sectoral proximity (relatedness) and the quality of institutions to better understand their effects on diversification dynamics and their potential consequences for regional development. Following up on the challenge to distinguish formal from relatively under-investigated informal institutions, an econometric analysis for the FP7-project *Smartspec* is applied to a European regional setting. The regional dimension is considered particularly relevant for Europe given the significant differences across regions in formal and informal institutional arrangements (Barca *et al.* 2012, p. 143): 'The EU is a prime example of how an international territorial system emerges out of increasing economic integration among nation states with relatively similar levels of development but with different social, institutional, and technological features in regions'. Cortinovis *et al.* (2016) therefore first investigate whether the hypothesis that sectoral relatedness or proximity is driving diversification processes does actually hold for EU regions. They then look more closely at the role of formal and informal institutions by focusing on both the direct effects of institutions over the acquisition of new industrial specialisations ('entrepreneurial discovery') and on the interaction between the regional institutional endowments and the levels of relatedness among different sectors in the economy. Finally, they analyse whether formal or informal institutions impact most on diversification processes and performance, because informal rules may have more influence on economic and social outcomes in certain regional societies.

Concerning formal institutions, Cortinovis *et al.* (2016) argue that the quality of government may also facilitate the acquisition of specialisations in new sectors. Within a clearly established and inclusive set of rights and rules, firms and individuals are able to pursue their economic interests. With the lower associated risks and uncertainties in such environments, local actors strive for better standards of living by being more entrepreneurial, more innovative and by being better positioned to invest in new activities. Although this holds for indigenous economic actors, it is also highly relevant for foreign ones. In particular, the capacity of an economy to attract and benefit from foreign investment critically hinges upon its institutional settings. A sound formal institutional framework might help to facilitate and encourage a significant amount of investment, the acquisition of new-to-the-region skills by FDI, and the importing of capabilities through productivity and knowledge spillovers to host-region firms. Policies implemented by well-functioning governments help to make local actors better able to take advantage of the inflow of new ideas, products and knowledge which then help with diversifying and enlarging the regional industrial portfolio by creating new entrepreneurial discovery processes.

With respect to informal institutions, or social capital, Cortinovis *et al.* (2016) introduce the level of trust and involvement of people in associational life within EU regions using the European Values Study database, which contains survey data on the social attitudes and values of people at the regional level (Beugelsdijk & van Schaik 2005). Both formal institutions and informal institutions are found to be of crucial importance in Cortinovis *et al.* (2016) in relation to the capacity of European regions to economically diversify over time and to the related growth and creation of new innovative market niches. Studying the maps of formal institutions (formal regulation, quality of government) in Charron *et al.* (2014), and patterns of indicators for informal institutions (trust, social capital) in Beugelsdijk & van Schaik (2005), both of which are redrawn in Figure 9.2, we learn that CEE regions score particularly low on many of the indicators regarding growth-enhancing institutions, which magnifies and also causes the limited endogenous diversification and growth potentials of CEE regions.

Institutional arrangements in knowledge creation and organisation also influence how effective governance instruments can be applied in European regions. If in the past governments supported a handful of strategic sectors and cities, modern times require the identification of various groups of resources, the provision of a knowledge framework and flexible innovative policies for long-term growth to create and develop competitive local businesses. All available resources are currently required to be evaluated in cost-benefit terms (EC 2015).

These approaches can often be used efficiently within the existing framework of knowledge institutions (e.g., research institutes, universities, chambers of commerce, etc.) in which there are adequate investments in technologies for integration within international trade patterns, high-skilled workers, allied with entrepreneurship and flexible innovative policies to support and stimulate long-term growth (Figure 9.3). All these elements are highly dependent on the region's formal and informal institutional quality.

9.5 Growth Potentials of CEE Regions from FDI

Cities in CEE countries attract foreign capital simultaneously with but at a different rhythm from the endogenous development of local business environments. This aspect of the local economy is a double-edged sword. On the one hand, it can provide increased or improved employment, capital stock, infrastructure investments and better business network connections. On the other hand, it can make local economies dependent if the local business environment is unstable and/or poorly endowed in terms of capacities, human resources or capital stock.

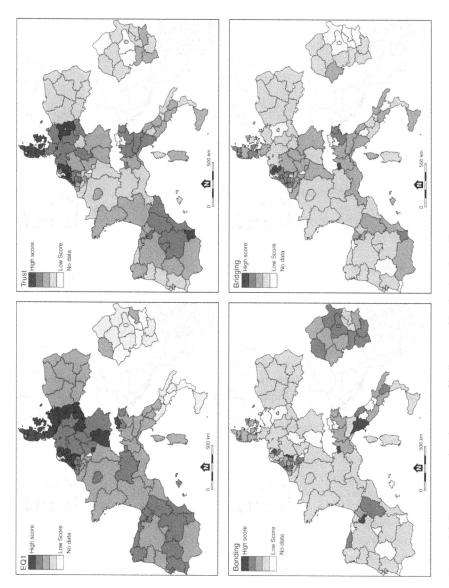

Figure 9.2 European regional scores of indicators of institutional quality.

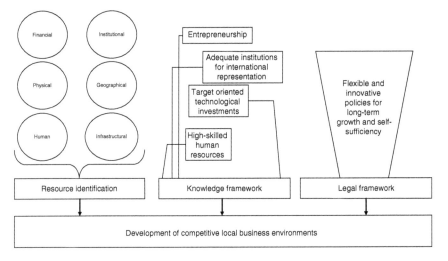

Figure 9.3 Smart specialisation in Central Eastern Europe.

It may be necessary to investigate whether exogenous growth potentials, such as foreign direct investment, really contribute to regional growth and diversification opportunities for CEE regions, and to identify what exactly is the role of formal and informal institutions in these processes. As suggested in earlier research with a general EU focus, the effects of institutions and FDI on local development may be considerable (Di Guardo *et al.* 2015, Ascani *et al.* 2015), yet a full analysis focused on CEE regions is still missing.

Recent member states joining the EU has meant increased trade opportunities for the newcomers while also transforming their own economies into more accessible new markets for the other EU members, some of which have higher growth rates. In addition, by joining the EU, newcomers have entered a new institutional reality of differently structured markets, with many more diversified, service-oriented economies where agglomeration economies are a key source of growth. The high regional and local competitiveness of Western Europe challenges CEE cities even further in their growth capacities (ESPON 2012). However, capital city regions in CEE countries have begun taking different development paths to other EU regions and have grown at a faster pace while changing their economic structure (Dijkstra *et al.* 2013). Although most CEE regions have experienced productivity growth in manufacturing industries, CEE capital city regions are converging at a faster rate due to their roles as business hubs and service oriented sectors (Dogaru *et al.* 2014). Yet, the competitive advantage of a region is not only dependent on the present sectors but also on the predominant type of activities within. As indicated by Chapman and Meliciani (2012), the spatial clusters of white collar labour and headquarters functions supplemented by a dynamic service sector can lead to renewed self-sufficient growth systems.

The presence of firms with intermediate activities and groups of service functions in cities increases the importance of functional rather than sectoral specialisation at the regional level (Duranton and Puga 2005). In this view, CEE cities have a potential for new markets as their strategic EU peripheral geographic position make them a bridge between EU members and the rest of Europe (Ascani *et al.* 2015). However, such opportunities should be seen as being primarily related to medium-term growth and capital stock investments, while long-term growth strategies imply high-skilled human resources and high-end functions. In terms of urban rankings, firms target metropolitan areas for high-end functions as there is a constant need for face-to-face communication, highly trained human capital and demand. Looking at locational life-cycles of investments it can also be observed that headquarters and high-end functions are located in larger cities and that production plants and low-end service functions position themselves in more peripheral areas and cities due to factor cost considerations. In this low-end part of the process direct contact with the final market is less significant. While empirically investigating this hypothesis, Dogaru *et al.* (2014) find that an overwhelming number of medium-sized cities in CEE countries accommodate this last type of firms focus on the last part of the life-cycle process. Although specifically second-tier cities can be characterized by having resources that are not fully exploited (especially in specialised knowledge in higher education), thereby showing potential for one-step better opportunities (Dogaru *et al.* 2014), the attraction of higher level functions is actually limited.

The selective positions of CEE regions in FDI attraction are based on the managerial decisions of multinational corporations (MNCs) (Defever 2012). As the literature in economic geography, international business and international economics shows, for reasons of risk reduction from a foreign business perspective, multinational location choices are based upon a region's local attractiveness in terms of its economic location factors or simply by imitation of the past behaviour of other similar MNCs. Burger *et al.* (2013) summarise the arguments of firms in the FDI literature and stress the fact that foreign business presence may be positive for the local environment due to skill and technology replication, as long as foreign employment does not replace indigenous activities (see also Furlan 2014; Oberhofer 2013). Under such conditions, local economies can also benefit from employment creation and capital injections or export increases. According to the eclectic OLI paradigm, firms go abroad for market expansion through ownership over products or processes, location or process division for costs or for know-how reasons through trade or networking (Dunning & Lundan 2008). The latest interpretation of the OLI framework includes both formal and informal institutions as an important factor in knowledge diffusion, mostly within but also among firms. According to Iammarino and McCann (2013), the institutionalisation of innovation through R&D investments in firms is one of the top catalysts in industrial competition. This particular advantage can be internalized by local businesses only if these have the human capital and capacity to assimilate and further develop it. Therefore, if CEE policy agendas target foreign investments for growth, a first priority may be the enhancement of the local human and technological capacity level within the indigenous business environment through national and local investments in the shape of incentives or loans.

Several aspects of FDI should also be considered to best capitalize on it at the CEE local level. Dunning and Lundan (2008) show that development and transfer of knowledge in MNEs is hierarchical in terms of the importance of affiliates (e.g., headquarters, distribution centres, production plants, etc.). Most investments in CEE regions target medium-low functions (Dogaru *et al.* 2014). For long-term growth it is essential that exogenous FDI is complemented by (and embedded in) endogenous growth opportunities created by a targeted policy plan for native firms to focus on higher-end functions supplying highly skilled human capital. In the past, MNEs chose to locate in CEE regions for multiple reasons, and given their horizontal and vertical orientation on the value chain organisation (Barba Navaretti & Venables 2004), the decision was based upon competitive advantages gained from increased sales and market access, as well as trade-related strategic advantages and lower transportation and factor costs associated with investing abroad, versus the increased coordination costs. Furthermore, MNEs also look for more foreign markets, efficiency increases, improved resources or enhanced strategic assets. In general, it can be expected that horizontal FDI will be drawn to locations with good market access, whereas vertical FDI will be drawn to places with lower factor costs, so without a tailored learning and investment scheme, the latter may remain dominant in the CEE patterns of FDI attraction.

Institutional quality is also a necessity in the CEE space, and Charron *et al.* (2014) show that CEE countries score poorly for this indicator. Such a context influences foreign investments but, most importantly, inhibits a healthy business and innovation environment at the local level. Agglomeration advantages fuelling economies of scale, employment and productivity are currently not directed towards the upgrading of local production structures for both endogenous and exogenous FDI developments in CEE regions. Focusing explicitly on agglomeration and specialisation advantages *and* diversification opportunities simultaneously is therefore essential for the research and policy agenda of CEE regions.

9.6 Whither Second-tier City Regions in CEE Countries?

Although agglomeration economies in the capital cities of CEE countries are already being developed and their costs (including negative externalities) are already high, these cities still benefit from the critical size requirement that obviously plays a dominant role in endogenous growth processes, driven by foreign investment decisions, diversification and entrepreneurial search processes alike. As much as capital cities differ in size from Bratislava and Ljubljana to Bucharest and Warsaw, second-tier cities differ in structure and sizes as well. Rotterdam (The Netherlands), Milan (Italy), Munich (Germany) and Barcelona (Spain) are somewhat at odds in terms of their size, agglomeration and functional structure in comparison with Timisoara (Romania), Krakow (Poland), Brno (Czech Republic) or Szeged (Hungary). Still, all these urban areas are also marked as being second-tier cities (Dijkstra *et al.* 2013). The often suggested functioning of such cities in polycentric urban networks that may collectively form a critical mass is frequently met with institutional and cognitive barriers between the cities – in CEE-countries perhaps even more than in the 'old' Europe (Dogaru *et al.* 2014). For such a policy strategy to be successful, the efforts of local and national governments must be focussed on working on improving the economic complementarities, infrastructure connections, trans-local service provision and a supra-regional strategy. This approach requires a strategy aimed at place-based development that takes into account the specialisation and diversification opportunities in larger nationally and more globally networked regions, as well as the region's position in interregional and international networks of trade, knowledge and FDI as growth factors. In order to create conditions for enhancing the economic performance of secondary city regions, the European Union advocates strong public interventions that aim at the creation of integrated, multi-level and participatory governance and structural reforms (EC 2015). In this section we focus on an important ingredient for a CEE second-tier cities strategy based on our research experiences in the FP7 *Smartspec* project.

After switching to a new economic path after 1989, for a long time, capital regions in CEE countries retained their leading roles by being highly internationally connected and having the most developed economies in their countries. However, following European integration, other cities and regions also joined the chart of nationally significant economic builders and these cities are now competing among themselves, as well as with the capitals. Second-tier cities are newcomers in the importance list. To grow sustainably and resiliently, these cities must support themselves primarily by mobilising local actors and resources. Self-sufficiency requires complex strategies for regions and cities by aiming mainly at 'smart' regional specialisations and growth, complemented by international networking and foreign investments. This regional profiling and competitiveness should no longer be an exclusive aim for EU (structural) funding, but primarily for enhancing the knowledge position and role of regions on the national and global map. Smaller cities need to focus on larger regional areas by working as a team for growth, building on the concept of 'borrowed size' as used in the literature on polycentric regions. Yet, the heterogeneity of these smaller cities in CEE countries results in both restrictions and opportunities for development. Regions and cities can be 'smartly' profiled together, focusing on specific sectors and complementary functions that are present (Dogaru *et al.* 2014). Important determining factors here are the presence of top sectors and functions, the levels of trade, FDI and knowledge-network connectedness, along with the presence of high-skilled workers, infrastructure, and capital. A place in such a system can be industrial, in those cases which have the related infrastructure such as production or assembling plants (e.g., Solaris automotive industry in Poznan), whereas others can be geographically dominated by rural production related to agriculture (e.g., Nitra in Slovakia); while others again may rely on activities such as tourism. In reality, however, second-tier cities in CEE regions are mostly industrial. Although the inner-cities are decorated with picturesque historic architecture, the outskirts are dominated by old industrial infrastructure that mainly supported the local economy in the past. Many of these sites have either been abandoned or bought and re-used by foreign firms. Thus, an overall vision and preferably an improvement plan is required because the majority of industries in Central Eastern Europe still show outdated technical facilities and processes with medium-low working functions.

Smart specialisation and related variety-based policy implies a local choice of one or two sectors and specialisation within each of them by creating new market niches. Nevertheless, in many cases, the innovation capacity is not feasible over the long term because local endowments are scarce. Such cases can therefore potentially benefit by inter-municipal clustering and positioning in (inter)national value chains. Complementing the economic branches in the vicinity can be profitable and lead to the gaining from knowledge externalities (Wintjes and Hollanders 2011). Ideally, such an agenda should also focus on the local opportunities stemming from the presence of financial capital, highly trained and skilled human resources, adequate institutions and flexible policies fostering international trade, simultaneously with the stimulation and support of entrepreneurship. At the same time, job opportunities within a burgeoning labour market have to be increased within the commuting areas. Otherwise, the benefits of local advantages will spill over to the place that attracts more talent and human capital (brain drain), and the survival of start-ups must be supported by capital in a sound banking system. In Central Eastern Europe entrepreneurship is nurtured mostly in capital regions, and these first-tier cities are converging at a faster rate than other areas due to proximity to governments, better connection to international networks and the presence of high-skilled human resources and agglomeration economies within a knowledge and service-oriented economic environment. Other cities exhibit less diversity and longevity in entrepreneurship and the regional entrepreneurship development index (REDI) shows that although second-tier city regions have the ability for rapid resource mobilization, these are without significant profit results (EC 2013).

9.7 Conclusion: Multilevel Governance including EU and National Involvement

Jobs, labour market efficiency, entrepreneurship, governance and institutions, along with a focus on diversification and specialisation opportunities, are amongst the many ingredients that have to be captured simultaneously in CEE regional intervention strategies in order to be successful, because as yet market mechanisms often fail to provide locally sustainable outcomes. These interventions should come, on the one hand, from the cities themselves, and, on the other hand, from the national and European level. Second-tier city regions in CEE countries are supposed to open their internal structures for cooperation with other stakeholders, and following the Tripe Helix-type arguments, these engagements should be oriented especially towards potential economic and educational partners. They are also encouraged to open in a territorial sense towards their surrounding areas, aiming at uniting larger functional urban areas and allowing for the up-scaling of agglomeration economies. The task of national governments then is to establish the overarching governance reforms so as to initiate cooperation between local governments within the same urban area and to stimulate more regional decentralisation: regions with more planning independence would give increased power to secondary cities as centres of CEE regions. However, in CEE countries this decentralisation process has not yet been experienced at such levels. There is little expertise and, more importantly, the institutional and human resources are lacking. Consequently, future decentralisation policies should come in well-planned and safe steps to avoid generating unstable public institutional capacity regarding public safety or local healthcare systems, and especially those affecting smaller cities or rural areas within a region.

In the case of the Central East European secondary city regions little progress has been made so far regarding their own efforts towards having more open and flexible government policies (Dogaru *et al.* 2014). There is a clear need for more European involvement in redirecting attention and perhaps funding to secondary city regions. In this view, cohesion policy should partly shift its emphasis from compensating for deficient regional growth to encouraging secondary growth centres. Additionally, EU guidelines should emphasize the importance of more decentralised regional development.

The 'old' Western European development process is not necessarily an optimal recipe for growth in CEE regions. Rather, it definitely requires more of a place-based adaptation. Second-tier city regions in CEE countries have generally little technological readiness, few endogenous high-tech diversification opportunities and lack an overall central position in networks of foreign direct investment – an important (exogenous) development factor of regions and cities. Given the critical mass, structural change, knowledge endowments and physical accessibility that are needed simultaneously, a concomitant networked diversification and FDI-based development will be difficult. At present, second-tier city regions, and even some of the smaller CEE capital city regions, are not capable of offering all these factors at the same time in sufficient quantities. Above all, endogenous growth factors of economic structure and job opportunities need to be refocused as they are scarce and not ideally planned. Structurally strategic and sound institutional circumstances are needed to encompass a long-lasting growth framework. Implicitly, identifying key factors in building long-term viable, resilient and strategic growth pillars in these states can multiply their convergence rhythms towards Western Europe and the rest of the world.

Place-based development may be a centrepiece in emancipating CEE regions economically, yet they should explicitly complement people-based and network-based strategies. The common history of many CEE cities creates socio-economic regularities. Countries, regions and cities develop in similar ways economically and in terms of societal values. The Central Eastern European space is distinguished by tradition and adaptation.

Our recent analyses of diversification opportunities, FDI attraction and growth show that this space is below average in knowledge diffusion and absorptive capacity. The missing link in tightening *all* these results together in a strategic multilevel vision concerns the institutional framework. In fact, the CEE space shows considerably low institutional quality values. Here, both formal and informal institutions require a new long-term viable and socially responsible focus. More substantial and directed investments are needed in people, as are place- and network-based policies for long-term convergence with a large focus on institutions and institutional reform (EC 2015). The newly allocated structural funds can increase their efficiency if they are refocused on smart local, regional and network policies, by supporting those ex ante identified sectors which are regarded as being viable for diversification and in interaction with institutions (Rodriguez-Pose *et al.* 2013, Cortinovis *et al.* 2016). It is only with this focus that the suggested competitiveness opportunities of CEE second-tier city regions (Dijkstra *et al.* 2013) might be achieved. Leaving regional development only to the market will result in CEE countries' activities sorting themselves out increasingly in the capital regions, with large parts of CEE countries then facing structurally and substantially lower levels of cohesion.

Note

1   Missing data for Switzerland, Norway, Scotland and parts of Finland led to these regions' exclusion in the analysis of Corinovis *et al.* (2015).

References

Akçomak, S. & B. ter Weel (2009), Social capital, innovation and growth: evidence from Europe. *European Economic Review* 53: 544–567.

Arbia, G., M. Battisti & G. di Vaio (2010), Institutions and geography: Empirical test of spatial growth models for European regions. *Economic Modelling* 27: 12–21.

Ascani, A., R. Crescenzi & S. Iammarino (2015), 'Economic institutions and the location strategies of European multinationals in their geographical neighbourhood'. LSE Discussion Paper 97/2015.

Asheim, B., P. Cooke & R. Martin. (2006), *Clusters and regional development. Critical reflections and explorations*. London: Routledge.

Bachtler, J., C. Mendez & F. Wishlade (2013), *EU Cohesion policy and European integration. The dynamics of EU budget and regional policy reform*. Aldershot: Ashgate.

Barba Navaretti, G. & A. Venables (2004), *Multinational firms in the world economy*. Princenton, NJ: Princeton University Press.

Barca, F., P. McCann & A. Rodriguez Pose (2012), The case for regional development intervention: place-based versus place-neutral approaches. *Journal of Regional Science* 52: 134–152.

Beugelsdijk, S., & T. van Schaik (2005), Social capital and growth in European regions: an empirical test. *European Journal of Political Economy* 21: 301–324.

Boschma, R. & G. Capone (2015), Institutions and diversification: Related versus unrelated diversification in a varieties of capitalism framework. *Research Policy* 44: 1902–1914.

Breschi, S. & F. Lissoni (2009), Mobility of skilled workers and co-invention networks: an anatomy of localized knowledge flows. *Journal of Economic Geography* 439–468.

Breschi, S., F. Lissoni & F. Malerba (2003), Knowledge-relatedness in firm technological diversification. *Research Policy* 32: 69–87.

Burger, M., B. van der Knaap and R. Wall (2013), Revealed competition for greenfield investments between European regions. *Journal of Economic Geography* 13: 619–648.

Chapman, S. A. & V. Meliciani (2012), Income disparities in the enlarged EU: socioeconomic, specialisation and geographical clusters. *Tijdschrift voor Economische en Sociale Geografie* 103: 293–311.

Charron, N., Dijkstra L., & V. Lapuente (2014), Regional governance matters: quality of government within European Union member states. *Regional Studies* 48: 68–90.

Cortinovis, N. & F. van Oort (2015), Variety, economic growth and knowledge intensity of European regions: a spatial panel analysis. *The Annals of Regional Science* 55: 7–32.

Cortinovis, N., J. Xiao, R. Boschma & F. van Oort (2016), Frmal and informal institutions as drivers of regional economic diversification. Mimeo, Utrecht University.

Defever, F. (2012), The spatial organization of multinational firms. *Canadian Journal of Economics* 45: 672–697.

Dettori, B., E. Marrocu & R. Paci (2012), Total factor productivity, intangible assets and spatial dependence in the European regions. *Regional Studies* 46: 1401–1416.

Di Guardo, M., E. Marrocu & R. Paci (2015), 'The effect of local corruption on owner-ship strategy in cross-border mergers and acquisitions'. Paper presented at the ERSA Conference, Lisbon.

Dijkstra, L., E. Garcilazo & P. McCann (2013), The economic performance of European cities and city regions: myths and realities. *European Planning Studies* 21: 334–354.

Dogaru, T., M. Burger, B. Karreman & F. van Oort (2014), The geography of multinational corporations in CEE countries: perspectives for second-tier city regions and European cohesion policy. *Investigaciones Regionales* 29: 193–214.

Dogaru, T., M. Burger, B. Karreman & F. van Oort (2015), Functional and sectoral divi-sion of labour within Central and Eastern European countries: evidence from greenfield FDI. *Journal of Economic and Social Geography (TESG)* 106: 120–129.

Dunning J. H. & Lundan S. M. (2008), *Multinational exterprises and the global economy*. Cheltenham: Edward Elgar.

Duranton, G. & D. Puga (2005), From sectoral to functional urban specialization. *Journal of Urban Economics* 57: 343–370.

EC (2013), *REDI: The regional entrepreneurship and development index – Measuring regional entrepreneurship Final Report*, http://ec.europa.eu/regional_policy/sources/docgener/studies/pdf/regional_entrepreneurship_development_index.pdf.

EC (2015), 'Background paper for the Lagging Regions project'. Brussels: European Commission.

ESPON (2012), *SGPTD Second tier cities and territorial development in Europe: perfor-mance, policies and prospects Final Report*, http://www.espon.eu/export/sites/default/Documents/Projects/AppliedResearch/SGPTD/SGPTD_Final_Report_-_Final_Version_27.09.12.pdf.

Foray, D. (2015), *Smart specialisation. Opportunities and challenges for regional innova-tion policy*. London: Routledge.

Frenken, K. & J. Hoekman (2006), Convergence in an enlarged Europe: the role of network cities. *Tijdschrift voor Economische & Sociale Geografie* 97: 321–326.

Frenken, K., F. G. van Oort & T. Verburg (2007), Related variety, unrelated variety and regional economic growth. *Regional Studies* 41: 685–697.

Furlan, B. (2014), 'Employment effects of mergers and acquisitions: a continuous treat-ment approach'. Mimeo, University of Salzburg.

Gedajlovic, E., B. Honig, C. Moore, G. T. Pryne & M. Wright (2013), Social capital and entrepreneurship: a schema and research agenda. *Entrepreneurship Theory and Practice* 37: 455–478.

Glaeser, E. L., H. Kallal, J. Scheinkman & A. Shleifer (1992), Growth in cities. *Journal of Political Economy* 100: 1126–1152.

Gripaios, P., P. Bishop, T. Hart & E. McVittie (2008), Analysing the impact of Objective 1 funding in Europe: a review *Environment and Planning C* 26: 499–524.

Guastella, G. & F. van Oort (2015), Regional heterogeneity and interregional research spillovers in European innovation: modelling and policy implications. *Regional Studies* 49: 1772–1787.

Hall, P. A. & D. Soskice (2013), *Varieties of capitalism. The institutional foundations of comparative advantage*. Oxford: Oxford University Press.

Hartog, M, R. Boschma & M. Sotarauta (2012), The impact of related variety on regional employment growth in Finland 1993–2006: high-tech versus medium/low-tech. *Industry and Innovation* 19: 459–476.

Hoekman, J., K. Frenken & F. van Oort (2009), The geography of collaborative knowledge production in Europe. *The Annals of Regional Science* 43: 721–738.

Iammarino, S. & P. McCann (2013) *Multinationals and economic geography*. Cheltenham: Edward Elgar.

Jacobs, J. (1969), *The economy of cities*. New York: Random House.

McCann, P. (2015), *The regional and urban policy of the European Union. Cohesion, results-orientation and smart specialisation*. Cheltenham: Edward Elgar.

Marrocu, E., R. Paci & S. Usai (2013), Productivity growth in the old and new Europe: the role of agglomeration externalities. *Journal of Regional Science* 53: 418–442.

Melo, P.C., D. J. Graham & R. B. Noland (2009), A meta-analysis of estimates of agglomeration economies. *Regional Science and Urban Economics* 39: 332–342.

Moreno, R., R. Paci & S. Usai (2005), Spatial spillovers and innovation activity in European regions. *Environment & Planning A* 37: 1793–1812.

Muller B., Finka, M. & Lintz, G. (2005), *Rise and decline of Industry in Central Eastern Europe*. New York: Springer.

Neffke, F., M. Henning & R. Boschma (2011). How do regions diversify over time? Industry relatedness and the development of new growth paths in regions. *Economic Geography* 87: 237–265.

Oberhofer, H. (2013), Employment effects of acquisitions: evidence from acquired European firms. *Review of Industrial Organization* 42: 345–363.

Rodríguez-Pose, A. (2013), *Do institutions matter for regional development? Regional Studies* 47: 1034–1047.

Rodriguez-Pose, A. & E. Garcilazo (2013), 'Quality of government and the returns of investment: examining the impact of cohesion expenditure in European regions'. OECD Working Papers 2013/12.

Rosenthal, S. S. & W. C. Strange (2004), Evidence on the nature and sources of agglomeration economies. In: J. V. Henderson & J. F. Thisse (eds.), *Handbook of Regional and Urban Economics*. Amsterdam: Elsevier 2119–2171.

Thissen, M., F. van Oort, D. Diodato & A. Ruijs (2013), *Regional competitiveness and smart specialization in Europe. Place-based development in international economic networks*. Cheltenham: Edward Elgar.

Thissen, M., T. de Graaff & F. van Oort (2016), Competitive network positions in trade and structural economic growth: a geographical weighted regression analysis for European regions. *Papers in Regional Science* (forthcoming).

Van Oort, F., S. de Geus & T. Dogaru (2015), Related variety and regional economic growth in a cross-section of European regions. *European Planning Studies* 23: 1110–1127.

Wintjes R. & H. Hollanders (2011), *Innovation pathways and policy challenges at the regional level: smart specialisation*. Working paper. United Nations University Maastricht.

10 From Plan to Process

Exploring the Human Element in Smart Specialisation Governance

Mari Jose Aranguren, Mikel Navarro and James R. Wilson

10.1 Introduction

The notion of territorial strategy is currently undergoing a boom in popularity, alongside the re-emergence of debates around industrial policy (Rodrik, 2004; Valdaliso and Wilson, 2015; Wade, 2012; Warwick, 2013). New industrial policies recognise that it is important for territories to have concrete strategies to guide their economic development, which means making choices around which economic activities to support. Where they break from old industrial policies is in emphasising that making those choices is not the job of government alone, but must build new forms of private-public interaction. In Europe these debates have taken shape around the concept of smart specialisation strategies (Foray and Van Ark, 2008; Foray, 2013, 2014; McCann and Ortega-Argilés, 2015, 2016), which have been interpreted largely at regional level following the European Commission's push for all regions to design and implement 'research and innovation strategies for smart specialisation' (RIS3) (European Commission, 2011, 2012, 2014; McCann, 2015).

Regional smart specialization strategies have two key features. Firstly, they should prioritise investments in research, development and innovation within the region. These priorities should support strategic structural change in the economy that builds from existing strengths and responds to emerging opportunities. Secondly, they should identify which areas to prioritise through an entrepreneurial discovery process (EDP) that engages key regional stakeholders from business, government, research/university and civil society. While there is widespread agreement around the conceptual arguments underpinning both of these features, putting into practice a regional EDP is challenging because it places new demands on regional governance. The EDP requires open-endedness and flexibility, which implies a fundamental shift from writing fixed, government-led plans (that often remain on the shelf), to developing flexible, multiple-stakeholder processes capable of feeding an ongoing, evolving and shared strategy. These processes are both complex and sensitive because they involve many different agents at many different levels, and because ultimately they should determine important decisions around both public and private research and innovation investment priorities.

Governance, understood as the dialogue, engagement and coordination processes through which decision-making takes place, is therefore fundamental for operationalizing regional EDPs. In particular, the change from plan to process in the way that territorial strategy-making is approached raises questions around the 'human element' of governance relationships. For example: how to overcome the transience of the actual people involved in smart specialization governance processes as organisations change? How to foster the personal capacities and capabilities needed to lead and/or participate in these processes? or how to harness the power/relevance of different narratives and different individuals to speak to and engage different audiences (public, private, research)? In particular, the leadership of specific people and/or organisations plays a key role by injecting impetus or guidance into emerging smart specialization governance processes at different moments in time.

The aim of this chapter is to explore this often neglected human element of smart specialisation governance,[1] with a focus on what is required in terms of leadership to make the move from plan to process and to operationalise a regional EDP. To do so the chapter brings together elements from existing literature – on governance, place-leadership, the relevance of certain of Mintzberg *et al.*'s (1998) strategy schools, and the lubrication to relationships provided by different dimensions of social capital – to propose a set of considerations with regards the leadership requirements of EDPs. To explore these considerations in the current context of RIS3, the chapter takes advantage of the fact that European regions have been grappling intensively over the last two years with designing smart specialization strategies that fulfil the European Commission's requirements for innovation funding. Specifically, it juxtaposes the quite different experiences of two seemingly similar and neighbouring Spanish regions – the Basque Country and Navarre – as a practical basis for discussing the arguments that emerge from the literature analysis.

10.2 The Complex Process of Entrepreneurial Discovery

Ultimately smart specialisation is about selecting certain research and innovation activities over others for investment of public and private resources within the region. This includes both vertical prioritization relating to specific productive activities (biosciences or creative and cultural industries, for example), and horizontal prioritization relating to broader regional competences (innovation cooperation or policy evaluation, for example). Yet as recognised by Foray (2013) the key novelty is in vertical prioritization, and any prioritisation of activities that favour certain technologies, fields, and therefore firms, is inherently difficult. How to focus public STI investment in the region is ultimately a policy decision taken by government, with all of the political pressures that go with that decision. The challenge is therefore twofold: (1) how to inform this government decision from an EDP that brings together the diverse knowledge on capabilities and possibilities that is embedded and constantly evolving among the quadruple helix of business, government, research and civil society; and (2) how to ensure that the decisions and resource commitments of all of the components of the quadruple helix are well-aligned with the emerging priorities such that the strategy can be considered to be truly territorial (and not just a government investment strategy). Central to both challenges is the concept of governance.

Governance has risen relatively recently and rapidly to prominence in the social sciences (Jessop, 1998), where it has become a critical element in our understanding of economic development. It is by no means a straightforward concept, however, and is often confused as being narrowly associated with the decision-processes of government (Sugden *et al.* 2006). This misconception is particularly important for smart specialisation debates, given that governments are only one of the many agents that should engage in EDPs. Taking a broad view, then, governance refers to the emergence of some sort of order for coordinating socioeconomic activities among a whole range of actors (and their associated interests) (Kooiman and Van Vliet, 1993; Jessop, 1998; Aranguren *et al.* 2008). For Stoker (1998) the essence of governance is in mechanisms that do not depend on the authority or sanctions of government, which is in line with Kooiman and Van Vliet's (1993: 64) view of governance as 'the creation of a structure or an order which cannot be externally imposed'. Rather than being externally imposed by a single authority, the structure or order that characterises any particular governance setting should result from interaction among the range of different actors with a stake in the outcomes of the decisions to be taken in that setting.

It is no surprise therefore that governance is a central feature of smart specialisation debates, as reflected in its inclusion as one of six steps in the European Commission's (2012) *Guide to Research and Innovation Strategies for Smart Specialisation*. As the guide argues (p. 21), 'the fact that RIS3 is based on a wide view of innovation automatically implies that stakeholders of different types and level should participate extensively in their design'. Moreover it highlights the need to go beyond the usual triple helix, to include a fourth *civil society and demand* sphere of consumers, citizens and workers. The resulting quadruple helix should be involved in the governance processes behind the design and ongoing implementation (and evolution) of the RIS3, in what can be seen as an extension of the concern with governance in the concepts of innovation systems (Braczyk *et al.* 1998; Edler *et al.* 2003; OECD, 2005) or clusters (Karlsson, 2008; Pitelis *et al.* 2005), for example.

When analysing the governance of RIS3 *the* critical consideration is that different governance processes can result in different outcomes. Depending on who is involved, what form of interactions take place between them, and how power dynamics are exercised among them, the outcomes in terms of the coordination of socioeconomic activities – in this case the priorities a territory should target in research and innovation – will be different. Indeed, following Bailey *et al.* (2006), every agent or territorial system has a development path, and therefore a development strategy that is either explicit or implicit in shaping that path. In these strategies there are (conscious and unconscious) choices which orient the strategy towards different aims, meaning that the decision-making processes surrounding these choices must be at the heart of what is meant by governance and, in the context of RIS3, of what is meant by entrepreneurial discovery.

The need to understand the articulation of governance processes in practice is complicated by the multi-level nature of territorial relationships. While multi-level governance is by no means a new concern, it has not been a central concern in debates around RIS3, which has resulted in a failure to clearly recognise the different levels of analysis (and their articulation) required for a coherent regional strategy. Yet the new, dynamic forms of governance required for EDPs do not have the luxury of being able to develop within an isolated single-level territorial system. The rise of systemic approaches to innovation and the importance that this places on proximity-based relationships has corresponded with a decentralisation in the governance of science, technology and innovation (STI) policies in many places, with certain competences shifting from national to regional and local levels. This adds a significant element of complexity to the design, implementation and evaluation of these policies (Braun, 2008; OECD, 2011; Magro and Wilson, 2013), which is exacerbated further by a fragmentation and multiplication of agents. Indeed, it is common to find a lack of policy coordination among the range of different government departments that deal with STI policy issues, operating alongside different agencies responsible for different phases of the policy-making processes (design, implementation and evaluation), and involving different sets of agents from the innovation system in their processes (firms, universities, research centres, etc.). In this respect STI policy governance can be understood as a coordination of decision-making among three different layers – political, administrative and operative (Boekholt et al. 2002; Lindner, 2012, Magro et al. 2014) – each of which are also present at various territorial scales. Moreover, while such fragmentation of the involvement of 'government' in innovation policy governance is fairly widely recognised, the heterogeneity among actors within each of the other helices is often forgotten. Pierre and Peters (2000), for example, note differences between large multinational corporations and small firms, and there are likely to be similar differences between large universities and small research centres or consultancies, or between large multinational NGOs and small local NGOs. This heterogeneity, intertwined with the multi-level dimension, makes it problematic to consider government, business, research or civil society as 'one' when analysing their involvement in territorial strategy.

The scenario faced by regions seeking to develop and pursue a RIS3 is above all one of complexity, therefore, in which it is no easy task to establish governance mechanisms capable of involving the right set of agents from the right places and at the right moments. Hooghe and Marks (2003), for example refer to Scharpsf's law: the more jurisdictions, the more difficult the coordination and governance. Furthermore, the governance requirements of RIS3 are particularly challenging because an EDP implies a strategy that is *alive*, constantly evolving, and constantly engaging a broad range of agents in its definition, implementation and evaluation. This requires new, dynamic and networked forms of governance that break with the more static and hierarchical forms that governments and other agents are used to when making their formal strategic plans in relatively top-down processes. Indeed, in the same way that public policies are path dependent of previous ones, territorial strategies exhibit a strong path-dependent character (Valdaliso *et al.* 2014). Thus the approach with which institutions and policy-makers in a territory address the issue of strategy is highly influenced by the way in which territorial strategy was constructed in the past. To change from one approach to another requires the development of new capabilities among agents, and in particular it raises questions for the role of different types of leadership in these processes.

10.3 Leadership for Entrepreneurial Discovery

While there has been some recent acknowledgement of the significance of collaborative leadership for RIS3 (Martinez and Palazuelos-Martinez, 2014), it is an aspect that has been little explored. Yet Sotarauta (2009) has argued that as regional scenarios become more complex, regional development relies more heavily on leadership and network management; while this new complexity can't be controlled, it can be influenced (Sotarauta, 2010). In earlier work Sotarauta (2004) translated the distinction between deliberate and emergent strategies introduced by Mintzberg (1992, 1994) to debates on territorial strategy. Deliberate strategies are in line with what might be termed a classical view of territorial strategy, whereby a written plan is formulated, committed to and then executed. Emergent strategies, on the other hand, form spontaneously from the development of patterns in an array of diverse processes, which require alignment. Citing Linnamaa (1996), Sotarauta (2004: 24–25) defines an 'actor- and communication-centred approach' to regional strategy as a continuous process during which 'various goals and strategies of individual organisations are made as parallel as possible by communication and negotiation'.

In practice, territorial strategy tends to be the result of a combination of both deliberate and emergent processes, but in different weights from place to place, in different dimensions or components of the strategy, and at different moments in its development. What is more, each type of process requires different types of leadership. In this regard Collinge and Gibney's (2010b) distinction between *purposive* and *spontaneous* governance is useful. While the former is related to a direct leadership from government policy, the latter refers to an indirect leadership or meta-governance in which leadership creates the conditions (incentives, structures, etc.) for complex governance relationships to flourish. While purposive leadership predominates in the traditional practice of government-led plans for innovation and competitiveness, the styles, forms and approaches of leadership required for spontaneous governance take on greater importance in a territorial EDP involving the entire quadruple helix. In particular, a greater degree of systemic leadership is required that is capable of somehow bringing together the different individual (and purposive) leaderships that may be established not just by government actors, but by a range of other agents in their own domains (leading firms or clusters, universities, civil society groups, etc.).

Another way of looking at this is that as governance scenarios become more complex the questions of *how* and *who* become more important than the question of *what* (Sotarauta, 2009). This line of argument finds a parallel in the territorial strategy framework developed by Navarro *et al.* (2013), which draws on a range of literature from business strategy, territorial strategy and science and technology policy to distinguish three questions that a territorial strategy should answer; *what for*, *what*, and *how/by whom*.[2] Aranguren and Larrea (2015) have delved deeper into the *how/by whom* question. Specifically, they argue that three of the strategy schools identified by Mintzberg *et al.* (1998) – the learning, cultural and power schools – are particularly relevant for how territorial strategy takes place. On the one hand the EDP is a perfect fit with the key premise of the learning school; that 'strategy-making must above all take the form of a process of learning over time, in which, at the limit, formulation and implementation become indistinguishable' (Ibid.: 208). On the other hand, the EDP is characterised by the social interaction based on shared beliefs and understanding that is central to the cultural school, and takes place in the context of conflicting interests that will inevitably lead to the types of political behaviours analysed by the power school (Ibid.).

Given its acknowledged importance as a lubricant for the interactive relationships central to the learning, cultural and power schools, the concept of social capital (Putnam, 1993; Fukuyama, 1995; Nahapiet and Ghoshal, 1998) presents itself as an important departure point for a deeper understanding of the leadership requirements of EDPs. While the concept remains somewhat fuzzy (Inkeles, 2000), Nahapiet and Ghoshal's (1998) distinction between three dimensions of social capital – structural, relational and cognitive – is useful. The structural dimension emphasises the importance of *creating spaces* to enable dialogue, sharing of information/experiences and making explicit areas of conflict or consensus. In the EDP such spaces are critical for uncovering the knowledge (or strategic intelligence) around existing capabilities in the region and around opportunities available from combining those capabilities. These spaces also play a key role in *generating a shared vision* of the strategy – what for, what, and how/by whom – among diverse agents and clarifying the roles of each agent in that vision; the cognitive dimension of social capital. For the strategy to be sustainable then the shared vision itself must develop in a way that is mutually beneficial and that balances benefits to different agents over the short and long term, a challenge that relies on *behaviours of reciprocity and trust*; the relational dimension of social capital.

For the ongoing process of learning that is necessary for the aims, content and process of a regional strategy to be 'discovered', leadership requirements will therefore be diverse. Above all we can talk of what Sotarauta *et al.* (2012) define as 'knowledge leadership'. A region is a complex system and in a complex system the knowledge necessary to overcome challenges and take advantage of opportunities is distributed, and not only among different territorial actors, but at a global level. It is useful therefore to distinguish the emergence of individual 'leaders' – key figures in the government, business, university or civil society fields – as playing roles within an overall 'leadership' of the territorial strategy. Indeed, a territorial strategy cannot (or should not) be led by one individual leader. Rather, different leaders should come together in the development of a multiplicity of quadruple helix partnerships that respond to different strategic challenges and/or opportunities and guide the evolution of the strategy as a whole. There are different roles to play within this. Leaders with a systemic vision are needed to create the interaction spaces and inspire involvement in those spaces; and leaders with an understanding of processes and with capabilities to nurture all important trust and reciprocity are needed to manage those spaces in ways that facilitate the emergence of opportunities and the generation of a shared vision. Leaders with knowledge of specific fields (sectors, technologies, scientific fields, product markets) are also needed to identify specific opportunities from combining regional capabilities, and to galvanise the right set of agents in developing them.

On the one hand these different roles are similar to the distinction between 'policy generalists, persons of substance and persons of process understanding' identified by Sotarauta (2010) or to Terry's (1993) distinction between 'content visionaries' and 'process visionaries' (as cited by Mabey and Freeman (2010: 512)). On the other hand, their reliance on each other and their necessary configuration to generate a regional EDP points to the concept of shared leadership that has become popular in the leadership literature (Conger and Pearce, 2003; Fletcher and Kaufer, 2003; Pearce and Conger, 2003). According to Pearce and Conger (2003: 1) shared leadership is 'a dynamic, interactive influence process among individuals in groups for which the objective is to lead one another to the achievement of group or organizational goals or both.' Rather than relying on downward hierarchical influence, shared leadership is based on a mixture of downward, upward and horizontal influence. This mix would appear particularly relevant at regional level, where there can be no one hierarchical leader setting a strategy and imposing downward influence for its execution.[3] Yet while lessons can be learned for territorial leadership from the organisational or business literature, care must be taken in how they are translated given the notable differences related to complexity, temporal scale, motivations, etc. (Collinge *et al.* 2010; Gibney, 2011; Gibney *et al.* 2009). With this in mind, a number of considerations for the specific shared leadership or mix of leadership styles, forms and approaches likely to be required by regional EDPs can be highlighted.

Firstly, there is an underlying need for the development of new collaborative habits among both public and private agents. In particular leaders need to establish the region as a frame of reference for their thinking and their decisions, alongside an already existing frame of reference (their firm, university, government department, etc.). Stough (2001: 35), for example, defines territorial leadership as the 'tendency of a community to collaborate among sectors (different groups) in a sustainable and decided way to increase the economic outcome of a region'. This implies that 'formal leaders find themselves representing places as well as / rather than organisations' (Gibney, 2011: 616), and would suggest that a *dualism in reference frame*, and the ability to effectively manage that dualism, is a key characteristic of the individual leadership required for territorial strategy-making. Moreover, it seems likely that a certain indirect leadership or spontaneous governance (Collinge and Gibney, 2010b) on the part of government should play a role in creating the conditions whereby such dual leaderships can emerge and thrive.

The distinction made by Stimson *et al.* (2009) between 'leaders' and 'entrepreneurs' in regional development also seems to be relevant. While leaders and entrepreneurs share certain characteristics (both should seek to innovate and assume risks, for example), the motivation and behaviour of the entrepreneur is more individualistic than that required of a leader.[4] Similarly, while the engagement of people from all parts of the quadruple helix with ideas and willing to take risks is undoubtedly critical for a regional EDP, it is the willingness and ability to put specific aims and concerns not shared by others to one side and think in terms of the region that distinguishes leaders in this process. This relates also to the concept of ownership of the strategy, which should be regional, and not belonging to any one agent. This doesn't imply that governments, firms, universities etc. do not have their own strategies, but that leadership of a regional strategy implies thinking beyond those specific frames of reference and putting certain interests to one side where necessary.

A second consideration is that different leadership competences are necessary at different stages of the development of a regional strategy. With regards network management, for example, Klijn *et al.* (2010:5) argue that there are some phases in which 'institutional design' is more important and others that correspond more with a 'management process'.[5] Similarly, Harmaakorpi and Niukkanen (2007) argue the necessity for different types of 'regional development network', each of which requires a different type of leadership. This argument could be extended to the different dimensions or components of a territorial strategy. As STI prioritizations are identified in a RIS3, for example, there will also be moments when leadership based on knowledge of specific content comes to the fore. The different competences required at different stages and in different components of the strategy are not typically held by the same actor or organization, implying *a mix and rotation of leadership*, with different agents playing different roles at different times. It is important therefore that each actor identifies the moments when its role could be critical and assumes responsibility, and likewise identifies the moments where it should step back and let others with different competences lead.

Finally, there is the important question of from where different individual leaderships emerge, given that different roles are likely to suit more or less different profiles from the quadruple helix. Here the above reflections on the requirements with respect to different moments and components of the process can guide us. For example, it is more likely that government or government agencies have the capacities to play the systemic leadership role required for process design and for creating base conditions for engagement of other agents, and here too academic institutions may play an important role (Aranguren *et al.* 2016; Goddard *et al.* 2013). When the strategy process is in a phase where specific prioritizations are being explored and experimented, the necessary knowledge leadership is more likely to be found in technology centres, universities, leading firms or clusters of firms (Aranguren and Wilson, 2013; European Commission, 2013). The *source of leaders* is likely to vary significantly region-by-region, however, according to the capacities of regional governments and the presence (or not) of universities, firms, clusters and other institutions with the capacities to play different leadership roles.

10.4 Shaping RIS3 in the Basque Country and Navarre

For the 2014–2020 period of European regional development funding the European Commission introduced an *ex-ante* condition that requires all EU member states and regions to have a RIS3 in place before their operational programmes are approved (European Commission, 2014). The formal responsibility to comply lies with member states, and there has been diversity in the degree of implication at regional level in accordance largely with the degree of policy autonomy that regions in different countries are afforded. Spanish regions have among the highest levels of policy autonomy in Europe and in Spain the processes of preparing RIS3 have been led at the regional level. In this context the cases of the Basque Country and Navarre make for an interesting comparison given that they are neighbouring regions that share the highest levels of decentralization in Spain (unlike other Spanish regions they have their own tax-collection powers). From the outside they also look very similar, sharing similar economic performance, innovation performance, sector specialization (in manufacturing) and export orientation (see Table 10.1). Both regions have also been relatively forward-thinking in terms

Table 10.1 A summary comparison of the regions of the Basque Country and Navarre

	Basque Country	*Navarre*
Population (size)	Medium (2.2 million)	Small (0,6 million)
Density and urbanization	High density	Low density, but population concentrated around the capital
Population growth	Stability and little immigration	Dynamism linked to immigration
Population 65 years or more	High rate	Average rate
Decentralization	Highest	Highest
General quality of government	Medium-high (above Spanish average)	Medium-low (below Spanish average)
Sectoral specialisation	High in industry, KIBS & ICT	Very high in industry
Manufacturing specialisation	Very high in basic metals, transport equipment, machinery	Very high in transport equipment, food & drinks
Export orientation	Medium-low (1.5 of Spanish average)	Medium-high (double Spanish average)
Firms size	Medium (above Spanish average, due to industrial specialisation)	Medium-high (double Spanish average, due to industrial specialisation & MNCs)
Innovation system	Innovation follower (RIS2014), with strong business R&D and technological infrastructures, and weak universities	Innovation follower (RIS2014), with strong business R&D and universities
Economic performance	High productivity, medium labour participation, high unemployment (but lowest in Spain) and very high per capita GDP (highest in Spain)	High productivity, medium labour participation, high unemployment (but second lowest in Spain) and very high per capita GDP (second highest in Spain)

Source: *Own elaboration. See Appendix 10.1 for a detailed statistical comparison of the two regions on which this summary is based.*

of innovation policy, and have been heavily active in European discussions and forums around RIS3 from the beginning.[6]

Yet there are important differences between the regions with respect to each of the elements of the quadruple helix. These differences can be observed to have shaped the design of their RIS3 and they continue to shape the ongoing implementation of their RIS3. The authors have strong knowledge of the Basque case, having studied the competitiveness of the Basque region for many years,[7] and having played an active role in discussions with government and other agents around the design and then implementation of the RIS3 from 2013 through to early 2016. In the case of Navarre, along with analysis of secondary sources,[8] the authors conducted a dozen in-depth interviews with key players in the RIS3 process during July 2014 to analyse the design phase of their RIS3. They have subsequently been engaged in a series of follow-up interviews, meetings and workshops during 2015, and in early 2016 they have supported the Government of Navarre in the revision of its RIS3, all of which has enabled them to follow progress in the RIS3 implementation. The remainder of this section reports the key quadruple helix differences between the two regions that can be seen to have influenced in the design and implementation of their respective RIS3.

With regards the government sphere of the quadruple helix, there are some significant differences between the two regions that have impacted on the RIS3 process (Table 10.2). While the two regions share one of the highest levels of policy autonomy in Europe, the scenario in the Basque Country is far more complex in terms of both multilevel governance and the articulation of different government departments with competences in R&D policy. On the other hand, Navarre is characterized by a greater degree of political instability and poorer perceptions of quality of government. While both have a long trajectory of making regional plans, Navarre has tended to pursue more traditional and less sophisticated horizontal policies and bottom-up processes, and even though both have sought to establish new institutions in recent years to support innovation and promote the infusion of external expertise, the Basque Country has been more prone to the creation of structures and Navarre to develop informal relationships.

There are also important differences in the other elements of the quadruple helix (Tables 10.3–10.5). While the regions have quite distinct university and scientific research systems, both in structure and quality, in both cases these have not played a leading role in territorial strategy processes for different reasons. In the technological system of both regions there is a network of technology centres which work directly with industry, more integrated and stronger in the Basque case. Despite some similarities stemming from their industrial specialisation and the strong presence of social or cooperative enterprises in both regions, business itself exhibits different characteristics across the regions. Basque Country business is more diversified and also more endogenous, with very little foreign ownership, and with a strong associational culture. There is also more of a tradition of business involvement in territorial strategy in the Basque country, with the long-standing cluster policy having supported the development and

Table 10.2 Government in the Basque Country and Navarre

	Basque Country	*Navarre*
Multilevel	Regional, provincial, county and municipal.	Regional.
Departments	9 (several with R&D competences).	8 (R&D competences more concentrated).
Autonomy level	One of highest in EU (high in tax & R&D&I).	One of highest in EU (high in tax & R&D&I).
Government quality	Good general image & good capabilities in R&D&I policies.	Bad general image, but acceptable capabilities in R&D&I policies.
Political stability	Rotating since 2008 after long period of stability. Currently a minority in government, but consensus of almost all parties on industrial & R&D&I policy.	Same party in power from 1996 to 2015: in coalition in 2011–2012, and afterwards in minority, with severe institutional & political crisis that affected the management of the RIS3 strategy. New government from late 2015, resulting from a coalition of Basque nationalistic and left-wing movements, which prompted changes in the content and management of the RIS3 strategy.
Elected officials and bureaucracy	Elected officials mainly related to ruling party. Elected officials & bureaucracy involved in RIS3.	Until the current government, second level of elected officials very often coming from bureaucracy, easing continuity & communication.
Legacy of plans	Long history of plans & strategies. Active role of government in emergence & development of new thematic activities (bio, nano, etc.).	Long history of plans & strategies, without thematic priorities until 2010. Less active role of government & a more bottom-up process.
Innovation agency	The innovation agency Innobasque, created in 2007 and formally a PPP but mainly funded by the government, acts as secretariat of the RIS3 process and fulfils a range of tasks requested by government. In the implementation phase this includes facilitating the establishment of pilot groups to develop each of the RIS3 thematic priorities, and evaluating the progress of the strategy.	A new public-private organization, the Moderna Foundation, was created in 2011 to develop the RIS3 of Navarre. Since 2012, their functioning was hindered by the severe economic, institutional & political crisis of the government. The new government has closed Moderna and transferred its personnel to Sodena (a public economic development agency), and plans to create a new governance platform for quadruple helix agents.

(Continued)

Table 10.2 Continued

	Basque Country	Navarre
External experts	In 2006 the Basque government supported the creation of Orkestra, a research institute with a mission to support Basque competitiveness by means of research and interaction. Orkestra is linked to the university & independent from government; personnel have academic backgrounds, but are action oriented & work in international knowledge networks. Currently many of their reflections feed the Basque RIS3. From 2010 onwards, experts external to the region (OECD, Kevin Morgan, …) have reviewed the innovation system and the R&D&I strategy.	Although Navarra has a good consultant in innovation policy, a small think-tank on competitiveness and university departments of economics and business, they lack either academic profile, orientation, resources and/or structures to assist properly the RIS3 process. The initial process of the Moderna Plan was partly conducted with external professional consultants. Afterwards, the external experts have acted on demand of the European Commission or linked to the SmartSpec project. The new government has reached a collaboration agreement with the UPNA (the public university of Navarre) and Orkestra, to develop intelligence for the RIS3 project.

Source: *Own elaboration based on authors' knowledge through involvement in processes, interviews with key regional stakeholders and a review of RIS3 and other documents.*

engagement of cluster associations (Aragón *et al.* 2014; Aranguren *et al.* 2014). In contrast, in Navarre the Government has supported a model of social partnership based on dialogue and agreement between employer and worker associations. Finally, with regards the civil society sphere the main difference is that in Navarre both major political parties and employer and worker associations are present in the governing bodies of the Moderna Foundation (the organisation that was responsible for the RIS3 strategy), while they watch from the side-lines in the Basque case.

Having made a comparative analysis of each element of the quadruple helix, Table 10.6 compares the main characteristics of the resulting RIS3 as they currently stand (and bearing in mind that RIS3 is an ongoing process). There are similarities in terms of the starting point for the current RIS3 process; an existing plan that had been approved prior to the requirement for a RIS3 by the EU and that identified certain priorities. However, the differences are more significant: in how the RIS3 is integrated in a more general socio-economic development strategy; in how the priorities were initially arrived at; in the priorities themselves; and in what was the response to the requirement for a RIS3 coming from the EU and what has happened subsequently in terms of the EDP.

Table 10.3 Universities and knowledge organisations in the Basque Country and Navarre

	Basque Country	*Navarre*
Legal status & size	One large public university (UPV-EHU: 42,000 students) & two private universities (UD: 13,000 students; MU: 3,000 students).	One public university (UPNA: 8,000) & one private university (UN: 11,000).
Quality of universities	Overall, medium: UPV better in R&D; UD in teaching; MU in third mission.	Overall high: UN one of the best in Spain & UPNA medium-high.
Role in territorial strategy	Government strategies have prioritized technology & tend to mistrust the university. The public university has governance and incentive problems that impede a proactive approach to territorial strategy.	The dominant private university pursues its own strategy (with implications for Navarre). The potential role of the public university has not been considered, partly due to the huge influence of UN and to its governance and incentive problems.
Other scientific research centres	The regional government has created several centres because of mistrust of the university and given that Spanish public research centres are located outside of the region.	There are some created in collaboration with the Spanish government in the specialisation areas of Navarre, and some others linked to the universities.
Technological centres	They constitute one of the main strengths of the Basque innovation system. In the 1980s and 1990s they were the key actors, although recently the regional government has also supported other actors (e.g. research centres).	They have been created to bridge the distance between universities & industry, but they have not succeeded in that. There is currently a network of technological centres, but not as strong as the Basque one & in need of concentration.

Source: *Own elaboration based on authors' knowledge through involvement in processes, interviews with key regional stakeholders and a review of RIS3 and other documents.*

10.5 Discussion of the Human Element of Entrepreneurial Discovery Processes

The earlier literature analysis explored the often missed human element that is central to processes of territorial strategy-making. In particular, reflections on the literature led to the identification of three considerations with regards the leadership of RIS3: a dualism in reference frame among leaders; a mix and rotation of leadership; and the likely different sources of leaders. These three considerations can be

Table 10.4 Business in the Basque Country and Navarre

	Basque Country	Navarre
Ownership	Scarce penetration of foreign capital, although significant internationalisation of Basque Firms. Important presence of cooperative companies.	Big presence of foreign capital (13 out of 27 top Navarre firms are foreign-owned). In contrast, despite the high export ratio, few firms from Navarre have plants abroad. Presence of social economy and cooperative firms.
Representation of firms	Employer associations have lost prominence & direct representation of large firms, business groups or representation via cluster associations has increased, playing an important role in territorial strategy processes.	Business associations play an important representative role (social partnership model), but cluster associations are weak. Large firms and MNCs typically don't want participate in territorial strategy processes.
Diversity	The economy and industry are quite diversified.	The economy and industry is much more concentrated.

Source: *Own elaboration based on authors' knowledge through involvement in processes, interviews with key regional stakeholders and a review of RIS3 and other documents.*

related in various ways to the differences in how the RIS3 process has taken shape between the Basque Country and Navarre as described in the previous section of the chapter. This concluding discussion aims to bring together both sets of insights to reflect on the human element that is central to smart specialisation governance.

A first set of reflections refer to *implications from the context in which RIS3 develops*. The cases of the Basque Country and Navarre serve to highlight the differences in context between regions in terms of the characteristics of their quadruple helix, an aspect that is clearly conditioning the development of their RIS3. Moreover, this specificity of context conditions not only the objectives of the strategy and the types of activities that are prioritized, but also the governance processes and leadership necessary to activate EDPs. There are several aspects of regional context that might be important in this regard, of which the case analysis points especially to those related to the complexity that characterises the region's quadruple helix – the aforementioned Scharpsf's law in practice – and the stability and quality of regional institutions.

When it comes to RIS3, regional complexity refers primarily to the government administration (departments and government agencies involved, levels of government that operate in the region) and the innovation system (knowledge agents and other intermediary institutions). Along with the number of different agents involved in governance processes, the degree to which each of their roles are well-established and clear and the sophistication of established coordination mechanisms between them will all condition the development of a RIS3. There are also other characteristics highlighted by the Basque and Navarre cases that

Table 10.5 Civil society in the Basque Country and Navarre

	Basque Country	*Navarre*
Political parties	They don't participate explicitly in the development of territorial strategies and policies. Their input is limited to discussing proposed plans in the Parliament.	Until 2015 the two main parties participated in the governing bodies of the current RIS3, excluding the others. The process has become politicised, creating confusion about the role of representative political democracy.
Trade unions	Unions are strong in the Basque Country, but since the early 1990s they don't take part in industrial policy.	Along with the regional employer association, the two main unions take part in the governing bodies of the current RIS3. There has been a culture of dialogue and agreement between the main employer & worker associations. Some complaints that this defended more the existing rather than the emergent system, and excluded other trade unions.
Other agents	There is a strong associational movement in the Basque Country, but these associations are not involved in the current RIS3.	Other associational movements in Navarre are hardly involved in the current RIS3. The type of relationship with the Basque Country is a divisive issue in Navarre.

Source: *Own elaboration based on authors' knowledge through involvement in processes, interviews with key regional stakeholders and a review of RIS3 and other documents.*

might be associated with scenarios of greater or lesser complexity in the articulation of governance. These include: (1) the size of the region and the concentration of the population (the proximity associated with smaller size and concentration of population around the capital in the case of Navarre can be seen to ease governance relationships); (2) the concentration of economic activity (coordination can be seen to be simpler in the Navarre case, where industry is more concentrated in a few sectors and knowledge therefore more homogenous); (3) the types of firms (establishing a regional frame of reference for decisions is observed to be more difficult in the Navarre case, where there is a greater presence of large, multinational firms owned by foreign capital); and (4) the associational culture and existing social capital of the region (the density, variety and quality of existing networks present in the Basque Country can be seen to facilitate governance relationships with a regional frame of reference). In this respect, the number of potential variables means that talking about the degree of regional complexity can be disingenuous because all regions are complex in different ways. It makes more sense to talk about types of regional complexity, and the cases of the Basque Country and Navarre illustrate well how different scenarios can be complex in

Table 10.6 RIS3 in the Basque Country and Navarre

	Basque Country	Navarre
Starting point for the process in 2013	Existing 'Plan for Science, Technology and Innovation (PCTI) 2015', approved in 2012. New ruling party in government. Significantly fewer resources than those estimated in the PCTI-2015. Expert criticism of PCTI-2015 for lack of focus on thematic priorities.	Existing Moderna Plan for a 'new economic development model', approved in 2010. Severe institutional, political and economic crisis paralyzing government, both in resources and initiatives since 2012.
Response to the requirement for a RIS3 by the EU	Initially, to claim that the PCTI-2015 is the Basque RIS3. Then, taking advantage of the requirement, to design a new plan, the PCTI-2020 as the Basque RIS3, focusing more on thematic priorities.	To claim that the Moderna Plan is the Navarre RIS3, and that this plan already contains thematic priorities and integrates Quadruple Helix agents.
Extent of the focus on thematic priorities	Three 'thematic priorities': Biosciences-health, energy, advanced manufacturing. Four 'opportunity niches': Food, creative & cultural industries, urban habitat, environmental ecosystems. Priorities can be considered frames of reference rather than accurate priorities. In the implementation phase pilot groups have been established in each of the 7 areas to identify and explore specific niches and concrete projects.	Thematic priorities are an attractive arrangement of almost all the strengths and potentially interesting activities of Navarre, hardly excluding anything. Due to this lack of focus, the Moderna plan was initially rejected by the EU.
Analytical basis	Thematic priorities were set during the design phase from detailed evidence collected by government with the support of external consultants and advice, taking into account previous prioritizations, the economic context, and existing/potential capabilities.	The election of thematic priorities was the result of both statistical analysis and a process of consulting with a wide range of agents from the quadruple helix. The search for consensus led to excluding nothing.
Balance between traditional and emergent activities and roles of government	While previous plans prioritized the emergence of new activities (bios and nanos), the current process gives more weight to activities with undeniable existing strengths. Government has traditionally played a key role in targeting emergent activities, with business more prominent in developing existing activities.	Until the Plan Moderna vertical priorities had not been identified. Moderna's main goal was to change the economic model, but after 2011, with the government in crisis and no capabilities in the private sector, new activities were not launched or supported.

Table 10.6 Continued

	Basque Country	Navarre
Entrepreneurial discovery process	In the design of the RIS3 prioritizations were discussed largely within government, and in formal and general terms with business, knowledge and territorial agents in the Basque STI Council. In the implementation phase different government departments are leading the development of each priority, and an entrepreneurial discovery process is being established through pilot groups of quadruple helix agents focused on deepening each priority.	As Moderna Plan was approved in 2010, there has been time to advance in the development of the thematic priorities. The initial design for it was sensible, but the lack of resources and political and institutional crisis hindered its effective implementation. No significant EDP can be mentioned.

Source: *Own elaboration based on authors' knowledge through involvement in processes, interviews with key regional stakeholders and a review of RIS3 and other documents.*

different ways, which in turn generates different leadership requirements for territorial strategy processes.

In the Basque Country, the type of complexity (lots of agents at multiple levels; poly-centric geography; diversified industry with heterogeneous knowledge bases) suggests that the systemic leadership role will be especially difficult, although there are also existing characteristics (largely endogenous firms; strong associational culture) that make it easier to establish forms of process leadership with a regional frame of reference. This can be seen to have played out in the RIS3 process, where the design phase was not highly participative, and the reluctance from regional government to lose control in wider stakeholder processes reflected the acknowledged complexity of doing so. There was also some tension around leadership of the RIS3 between government departments, which resulted in leadership being assumed by the Presidency department and a fairly top-down elaboration of the new plan. However, at the same time this process also arguably reflected a confidence that the strong existing regional frame of reference and associational culture in the region would make it easier for process leadership and content leadership to emerge at a later stage, and there are signs in the implementation phase that this is proving to be the case. The initially strong government leadership is evolving into a shared leadership with other quadruple helix agents in the context of the pilot groups established around each priority.

Broadly speaking the Navarre case demonstrates an opposite scenario in terms of regional complexity, and this is reflected in quite different outcomes (to date) of its RIS3 process. The Navarre RIS3 appeared to be neater and more complete following the design phase, having integrated consultation processes with most of the relevant agents. This was much easier to achieve than in the Basque case given the lower number of agents to be involved, and the clearer articulation of competences within the regional government. However, following this initial design phase there was an acute lack of resources to support the development of the processes that had been initiated and a political and institutional crisis that prevented the government from assuming leadership. Moreover, in contrast to the Basque case, the less formal structures among agents and lower associational culture (for example, absence of strong clusters), have made it more difficult for the process and content leadership required for the implementation phase to emerge among other actors.[9]

The stability and quality of regional institutions is the other element of context that emerges as particularly important in the case analysis. A difference in general institutional quality between the two regions is reflected in their relative performance in Charron *et al.*'s (2012) index (see Table 10.1). It is important, however, to make a distinction between confidence in government at a general level and the capacity of government to manage specific policies. The trajectory of Navarre in this latter respect, reflected in the early trajectory of its RIS3 process (advanced as it was in terms of European developments in this area), suggest that the two need not go hand-in-hand. However, the political instability that characterised Navarre from 2012 until the end of 2015 led to the RIS3 process becoming politicised, resulting in a paralysis effect that is only now starting to release its hold under a new government. This would suggest that political stability of some degree (whether through a political majority or a stable coalition between political forces) is a prerequisite for the effective functioning of the processes that are central to RIS3.

A second set of reflections refer to the *implications associated with the shift from planning to process*. Here we can see that path dependency plays an important role. As a general argument different regions typically have quite different experiences in the construction of territorial strategies, which conditions their existing leadership capacities for igniting EDPs and making the required shift from plan to process. In particular, there is an important issue of perceptions; of what is understood within the region by strategy. In this sense the third step for articulating a RIS3 in the *RIS3 Guide* (European Commission, 2012) refers to the importance of having a clear and shared vision of the future development of the region around which stakeholders can be engaged. This is commonly interpreted as a common vision of the direction that the region should take, but there is a strong argument that a common vision is also required around how stakeholders should engage in the strategy process. For example, until the recent establishment of pilot groups (once priorities had already been determined) in the Basque case, the sense of security provided by the development of a government plan (the PCTI-2020) can be seen to have created a barrier to the opening up of a wider EDP. In the case of Navarre, in contrast, previous plans had emerged from more bottom-up processes tackling quite broad thematic priorities, which can be seen to have eased the stakeholder processes underlying the Moderna Plan, resulting in broader stakeholder involvement in an EDP from the beginning, before the political instability paralyzed the process. An implication is that different types of leadership – more or less disruptive – will be required not only in different phases of the strategy but also in function of existing regional inertias and perceptions.

These arguments are also related to the ownership of the strategy, where there is a key distinction to be made between territorial strategy and government strategy. RIS3 is about the former but has been interpreted in many regions largely as the latter. While it is to be expected that different agents in the region (government, firms, universities, clusters, civic associations, etc.) have their own strategies, individual leaders must be capable of developing a dual reference frame that positions these strategies alongside an overall territorial strategy and puts specific interests to one side at certain moments. Both cases studied here illustrate the existence of important, though different, barriers to doing that: in the case of Navarre the lack of participation of large firms, the pursuit of its own strategy by the dominant university, and the politicised involvement of the main political parties in the process; in the case of the Basque Country the reluctance of government to cede control of its planning process in the early stages, despite the existence in the region of forms of leadership among certain agents (clusters, for example) that had previously demonstrated a dual reference frame. Juxtaposing the two cases also suggests that it is easier to secure ownership among the other elements of the quadruple helix in the implementation phase when senior government officials have been strongly implicated in the design phase (the Basque case), than the other way around (the Navarre case). While the implementation of the Basque RIS3 appears to be engaging a wider range of agents from a government-led starting point, it is proving more difficult to secure government support for implementation of the Navarre RIS3 that was designed with broad quadruple-helix participation but relatively limited involvement of government civil servants.

Finally, much of the above discussion points to specific *implications in terms of the required mix of leadership capabilities*. A clear conclusion is that both existing leadership capabilities and current leadership requirements will depend on the specific context of the region and the previous experiences of constructing territorial strategies, as well as on the type of strategy that is being pursued (for example, a strategy based primarily on horizontal priorities is not the same as one based on clear vertical priorities). Thus the mix of new leadership capabilities to be developed will vary from region to region; in some regions the need will be greater for systemic leadership, in others for process leadership, and in others still for content leadership. Moreover, these requirements will necessarily evolve with the life of the strategy. In the case of Navarre, for example, while the Moderna Foundation played a key leadership role in the design of the RIS3, it struggled to assume the leadership to manage the subsequent processes and their tensions and has ultimately been disbanded. In this sense participation in RIS3 processes is punctual, not continuous, and a key requirement for all forms of territorial leadership is to know and accept when to step forward and when to step back. Indeed, in the case of the Basque Country it could be argued that process and content leadership are much better developed among a wide range of agents, but the capabilities to ignite the processes in a regional frame are too concentrated in one agent (government). Leadership for RIS3 depends above all on specific context, therefore, and on finding the right *leadership mix* for that context.

Notes

1   There is a widespread perception that the 'human element' of how policies are designed, including leadership considerations, has been neglected in regional studies literature (Collinge and Gibney, 2010a; Gibney, 2011; Karlsen and Larrea, 2012; Sotarauta, 2005; Sotarauta and Mustikkamaki, 2012; Stimson *et al.* 2009; Stough, 2003), and Gibney (2011) also notes that *vice versa* the leadership literature has not taken on board the place dimension.
2   See also Valdaliso and Wilson (2015) for the further development of this framework and its application to a set of regional cases from around the world.
3   Indeed, this is likely to be even more so at regional level than at national level, where Harmaakorpi and Niukkanen (2007), for example, note that strategies have tended to be more hierarchical.
4   Benneworth (2007) also makes a distinction between 'institutional leaders' and 'institutional entrepreneurs', the former of which are argued to be leaders in that they commit to taking more risks, while the latter respond to the new opportunities that emerge from this by proposing new activities.
5   This is in line with the distinction between the roles of leader and manager in the organisational leadership literature (Colvard, 2008), a distinction that is also recognised in analysis of territorial leadership (Gibney *et al.* 2009; Harmaakorpi and Niukkanen, 2007). It also relates to the distinction between steering (setting goals and making priorities) and coordination (coordinating resources to support the pursuit of these goals) made by authors such as Pierre and Peters (2000).
6   In both cases the Basque Country more prominently than Navarre.
7   See, for example, Orkestra (2007, 2009, 2011, 2013, 2015).
8   See, for example, Bayona *et al.* (2005), Bergera and Arive (2011), Erro and Navarro (2011), Harmaakorpi (2013) and Moderna (2011).
9   As Metcalfe (1994: 278) states: 'Makeshift arrangements, informal contacts and ad hoc personal network cannot provide the degree of continuity and resilience required […] Policy co-ordination must be managed in order to be effective'.

References

Aragón, C., Aranguren, M-J., Iturrioz, C. and Wilson, J. R. (2014). A Social Capital Approach for Network Policy Learning: The Case of an Established Cluster Initiative, *European Urban and Regional Studies*, 21(2): 128–145.

Aranguren, M-J. and Wilson, J. R. (2013). What can experience with clusters teach us about fostering regional smart specialisation, *Ekonomiaz*, 83: 126–145.

Aranguren, M-J. and Larrea, M. (2015). Territorial strategy: Deepening in the 'how', in Valdaliso, J-M. and Wilson, J. R. (Eds.) *Strategies for shaping territorial competitiveness*, Oxford: Routledge.

Aranguren, M-J., Iturrioz, C. and Wilson, J. R. (Eds.) (2008). *Networks, Governance and Economic Development: Bridging Disciplinary Frontiers*, Cheltenham: Edward Elgar.

Aranguren, M-J., De La Maza, X., Parrilli, M. D., Vendrell-Herrero, F. and Wilson, J. R. (2014). Nested methodological approaches for cluster policy evaluation: an application to the Basque Country, *Regional Studies*, 48(9): 1547–62.

Aranguren, M-J., Guibert, J-M, Valdaliso, J-M. and Wilson, J. R. (2016). Academic institutions as change agents for territorial development, *Industry and Higher Education*, forthcoming.

Bailey, D., De Propris, L., Sugden, R. and Wilson, J. R. (2006) Public Policy for European Economic Competitiveness: An Analytical Framework and a Research Agenda, *International Review of Applied Economics*, 20(5): 555–572.

Bayona, C. (Ed.), Navarro, M., Goñi, S. and Merino, J. (2005). *Sistema de Innovación y competitividad en Navarra. Una comparación con el País Vasco*. Eusko Ikaskuntza, Donostia (available at: http://www.euskomedia.org/PDFAnlt/mono/idnav/00007302.pdf).

Benneworth, P. (2007). Leading innovation: Building effective regional conditions for innovation, NESTA research report, NESTA, London.

Bergera, M. and Arive, M. (2011). *Regional Innovation Monitor Regional Innovation Report (Region of Navarre)*, European Commission, Brussels (available at: http://www.rim-europa.eu/).

Boekholt, P., Arnold, E., Deiaco, E., McBibbin, S., Simmons, P., Stroyan, J. and Mothe, J. (2002). The Governance of Research and Innovation. An international comparative study. Synthesis Report, Technopolis Group, Brussels.

Braczyk, H-J., Cooke, P. and Heidenreich, M. (Eds.) (1998). *Regional Innovation Systems: The Role of Governance in a Globalized World*, London: UCL Press.

Braun, D. (2008). Organising the political coordination of knowledge and innovation policies, *Science and Public Policy*, 35(4): 227–239.

Charron, N., Lapuente, V. and Dijkstra, L. (2012). 'Regional governance matters: A study on regional variation in quality of government within the EU', *Regional Policy Working Papers WP01/2012*, European Commission, Brussels.

Collinge, C. and Gibney, J. (2010a). Connecting place, policy and leadership, *Policy Studies*, 31(4): 379–391.

Collinge, C. and Gibney, J. (2010b). Place-making and the limitations of spatial leadership: reflections on the Øresund, in Collinge, C., Gibney, J. and Mabey, C. (Eds.) *Leadership and Place*, Oxford: Routledge.

Collinge, C., Gibney, J. and Mabey, C. (2010) Introduction, in Collinge, C., Gibney, J. and Mabey, C. (Eds.) *Leadership and Place*, Oxford: Routledge.

Colvard, J. E. (2008). Developing future leaders, in Morse, E. E. and Buss, T. F. (Eds.) *Innovations in public leadership development*, New York: M. E. Sharpe, Inc.

Conger, J. A. and Pearce, C. L. (2003). A landscape of opportunities. Future research on shared leadership, in Pearce, C. L and Conger, J. A. (Eds.) *Shared leadership: Reframing the hows and whys of leadership*, Thousand Oaks: Sage Publications.

Edler, J., Kuhlmann, S. and Smits, R. (2003). New governance for innovation: The need for horizontal and systemic policy coordination, Fraunhofer ISI Discussion Papers Innovation System and Policy Analysis, No. 2/2003, Fraunhofer ISI, Karlsruhe.

Erro, A. N. and Navarro, M. (2011). El sistema de innovación en Navarra. Un ejercicio de diagnóstico y benchmarking. *Orkestra Working Paper Series in Territorial Competitiveness* No. 2011-R03 (CAS) (available at: www.orkestra.deusto.es).

European Commission (2011). *Regional Policy for Smart Growth in Europe 2020*, Brussels: European Commission.

European Commission (2012). *Guide for Research and Innovation Strategies for Smart Specialization (RIS3)*, Brussels: European Commission.

European Commission (2013). *The role of clusters in smart specialisation strategies*, Brussels: European Commission.

European Commission (2014). *National/Regional Innovation Strategies for Smart Specialisation (RIS3), Cohesion Policy 2014–2020 Factsheet*, Brussels: European Commission.

Fletcher, J. K. and Kaufer, K. (2003). Shared leadership. Paradox and possibility, in Pearce, C. L and Conger, J. A. (Eds.) *Shared leadership: Reframing the hows and whys of leadership*, Thousand Oaks: Sage Publications.

Foray, D. (2013). The economic fundamentals of smart specialisation, *Ekonomiaz* 83(2), 54–81.

Foray, D. (2014). *Smart Specialisation: Opportunities and Challenges for Regional Innovation Policy*, Oxford: Routledge.

Foray, D. and Van Ark, B. (2008). Smart specialisation in a truly integrated research area is the key to attracting more R&D to Europe, in *Knowledge for Growth: European Issues and Policy Challenges*, p.28, Brussels: European Commission.

Fukuyama, F. (1995). *Trust: The social virtues and the creation of prosperity*, New York: Free Press.

Gibney, J. (2011). Knowledge in a "Shared and Interdependent World": Implications for a Progressive Leadership of Cities and Regions, *European Planning Studies*, 19(4): 613–627.

Gibney, J., Copeland, S. and Murie, A. (2009). Toward a "new" strategic leadership of place for the knowledge based economy, *Leadership*, 5(1): 5–23.

Goddard, J., Kempton, L. and Valance, P. (2013). Universities and Smart Specialisation: challenges, tensions and opportunities for the innovation strategies of European regions, *Ekonomiaz*, 83, 83–102.

Harmaakorpi, V. (2013). Expert Assessment Smart Specialisation Navarre. Susinno Ltd, Lahti.

Harmaakorpi, V. and Niukkanen, H. (2007). Leadership in different kinds of regional development networks, *Baltic Journal of Management*, 2(1): 80–95.

Hooghe L. & Marks, G. (2003). Unraveling the Central State, but How? Types of Multi-Level Governance. *American Political Science Review*, 97(2): 233–243.

Inkeles, A. (2000). Measuring social capital and its consequences, *Policy Science*, 33: 245–268.

Jessop, B. (1998). The rise of governance and the risks of failure: the case of economic development, *International Social Science Journal*, 50(155): 29–45.

Karlsen, J. and Larrea, M. (2012). Emergence of shared leadership in the Basque Country, in Sotarauta, M., Horlings, L. and Liddle, J. (Eds.) *Leadership and Change in Sustainable Regional Development*, Oxford: Routledge.

Karlsson, C. (2008). *Handbook of research on cluster theory*, Cheltenham: Edward Elgar.

Klijn, E. H., Steijn, B. and Edelenbos, J. (2010). The impact of network management on outcomes in governance networks, *Public Administration*, 88(4): 1063–1082.

Kooiman, J. and Van Vliet, M. (1993). Governance and the public management, in Eliassen, K. A. and Kooiman, J. (Eds.) *Managing Public Organisations: Lessons from Contemporary European Experience*, London: Sage.

Lindner, R. (2012) Cross-sectoral coordination of STI policies: Governance principles to bridge policy-fragmentation, in Fraunhofer ISI (Ed.), Innovation Systems Revisited: Experiences from 40 years of Fraunhofer ISI Research, Fraunhofer Information, Stuttgart.

Linnamaa, R. (1996). Paikallinen elinkeinopolitiikka LED-ideologian toteuttamisvälineenä, in Haveri, A., Linnamaa, R. and Siirilä, S. (Eds.) Puheenvuoroja aluekehityksestä. Tampereen yliopisto, Aluetieteen laitos, Tampere.

Mabey, C. and Freeman, T. (2010). Reflections on leadership and place, *Policy Studies*, 31(4): 505–522.

Magro, E. and Wilson, J. R. (2013). Complex innovation policy systems: Towards an evaluation mix, *Research Policy*, 42(9): 1647–1656.

Magro, E., Navarro, M., Zabala-Iturriagagoitia, J. M. (2014). Coordination-mix: the hidden face of STI policy, *Review of Policy Research*, 31(5) 367–389.

Martinez, D. and Palazuelos-Martinez, M. (2014). Breaking with the past in smart specialisation: A new model of selection of business stakeholders within the entrepreneurial process of discovery, *S3 Working Paper Series*, No. 04/2014, IPTS, Seville.

McCann, P. (2015). *The Regional and Urban Policy of the European Union: Cohesion, Results-Orientation and Smart Specialisation*, Cheltenham: Edward Elgar.

McCann, P. and Ortega-Argilés, R. (2015). Smart Specialisation, Regional Growth and Applications to EU Cohesion Policy, *Regional Studies*, 49(8): 1291–1302.

McCann, P. and R. Ortega-Argilés (2016). Regional competitiveness, policy transfer and smart specialization, in R. Huggins and P. Thompson (eds), *Handbook of Regions and Competitiveness: Contemporary Theories and Perspectives on Economic Development*, Cheltenham: Edward Elgar.

Metcalfe, L. (1994). International policy co-ordination and public management reform. *International Review of Administrative Sciences*, 60: 271–290.

Mintzberg, H. (1992). Opening Up the Definition of Strategy, in Quinn, J. B., Mintzberg, H. and James, R. M. (Eds.) *The Strategy Process – Concepts, Contexts and Cases*, new Jersey: Prentice-Hall International.

Mintzberg, H. (1994). *The Rise and Fall of Strategic Planning – Reconceiving Roles for Planning, Plans, Planners*, New York: The Free Press.

Mintzberg, H., Ahlstrand, B. and Lampel, J. (1998). *Strategy Safari*, New York: The Free Press.

Moderna (2011). New Economic Development Model for Navarra: Executive Summary, Moderna, Pamplona (available at: http://www.modernanavarra.com/wp-content/uploads/ExecutiveSummary.pdf).

Nahapiet, J. and Ghoshal, S. (1998). Social capital, intellectual capital and the organizational advantage, *Academy of Management Review*, 22(2): 242–266.

Navarro, M., Valdaliso, J. M., Aranguren, M. J., and Magro, E. (2013) A holistic approach to regional strategies: The case of the Basque Country, *Science and Public Policy*, doi: 10.1093/scipol/sct080.

Navarro, M., Gibaja, J. J., Franco, S., Murciego, A., Gianelle, C., Hegyi, F. B. and Kleibrink, A. (2014). Regional benchmarking in the smart specialisation process: Identification of reference regions based on structural similarity. *S3 Working Paper Series* n° 03/2014 (paper and database available at http://s3platform.jrc.ec.europa.eu/regional-benchmarking-tool).

OECD (2005). Governance of innovation systems: Synthesis report', Geneva: OECD Publishing.

OECD. (2011). Regions and Innovation Policy, *OECD Reviews of Regional Innovation*, OECD Publishing, Paris.

Orkestra (2007). Competitiveness Report of the Basque Country: Towards a unique value proposition, Deusto Publications, Bilbao.

Orkestra (2009). Second Report on the Competitiveness of the Basque Country: Towards an innovation-based competitive stage, Deusto Publications, Bilbao.

Orkestra (2011). The Basque Country Competitiveness Report 2011: Leading the New Complexity, Deusto Publications, Bilbao.

Orkestra (2013). The Basque Country Competitiveness Report 2013: Productive Transformation for Tomorrow, Deusto Publications, Bilbao.

Orkestra (2015). The Basque Country Competitiveness Report 2013: Productive Transformation in Practice, Deusto Publications, Bilbao.

Pearce, C. L. and Conger, J. A. (2003). All those years ago. The historical underpinnings of shared leadership, in Pearce, C. L and Conger, J. A. (Eds.) *Shared leadership: Reframing the hows and whys of leadership*, Thousand Oaks: Sage Publications.

Pierre, J. & Peters, B. G. (2000). *Governance, Politics and the State*. New York: San Martin's Press.

Pitelis, C., Sugden, R. and Wilson, J. R. (Eds.) (2005). *Clusters and Globalisation: The Development of Urban and Regional Economies*, Cheltenham: Edward Elgar.

Putnam, R. (1993). *Making democracy work: Civic traditions in modern Italy*, Princeton: Princeton University Press.

Rodrik, D. (2004) Industrial policy for the twenty-first century. Kennedy School of Government Working Paper, RWP04-047.

Sotarauta, M. (2004). Strategy Development in Learning Cities. From Classical Rhetoric towards Dynamic Capabilities, Sente Working Papers 8/2004, Research Unit for Urban and Regional Development Studies, University of Tampere, Tampere.

Sotarauta, M. (2005). Shared leadership and dynamic capabilities in regional development, in Sagan, I. and Haikier, H. (Eds.) *Regionalism contested: Institutions, Society and Governance*, Cornwall: Ashgate.

Sotarauta, M. (2009) Power and influence tactics in the promotion of regional development: An empirical analysis of the work of Finnish regional development officers, *Geoforum*, 40: 895–905.

Sotarauta, M. (2010) Leadership and governance in regional innovation systems, in Eriksson, A. (Ed.) *The Matrix – Post Cluster Innovation Policy*, Vinnova Report VR 2010:10, Vinnova, Stockholm.

Sotarauta, M. and Mustikkamaki, N. (2012). Strategic leadership relay. How to keep regional innovation journeys in motion?, in Sotarauta, M., Horlings, L. and Liddle, J. (Eds.) *Leadership and Change in Sustainable Regional Development*, Oxford: Abingdon.

Sotarauta, M., Horlings, L. and Liddle, J. (2012). Leadership and sustainable regional development, in Sotarauta, M., Horlings, L. and Liddle, J. (Eds.) *Leadership and change in sustainable regional development*, Oxford: Routledge.

Stimson, R., Stough, R. R. and Salazar, M. (2009). *Leadership and Institutions in Regional Endogenous Development*, Cheltenham: Edward Elgar.

Stoker, G. (1998), Governance as theory: five propositions, *International Social Science Journal*, 50(155); 17–28.

Stough, R. (2001). Endogenous growth theory and the role of institutions in regional economic development, in Johansson B., Karlsson, J. B. C., Stough R. (Eds.) *Theories of endogenous regional growth: Lessons for regional policies*, Berlin: Springer.

Stough, R. (2003). Strategic management of places and policy, *The Annals of Regional Science*, 37: 179–201.

Sugden, R., Wei, P. and Wilson, J. R. (2006) Clusters, Governance and the Development of Economies: A Framework for Case Studies, in Pitelis, C., Sugden, R. and Wilson, J. R. (Eds.) *Clusters and Globalisation: The Development of Urban and Regional Economies*, Cheltenham: Edward Elgar.

Terry, R. W. (1993) *Authentic leadership: Courage in action*, San Francisco: Jossey-Bass.

Valdaliso, J.-M., Magro, E., Navarro, M. Aranguren, M-J. and Wilson, J. R. (2014). Path dependence in policies supporting smart specialisation strategies: Insights from the Basque case, *European Journal of Innovation Management*, 17(4): 390–408.

Valdaliso, J.-M. and Wilson, J. R. (Ed.) (2015). *Strategies for shaping territorial competitiveness*, Oxford: Routledge.

Wade, R. (2012). Return of industrial policies, *International Review of Applied Economics*, 26(2): 223–39.

Warwick, K. (2013). Beyond industrial policy: emerging issues and new trends, *OECD Science, Technology and Industry Policy Papers*, 2.

APPENDIX 10.1 Statistical comparison of the Basque Country and Navarre

		Basque Country	Navarre	Spanish regions (average)	EU regions (average)
Geo-demographic profil	Area (square kilometer) (2013)	7,235	10,390	29,762	21,064
	Density (inhabitants per km²) (2013)	300,9	61,8	166,6	308,0
	Population in cities and commuting zones (%)	80,0	71,2	70,6	60,8
	Population (thousands; 2013)	2,177	639	2,739	2,411
	Population (percentage change) (1990–2013)	2,9	23,1	20,3	6,5
	Percentage of population of 65 years or more (2011)	20,0	18,1	17,2	17,4
Sectoral distribution of total employment (%; 2012)	Agriculture, forestry and fishing (A)	1,3	3,6	5,2	6,6
	Industry (except const.) (B–E)	21,0	25,5	15,3	17,4
	Construction (F)	6,1	6,7	7,3	7,3
	Trade, hotel & restaurants, and transport (B–I)	23,4	23,4	28,5	23,8
	Information and communication (J)	3,3	2,6	2,3	2,4
	Financial and insurance activities (K)	2,8	2,2	2,2	2,5
	Real estate activities (L)	0,4	0,4	0,5	0,7
	Professional, scientific and technical activities (M–N)	11,1	7,9	8,9	7,9
	Public administration (O–Q)	23,5	22,1	22,4	24,4
	Arts, entertainment and recreation (R–U)	7,3	6,5	7,5	5,0
Sectoral distribution of manufacturing employment (%; 2011)	Mining and quarrying (05–09)	3,8	5,3	11,2	12,0
	Food, drinks and tobacco (10–12)	6,0	21,5	20,7	15,4
	Textiles, apparel and leather (13–15)	0,9	2,5	5,2	6,0
	Wood, paper and printing (16–18)	6,2	6,4	7,2	8,1
	Chem, pharm, rubber, plastic and refined petroleum (19–22)	8,9	6,9	8,6	9,6
	Non-metallic mineral products (23)	3,7	4,5	4,7	4,1
	Basic metals and metal products (24–25)	26,8	10,9	14,6	13,2
	Electric, electronic, computer and optical equipment (26–27)	8,1	5,4	4,0	6,8
	Machinery (28)	12,0	7,2	4,5	6,3
	Transport equipment (29–30)	18,4	23,3	9,1	8,4
	Other manufacturing (31–33)	5,2	6,1	10,3	10,0

Firms	Exports (% GDP)	22,0	29,6	14,6	27,8
	Average firm size (number of workers)	16,5	19,2	11,3	16,5
RIS 2014 (normalized values)	Population with tertiary education	0,97	0,77	0,61	0,48
	R&D expenditure in the public sector	0,31	0,37	0,35	0,36
	R&D expenditure in the business sector	0,53	0,51	0,29	0,34
	Non-R&D innovation expenditures	0,14	0,16	0,21	0,32
	SMEs innovating in-house	0,40	0,49	0,27	0,41
	Innovative SMEs collaborating with others	0,37	0,32	0,19	0,34
	EPO patent applications	0,24	0,31	0,15	0,25
	SMEs introducing product or process innovations	0,42	0,54	0,33	0,44
	SMEs introducing marketing or organizational innovations	0,21	0,30	0,21	0,38
	Employment in knowledge–intensive activities	0,65	0,55	0,41	0,50
	Sales of new to market and new to firm	0,62	0,66	0,52	0,45
Economic performance	GDP per inhabitant (PPS) (2011)	32.500	31.100	24.153	23.465
	GDP per worker (PPS) (2011)	79.162	74.959	65.043	58.113
	Employment rate (% over population) (2013)	40,1	40,4	36,7	43,1
	Unemployment rate (2013)	16,6	17,9	24,7	11,7
Institutions	Decentralization index	58,0	58,0	58,0	47,4
	Quality of governmental institutions	0,67	0,17	0,19	0,05

Source: Eurostat and Navarro *et al.* (2014). Own elaboration.

11 Entrepreneurship, Networks and Recombinant Open Innovation

Lessons for Regional Policy

Robert Huggins

11.1 Introduction

Innovation is commonly acknowledged to be a principal means by which regions foster economic growth and competitiveness (Capello and Nijkamp 2009; Harris 2011). At the same time, it is increasingly suggested that entrepreneurship is also a key source of such growth (Audretsch *et al.* 2006). Alongside these perspectives there is a growing school of thought which suggests that the networks facilitating flows of knowledge within and across regions are a key source of innovation and growth (Huggins and Izushi 2007). Furthermore, regions are increasingly considered to be important sources of economic development and organisation in a globalised economy (Malecki 2007), the innovation that entrepreneurship has the capacity to spawn, is increasingly considered to be a key factor underpinning the future growth trajectories of regions (Fritsch and Mueller 2004). The ability of regions to gain from the positive effects of entrepreneurship is likely to more than partly depend on their capability to turn knowledge into regional innovation and growth through the creation and dissemination of this knowledge (Audretsch and Keilbach 2008). The innovation systems literature, especially the regional variety literature, highlights the flow of knowledge across organisations as a crucial factor for effective innovation (Cooke *et al.* 2011).

Based on the rise of endogenous models of economic growth, the sources of regional economic growth are increasingly considered to be based on the role that the production, distribution and use of knowledge play within and across regional economies (Antonelli *et al.* 2011). The knowledge-based economy is generally considered to consist of the sphere and nexus of activities and resources which are centred on, and geared towards, innovation (Romer 2007). With increasing globalisation, it can be argued that the regional level has become more important than nations in promoting and understanding innovation and economic growth (Scott and Storper 2003). Furthermore, entrepreneurship itself has a pronounced regional dimension, with differences in regional start-up rates, as well as differences in the success of start-ups and entrepreneurial attitudes, all indicating the role of the regional environment in fostering entrepreneurship (Fritsch and Wyrwich 2014). Regions, therefore, can become 'incubators of new ideas' and provide opportunities for entrepreneurship to take place, as well as for discovering valuable new knowledge (Huggins and Williams 2011).

Given the acknowledged central role of regional spaces in promoting economic development, the aim of this chapter is to focus on three contemporary determinants of development at the regional level: entrepreneurship; networks, and open recombinant innovation. Drawing on examples from Silicon Valley; Taiwan and Finland, it is argued that an open networked environment, built upon global knowledge search mechanisms, is central to fostering innovation and entrepreneurship, and subsequently regional competitiveness. In particular, it highlights how the open model of economic development adopted by Taiwan fares when compared with the closed model associated more with Finland. Also, it indicates how the enduring success of Silicon Valley has occurred through processes of networked connectivity and recombinant innovation.

11.2 Entrepreneurship and a Network-Based View of Innovation

Entrepreneurship forms a part of endogenous modes of economic development consisting of activities, investment and systems arising and nurtured within a region, as opposed to being attracted from elsewhere (Ghio *et al.* 2014). As part of these modes, the capability of entrepreneurs to influence economic development is related to their capacity to access and exploit knowledge and generate innovation. Entrepreneurship is increasingly recognised as a crucial element in fostering economic growth (Carree and Thurik 2006). Romer (2007, p. 128) emphasises the role of entrepreneurship by stating that 'economic growth occurs whenever people take resources and rearrange them in ways that are valuable … [It] springs from better recipes, not just more cooking'. In general, the process of entrepreneurship is widely considered to stimulate competition and drive innovation (Powell 2007).

Within endogenous models of regional growth, knowledge is considered to spillover to other organisations, resulting in the generation of increasing returns, principally via innovation (Capello and Nijkamp 2009). Such knowledge, however, is not considered to be a purely public good, but one that is at least partially excludable – such as through the use of intellectual property rights – given that organisations often consider there to be incentives for investing in its creation. Similarly, models seeking to explain innovation outputs, such as patents, are based on a knowledge production function in which organisations (i.e. firms) intentionally pursue new economic knowledge as a means of generating innovation (Audretsch 2000). This pursuit is generally considered to consist of the appropriation and exploitation of the knowledge spilling over from other organisations (other firms, universities and the like). Despite these theoretical developments, endogenous growth theorists throw little light on the mechanisms by which knowledge is transmitted across firms and organisations (Storper and Venables 2004), suggesting the need for a better understanding of the role of investments in spillover conduits in generating innovation and growth (Audretsch and Feldman 1996). Emerging theories of the firm such as the knowledge-based view (Grant 1996) and extensions of the resource-based view (Lavie 2006) recognise that the need to access knowledge is a key reason why firms build or enter networks with other organisations. These networks concern the interactions, relationships and ties existing between firms, and may arise through the need to access new technology, skills or expertise in order to keep pace with competitors (Ahuja 2000).

Networks in this context consist of the interactions and relationships organisations (principally firms) utilise to access knowledge beyond their market relationships. In other words, these networks consist of the means by which knowledge flows across organisations beyond simply the direct purchasing of it. As others have noted, networks of this kind generally come into being due to markets for knowledge being rare, since – with the exception of knowledge protected by property rights, such as patents and copyrights – they are difficult to create due to the inherent asymmetry in the existing knowledge base of buyers and sellers (Arrow 1971; Malecki 2010). Networks are increasingly found to act as a conduit facilitating the flow of skills, expertise, technology, R&D and the like (Weterings and Ponds 2009). Networks, therefore, are an important aspect of the innovation process, with network scholars stressing that innovation is a complex process often requiring knowledge flow between organisations (Bergenholtz and Waldstrøm 2011). Increasingly, this process is viewed as a systemic undertaking, i.e. organisations no longer innovate in isolation but through a complex set of interactions with other organisations (Chesbrough 2003). It is through the networks underpinning these systemic processes that organisations access knowledge that they cannot, or do not wish to, generate internally.

In recent years, the term 'open innovation' has been coined to define the networked nature of innovation mechanisms. According to Chesbrough (2003, p. xxiv), open innovation is 'a paradigm that assumes that firms can and should use external ideas as well as internal ideas … as the firms look to advance their technology'. Although existing evidence has mainly focused on open innovation in the context of large corporations, it is likely that it is a phenomenon equally applicable to a strata of more entrepreneurial firms (Laursen and Salter 2006; Perkmann and Walsh 2007). Furthermore, it has been proposed that the investment in calculative relations through which organisations gain access to knowledge to enhance expected economic returns is itself a form of capital, which can be termed network capital (Huggins and Thompson 2014; 2015). The notion of network capital is a response to the increased recognition that inter-organisational networks can be considered a strategic resource for firms (Gulati 2007). Research stemming from the field of strategic management has proposed an extension of the resource-based view of the firm to account for external network capabilities (Lavie 2006).

11.3 Global and Local Connectivity

Knowledge spillovers are generally found to be greater in the presence of knowledge investments, and vice versa, with those regions possessing high knowledge investments experiencing a higher level of knowledge spillover – with interregional spillovers contributing significantly to regional knowledge production (Bathelt *et al.* 2004). A growing base of evidence suggests that knowledge is increasingly flowing across regional clusters, resulting in heightened global knowledge connectivity. It can be suggested, however, that although knowledge spillovers may take place across regions, it is usually through more selective routes (Audretsch and Lehmann 2005). For instance, the concept of 'temporary clusters', whereby strategic network building occurs through conferences, trade fairs, exhibitions and the like, highlights the importance of network capital and access to knowledge through global pipelines (Schuldt and Bathelt 2011).

In general, a key dimension of the knowledge spillover theory of entrepreneurship is geographic distance, with the general argument being that knowledge spills over more easily within regions than at a distance beyond them (Jaffe *et al.* 1993). This suggests that local firms may often be embedded in regional knowledge channels (Breschi and Lissoni 2009), with ready access to local public or private research institutes and universities being facilitated through local knowledge flow routes (Mueller 2006). However, while firms may benefit from local knowledge spillovers as an undirected and spontaneous 'buzz' (Storper and Venables 2004), they may also need to consciously build non-local 'pipelines' to tap into knowledge from outside their region (Bathelt *et al.* 2004).

These intra- and inter-regional network patterns indicate that the geographic location of entrepreneurial firms will influence the innovation output regions accrue from these networks. For example, if all the knowledge flowing through a network consists of firms and organisations based in the same region, it is likely that all the benefits will accrue to this region. If some firms and organisations are based in another region, it is likely that some of the benefits of this knowledge flow will also accrue to this other region. Therefore, it may well be the case that the knowledge flowing from organisations in this other region is more economically valuable (in terms of its superiority, excludability or miscibility) than that available in the focus region, with advantages in terms of the nature of the knowledge outweighing any disadvantages in terms of location (Belussi and Sedita 2012).

11.4 Recombinant Open Innovation and Silicon Valley

As the information revolution has greatly multiplied the types of potential solution to any technical problem, the chances that the best answer is reached by further development of the current one decrease. In developing new products, firms, therefore, rely less on internal units for whom pursuit of particular development paths has become an inviolable routine, and search out rather external partners whose practice is to scan for novel solutions. As a result, expedited of course by many other factors, we find the disintegration of the vertically integrated firm, and the concomitant growth of global supply chains in which suppliers all along the chain are expected to co-design, and continuously improve the performance of the products they provide their customers (Sturgeon, 2002; Sabel and Zeitlin, 2004).

With global competition and information technology creating a proliferation of new potential solutions and pathways, innovation has become unpredictable and recombinant, with multiple competing solutions with different strengths in different contexts. Hence, the progress of technology becomes unpredictable insofar as there can be no expectation that one good solution will lead by a natural progression to another. Counter intuitively, the more knowable the world as a whole becomes, the less confident we can be about the kind of knowledge that will prove useful in engaging its parts. By the same token, the more development depends on applying knowledge from domains traditionally unrelated to the industry's core activities, the less meaningful the idea of a technological frontier – it is everywhere and nowhere – and the less confident we can be that leadership today assures leadership tomorrow. In these circumstances it may well be more important to be able to search effectively across domains than to dominate the generation of ideas and technologies within any one of them (Saxenian and Sabel, 2008). Furthermore, as boundaries between sectors and domains become increasingly indistinct, a key is the capacity for firms and economies is to search effectively and recombine changing capacities rather than dominate a fixed subset of technology.

In the case of Silicon Valley, it has grown through increasing specialisation and repeated waves of recombination. As shown by Figure 11.1, productivity (value added) continues to rise with each successive wave of technology. Through processes of fragmentation and reintegration the blurring of industrial boundaries takes place from, for example, PC to internet to mobile web to the latest generation of web applications – web browsers, search engines, social networking – all of which are combining similar components including programming languages, protocols, standards, software libraries, productivity tools – into a common framework. In essence, there are no longer any fixed technology trajectories and 'catch-up' processes are too fast. In Silicon Valley, we see a continuous blurring of boundaries between previously distinct industries and sectors, and whilst we often think of the region as being made up on corporate giants – HP, Intel, Apple, Google, Facebook, Twitter – there is a remarkable amount of churn in the industrial system, with the majority of the region's largest 20 corporations in 1980s and

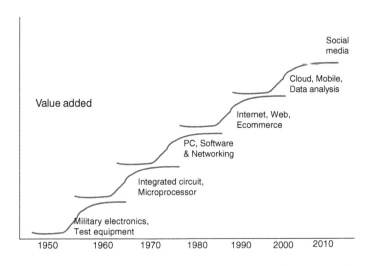

Figure 11.1 The evolution of innovative recombination in Silicon Valley.

1990s no longer on that list. Indeed, small firms collectively represent a major force in Silicon Valley's dynamics, and they have made, and will continue to remake, the regional economy (Huggins, 2008). Fundamentally, Silicon Valley's success stems from a regional ecosystem that is rich in high quality institutions that promote: entrepreneurial experimentation; open labour markets; firm specialisation; venture capital networks; collective learning; and regional adaptation.

Within Silicon Valley, firms of all sizes interact in the ecosystem, in which superior technology trumps business size, with innovation occurring in a highly decentralized environment, with the benefits of proximity – dense social and professional networks, informal information exchange, cross-firm collaboration, and serendipity – outweighing the high and rising costs of being in the ecosystem (Saxenian, 1994). Innovation, therefore, no longer occurs in isolated laboratories, but rather through collaborative co-development networks between increasingly specialist producers. Innovation at all stages of the production process is a highly iterative and non-linear process. Learning happens through continuing interactions facilitated by social networks and open labour markets, which allow know-how and information to circulate freely. It is possible to contribute to the formation of such an ecosystem, but it cannot be planned from the top down, and once it gets started, the strength of such a system is that it fosters unanticipated re-combinations of skill and technology, and multiple, often parallel, experiments with technology, organisation, markets, and so forth. Learning happens through trial and error, and often through failure. Failure is common, but it is not a stigma, and reflects a highly social process in which people learn through their own and others mistakes and in which the trust that grows from face-to-face interaction, and the serendipity that grows out of the free circulation of ideas and talent which create feedback loops.

Furthermore, the spatial differentiation of economic activity that is typically linked to industrial specialisation (another manifestation of heterogeneity) means that a focus on national indicators and institutions can obscure critical transformations that occur at the regional level. Likewise, the state, in both developing as well as in developed countries, is not a unified whole, but rather consists of multiple, differently organised, units with various political and economic resources, jurisdictions, and interests. It is precisely this heterogeneity that permits innovation and growth in specific industries that are located in a small number of urban areas or regions. Thus, economic and institutional change begins in certain locations and/or domains and advances through partial and incremental (micro-level) reforms that aggregate into larger-scale transformations with time (Kuznetsov and Sabel 2007; Saxenian and Sabel, 2008). A particular example of this is the role of Taiwanese diaspora in helping establish Taiwan as an open networked and economic successfully, and the following section draws a comparison between Taiwan's openness and a more 'closed' network economy as typified by Finland.

11.5 Comparing 'Open' Taiwan with 'Closed' Finland

At the end of the nineteenth century both Taiwan and Finland were de facto colonies, and suffered the forms of economic marginality typically associated with that status. Finland, having passed from Swedish to Russian sovereignty in 1809, only became independent from the Russia in 1917. Taiwan, having been occupied by Japan on and off since 1592 became a territory of that country in 1895, and came under the control of the Kuomintang (KMT), in flight from China, but was formally released from all Japanese claims in 1952. Economically, there are a number of commonalities in their evolution, and as recently as the 1960s both were small, economically marginal economies. Both came relatively late to industrialisation, and in the 1970s–1980s strong developmental states led to resource mobilisation in technology sectors, with heavy investments in R&D and universities, and a goal to catch up to 'global technological frontier'. By 1980 Finland was the economically stronger with a GDP per capita of US$8,609m compared with US$3,571 in Taiwan.

In the 1990s, both emerge as global ICT leaders with Finland creating and leading the mobile phone industry, and Taiwan dominating integrated circuit (IC design) and manufacturing, and electronic systems production. By 2000, in Finland Nokia pioneers technical and design innovation, with dizzying growth (40% world market for mobile phones), supported by a 'national' system of innovation, and expands production to India, Hungary, and China. Taiwan pioneers the IC foundry business, with state investment in IC and electronics research, and the expansion of production to the greater Shanghai region.

By 2000, both Finland and Taiwan could be viewed as parallel global models of ICT success, but their underlying trajectories differ dramatically, and this only becomes apparent in the mid–late 2000s. In Finland, a crisis in leading industries including ICT led to a deepening recession, and whilst Taiwan also suffered an economic downturn there was continued export growth. As result by 2010, Taiwan surpassed Japan, Korea, UK, France and Israel in GDP per capita, which stood at US$49,970, compared with US$34,454 in Finland. In the case of Finland, its problems can be viewed as stemming from the closed economic model associated with Nokia and its position and role within the national innovation system, and the lack of any mechanism for the exploration of new markets which reinforced refinements of existing technologies and the more extensive exploitation of existing markets.

National systems of innovation, including Finland's, were often designed with the idea of closing the gap between a country's capabilities in particular areas and the respective world technological frontier (Saxenian and Sabel, 2008). Such systems, however, become less useful as the 'boundary' begins to wander. In the worst case, the national system of innovation can actually impede progress by focusing attention, and fixing resources, on the problems that would have been central to an industry's domain if unanticipated connections to other bodies of knowledge had not rendered them irrelevant. The risk of this strategy is self-blocking entrenchment, and in the case of Finland, left Nokia, which was by far the most dominant economic actor, unprepared for boundary-blurring innovations introduced by Apple, Google, and others.

As a result of such entrenchment, organisational trajectories become very difficult to change due to the dominance of certain actors – such as engineering teams and product groups – who are locked-in to existing cognitive and organizational routines. In effect, Nokia went from boom to bust, and following the period in which it became a clear early innovator and mobile design pioneer, it continued to hone its mastery of complex supply chains and antennae technology. However, it has struggled to give commercial meaning to the idea – in a manner as compelling to it as to Apple, Samsung or Google – of the cell phone being a mobile portal to the internet. At the same time, its success in emerging markets entails relentless attention to lowering the costs of high-volume products, and so increases the pressures for and rewards to optimisation, making the re-direction of the organization, or even of some of its key parts, that much the harder.

In contrast to Finland, the role of institutional reform, the diaspora and international cross-cluster linkages have facilitated a process whereby Taiwan has economically forged ahead on the global stage. The diaspora has closely collaborated with the government to design institutions to support entrepreneurship and innovative search, and – in stark contrast to Finland – venture capital has become a powerful search network to identify and (re) combine parts of firms – financial, technical or marketing expertise, managerial talent, IP – to form ventures that in turn become nodes in networks for co-designing and building new products. By supporting a diverse portfolio of ventures and combining hands-on monitoring and mentoring with market selection, investors in Taiwan are thus institutionalizing a process of continuous economic restructuring – and learning about how to improve restructuring itself – that transforms the domestic economy by linking it to the most demanding and capable actors in global markets (Saxenian, 2006).

Entrepreneurship, vertical decomposition and the clustering of IC and electronic systems production has facilitated deepening specialisation and the co-design of components, subsystems, and periodic re-integration. The diaspora is instrumental in collaborative exploration and innovative recombination, and establishing the cross-regional collaboration, mutual upgrading and cross-cluster linkages between Taiwan and Silicon Valley. Firms in Taiwan which are shifting from vertical integration to collaborative exploration of new markets with outsiders have had to invent new forms of contracting, joint venturing and strategic alliances, including novel institutions in the form of search networks connecting actors, domestic and foreign, engaged in potentially complementary searches. These ongoing and myriad new organisational forms between hierarchies and markets, are changing the boundaries between the firm and its environment and perhaps even the very nature of the firm itself. Whilst Taiwan sought to imitate Silicon Valley in 1980s, and acted as a provider of low cost labour and components, the strong connections that have since formed have to led a relationship based on parity of esteem, as well as the co-creation of a venture capital industry, return entrepreneurship, cross-regional collaboration and innovation, and a reciprocal upgrading along value chain.

11.6 Connectivity across Clusters and Regions

In his classic 1955 article, Francois Perroux (1955) argued that in the end scale and innovation are the predictors of success, whereas Albert Hirschman (1958) recognized the role of interdependences and linkages across related sectors in achieving economic growth. The processes of consolidating and connecting knowledge clusters is a manifestation that these principles are re-emerging as key tenets of change in today's global economy. In particular, some of the world's most visible regional clusters are operating networks that are more open, as they seek new knowledge and the means to more efficiently exploit their existing knowledge base. In Silicon Valley, it is clear that cluster actors utilize the benefits of proximity to build and manage global-scale production networks (Sturgeon, 2003). The key aspect of these developments is that the knowledge base of the world's most advanced regional economies is no longer necessarily local, but positioned within global knowledge networks, connecting clusters and their actors (Wolfe and Gertler, 2004).

Furthermore, national innovation systems are becoming more 'leaky' over time, whereby 'the role of tacit knowledge and the spatial limits on knowledge spillovers have caused firms to locate R&D facilities where new knowledge is being created' (Carlsson, 2006, p. 65). As a result, regional policy making is quickly seeking to shift itself toward more open and connected systems, with those clusters able to renew themselves and evolve through innovation developing a morphological capacity to remain comparatively competitive through periods of national or global recession. In other words, clusters must themselves be subject to innovation, dynamic change, and evolving processes in much the same way that products have to change if they are to diminish the risk of having a short shelf life.

Although it is undoubtedly impossible to replicate or clone regions such as Silicon Valley, or any other knowledge cluster for that matter, there are many lessons that can be learned about how to improve the competitiveness of regional locations, in particular the role networks have played in making regions with strong clusters the centres of global growth. At the same time, it is important to recognise that such clusters should not be viewed as utopian because, like firms, the challenges involved in their creation and sustainability are contingent on a set of factors related to prevailing local and global forces. For instance, the past failure of many science parks as a policy response for generating high-technology activity can be strongly related to the fact that although they facilitated the co-location of companies, such policies ignored the processes through which this co-location could be activated into meaningful interaction and collaboration, particularly between industry and academia. It has long been argued that most science park developments are no more than high-tech fantasies, contributing little to increased links between industry and the academic world (Massey *et al.* 1992). At the same time, other types of regional cluster development policies directly mirror the incentive to develop networks between firms. They reflect the desire of firms to lower the transaction costs of traditional market exchanges or cumbersome hierarchies. Networks and clusters have both become increasingly important as firms downsize and outsource many of their noncore activities. The overall effect of this is an extension of the value chain, as firm specialization and resource concentration become the axis of competitive advantage acquisition. This specialization has rapidly pushed the value of network resources higher up the ladder of strategic resources employed by firms (Gulati, 1999).

A key lesson for most regions, especially the less competitive, is that the 'Silicon Valley recipe' of merely investing in ingredients such as technology parks, university research, engineers, venture capital, and incubators alone is unlikely to prove successful. Rather than seeking to replicate the components and ingredients of successful regions, a more fruitful approach is to connect with them through both firm-level and regional collaborations. In particular, there is need to nurture global and local open search networks, and to define and invest in distinct capacities through processes of experimentation. Diaspora potentially play an important role as global search networkers acting as bridging and boundary spanning agents, connecting to the 'global leading edge' and scanning for new markets, partners and solutions. Furthermore, evidence suggests that diaspora can support policymakers in defining strategy, transferring global 'best practice', linking to customers and partners, broker technology or institutional adoption, and overcome political opposition to reform (Saxenian, 2006).

11.7 Entrepreneurship and Regional Innovation Policy

In order for regions to compete effectively on the global stage, it is clear that regional entrepreneurs seeking to innovate are likely to benefit from the accumulation of network capital, which will facilitate better access to economically beneficial knowledge. However, entrepreneurs should be aware of the trade-offs that may exist between accessing knowledge that is relatively easy to source and absorb, and knowledge which may be more difficult to identify and integrate, but potentially offers far greater economic returns. Given this, entrepreneurs should ensure that management systems are in place to effectively search, screen and select the most appropriate knowledge to flow in and out of their firms. It is likely that in order to access the highest quality knowledge, entrepreneurs should seek to invest in a balanced portfolio of networks encompassing both local and more global geographic connections. However, this balance, and the success of firms in generating innovation, will be partly governed by the regional environment in which entrepreneurial firms are located. Similarly, the networks established by entrepreneurs are likely to impact upon the innovation capability and economic growth capacity not only of their home region, but also the performance of other regions where there are firms and organisations with which they network.

These practical implications for entrepreneurs raise a number of potential recommendations for future policy that can be said to operate at the nexus of regional innovation and entrepreneurship policymaking. Interestingly, Asheim and Isaksen (2003) argue that endogenous regional development is unlikely to occur holistically without public intervention to stimulate network formation. Nauwelaers and Wintjes (2003) classify regional innovation policies according to two core types: (1) system-oriented (regional) – principally network building and brokering, cluster development, innovation system development, cooperation and mobility and (2) firm-oriented – principally access to human capital (e.g. business support and advice), financial capital (e.g. risk capital, loans or subsidies) or physical capital (e.g. incubators, research and technology centres).

The latter firm-oriented policies are generally aligned with a range of recognised policies focused on promoting entrepreneurship in its broader context; that is, not simply in terms of business start-ups or small business growth (Huggins and Williams 2011). From the perspective of promoting the accumulation of effective network capital across entrepreneurial firms, both types are likely to be required to operate in tandem, with a need for coordination across policies (Nauwelaers and Wintjes 2003).

Regional rates of innovation and competitiveness are likely to be relatively high in those regions where entrepreneurial firms are able to establish networks facilitating access to a pool of high-quality knowledge. In regions with lagging rates of innovation, entrepreneurial firms are likely to face barriers in accessing such knowledge, especially through networks within their own region. This implies the need for policy intervention to be made available to entrepreneurial firms in regions with low rates innovation. More generally, across regions of all types there is a need to ensure the necessary support to help firms develop their capability to establish effective networks. For example, if entrepreneurs within a region are unable to assimilate knowledge from their internal base with that accessible from other organisations, there is a potential role for intervention in the form of innovation policies that act as an 'emulsifier' allowing different types of knowledge to be more effectively combined.

Similarly, policy should support firms to ensure they are capable of accessing the most appropriate and suitable knowledge for their innovation needs. In particular, policymakers need to become increasingly aware of the need for entrepreneurial firms to establish a portfolio of both sustained and more dynamic ephemeral knowledge sources. Without this balance, entrepreneurial firms run the risk of becoming locked into using outdated knowledge that undermines their innovative capabilities (Pittaway *et al.* 2004). Alongside this, there is a clear and ongoing requirement for regional policy to ensure sufficient absorptive capacity and human capital within the regional base of entrepreneurial firms (Cohen and Levinthal 1990; Zahra and George 2002). Therefore, regional innovation policies must be closely meshed with regional skills strategies to continue efforts to upskill the workforces and human capital of entrepreneurial firms – particularly with regard to management development – ensuring they are able to identify, absorb and transform into innovation the wealth of knowledge potentially available to them.

Furthermore, although entrepreneurial firms are unlikely to be able to bear the cost of full-time knowledge gatekeepers (Rychen and Zimmermann 2008; Belussi *et al.* 2010), more can be done to educate firms in the key principles of network management, as a feature of more general knowledge management practices. There are growing applied and professional disciplines related to the management of networks and knowledge flows, which should be supported through public policy. In particular, policy initiatives should widen their regional focus and embrace more spatially open and connected network systems. Efforts to internationalise the trading activities of entrepreneurial firms (Oviatt and McDougall 2005) should be complemented by a greater effort to internationalise their knowledge and innovation networks. Support should also be made available for engagement with global communities of practice. Communities of practice are becoming ever more international in their dimensions, and to remain innovative, entrepreneurial firms must become better integrated into their respective global villages (Bathelt *et al.* 2004).

Finally, regional policy can play a role in empowering entrepreneurial firms. Entrepreneurial firms are often fearful of engaging in knowledge exchange partnerships with larger firms, particularly multinationals, due to worries concerning the exploitation of their knowledge base without receiving appropriate levels of financial reward (Lechner and Dowling 2003; Huggins and Johnston 2010). Traditionally, the assertion of intellectual property has been seen as the key means by which entrepreneurial firms are able to protect their knowledge. However, due to increasing problems of asserting rights in many sectors (e.g. services) and the cost and time implications of patenting and licensing agreements (Hipp and Grupp 2005), this is not an option for all entrepreneurial firms, especially as larger firms are adopting open innovation strategies. To an extent, the traditional intellectual property support available to entrepreneurial firms is likely to become less relevant as open innovation and open sourcing become ever more prevalent business practices (Chesbrough 2003; von Hippel 2005), and new policy initiatives are required to support these firms in ensuring they are equitably treated when establishing joint knowledge-based ventures and strategic alliances with larger firms.

11.8 Conclusion

The observations made in this chapter are principally focused on explaining and understanding how networks promote and mediate the relationship between entrepreneurship, innovation and regional level economic outcomes. It is suggested that the innovation performance of entrepreneurs and subsequently the innovation and competitive performance of the regions in which they are located, is significantly related to investment in dynamically configured networks and search interactions and relationships. There are multiple mechanisms underlying the formation and development of networks by entrepreneurs and their firms, and it is through a range of complementary networks that firms are able to appropriately access and apply knowledge and subsequently develop innovative goods and services.

In terms of improving our understanding of the unevenness of rates of innovation and economic growth across regions, it can be proposed that regional innovation rates are a function of the interaction between the rate of entrepreneurship and the rate of network capital accumulation by entrepreneurs and their firms, as manifested by the capability to access external knowledge. This suggests that the interaction between rates of entrepreneurship and network capital should be more explicitly integrated into endogenous models of regional growth. For example, there is the potential for models to not only analyse knowledge spillovers from the perspective of the geographic space and distance over which such knowledge flows but also the 'network space' encompassing these flows. In this case, network space can be conceptualised as principally consisting of the structure of the relationships, interactions and ties underlying network capital, with emerging evidence suggesting that geographic space and network space are intertwined factors underlying the evolution of knowledge networks.

Acknowledgement

I am grateful to AnnaLee Saxenian who very kindly provided access to some of the case-study data and information utilised in this chapter. The usual disclaimers apply.

References

Ahuja, G. (2000). The duality of collaboration: Inducements and opportunities in the formation of interfirm linkages. *Strategic Management Journal*, 21(3), 317–343.

Antonelli, C., Patrucco, P., & Quatraro, A. (2011). Productivity growth and pecuniary knowledge externalities: An empirical analysis of agglomeration economies in European regions. *Economic Geography*, 87(1), 23–50.

Arrow, K. J. (1971). *Essays in the Theory of Risk-Bearing*. Amsterdam: North-Holland.

Asheim, B., & Isaksen, A. (2003). SMEs and the regional dimension of innovation. In B. Asheim, A. Isaksen, C. Nauwelaers, & F. Tödtling (Eds.), *Regional innovation policy for small-medium enterprises* (pp. 21–48). London: Edward Elgar.

Audretsch, D. B., & Feldman, M. P. (1996). R&D spillovers and the geography of innovation and production. *American Economic Review*, 86(3), 630–640.

Audretsch, D. B. (2000). Knowledge, Globalization, and Regions: An economist's perspective. In J. H. Dunning (Ed.), *Regions, Globalization, and the Knowledge-Based Economy* (pp. 63–81). Oxford: Oxford University Press.

Audretsch, D. B., & Lehmann, E. E. (2005). Does the Knowledge Spillover Theory of Entrepreneurship hold for regions? *Research Policy*, 34(8), 1191–1202.

Audretsch, D. B., & Keilbach, M. (2008). Resolving the knowledge paradox: Knowledge-spillover entrepreneurship and economic growth, *Research Policy*, 37(10), 1697–1705.

Audretsch, D. B., Keilbach, M., & Lehmann, E. E. (2006). *Entrepreneurship and Economic Growth*. Oxford: Oxford University Press.

Bathelt, H., Malmberg, A., & Maskell, P. (2004). Clusters and knowledge: Local buzz, global pipelines and the process of knowledge creation. *Progress in Human Geography*, 28(1), 31–56.

Belussi, F., & Sedita, S. R. (2012). Industrial districts as open learning systems: Combining emergent and deliberate knowledge structures. *Regional Studies*, 46(2), 165–184.

Belussi, F., Sammarra, A., & Sedita, S. R. (2010). Learning at the boundaries in an "Open Regional Innovation System": A focus on firms' innovation strategies in the Emilia Romagna life science industry. *Research Policy*, 39(6), 710–721.

Bergenholtz, C., & Waldstrøm, C. (2011). Inter-organizational network studies: A literature review. *Industry and Innovation*, 18(6), 539–562.

Breschi, S., & Lissoni, F. (2009). Mobility of skilled workers and co-invention networks: an anatomy of localized knowledge flows. *Journal of Economic Geography*, 9(4), 439–468.

Capello, R., & Nijkamp, P. (eds) (2009). *Handbook of Regional Growth and Development Theories*. Cheltenham: Edward Elgar.

Carlsson, B. (2006). Internationalization of innovation systems: A survey of the literature. *Research Policy*, 35, 56–67.

Carree, M., & Thurik, A. R. (2006). Understanding the role of entrepreneurship for economic growth. In M. A. Carree, & A. R. Thurik (Eds.), *The Handbook of Entrepreneurship and Economic Growth (International Library of Entrepreneurship Series)* (pp. ix–xix). Cheltenham: Edward Elgar.

Chesbrough, H. (2003). *Open Innovation: The New Imperative for Creating and Profiting from Technology*. Boston, MA: Harvard Business School Press.

Cohen, W. M., & Levinthal, D. A. (1990). Absorptive capacity: a new perspective on learning and innovation, *Administrative Science Quarterly*, 35(1), 128–152.

Cooke, P., Asheim, B., Boschma, R., Martin, R., Schwartz, D., & Tödtling, F. (Eds.) (2011). *Handbook of Regional Innovation and Growth*, Cheltenham: Edward Elgar.

Fritsch, M., & Mueller, P. (2004). The Effects of new business formation on regional development over time. *Regional Studies*, 38(8), 961–976.

Fritsch, M., & Wyrwich, M. (2014). The Long Persistence of Regional Levels of Entrepreneurship: Germany, 1925–2005. *Regional Studies*, 48(6), 955–973.

Ghio, N., Guerini, M., Lehmann, E. E., & Rossi-Lamastra, C. (2014). The emergence of the knowledge spillover theory of entrepreneurship. *Small Business Economics*, 44(1), 1–18.

Grant, R. (1996). Toward a knowledge-based theory of the firm. *Strategic Management Journal*, 17(S2), 109–122.

Gulati, R. (1999). Network location and learning: the influence of network resources and firm capabilities on alliance formation. *Strategic Management Journal*, 20(5), 397–420.

Gulati, R. (2007). *Managing Network Resources: Alliances, Affiliations, and Other Relational Assets*. Oxford: Oxford University Press.

Harris, R. G. (2011). Models of regional growth: Past, present and future. *Journal of Economic Surveys*, 25(5), 913–951.

Hipp, C., & Grupp, H. (2005). Innovation in the service sector: The demand for service-specific innovation measurement concepts and typologies. *Research Policy*, 34(4), 517–535.

Hirschman, A. O. (1958). *The Strategy of Economic Development*. New Haven, CT: Yale University Press.

Huggins, R. (2008). The evolution of knowledge clusters: Progress and policy. *Economic Development Quarterly*, 22(4), 277–4289.

Huggins, R. A., & Izushi, H. (2007). *Competing for Knowledge: Creating, Connecting and Growing*. London: Routledge.

Huggins, R., & Johnston, A. (2010). Knowledge flow and inter-firm networks: The influence of network resources, spatial proximity, and firm size. *Entrepreneurship and Regional Development*, 22(5), 457–484.

Huggins R., & Williams, N. (2011). Entrepreneurship and regional competitiveness: The role and progression of policy. *Entrepreneurship and Regional Development*, 23(9–10), 907–932.

Huggins, R., & Thompson, P. (2014). A Network-based view of regional growth. *Journal of Economic Geography*, 14(3), 511–545.

Huggins, R., & Thompson, P. (2015). Entrepreneurship, innovation and regional growth: a network theory. *Small Business Economics*, 45(1), 103–128.

Jaffe, A. B., Trajtenberg, M., & Henderson, R. (1993). Geographic localization of knowledge spillovers as evidenced by patent citations. *Quarterly journal of Economics*, 108(3), 577–598.

Kuznetsov, Y., & Sabel, C. (2007). *Towards a new open economy industrial policy: Sustaining growth without picking winners*. Washington, D.C.: World Bank Institute.

Laursen, K., & Salter, A. (2006). Open for innovation: the role of openness in explaining innovation performance among U.K. manufacturing firms. *Strategic Management Journal*, 27(2), 131–150.

Lavie, D. (2006). The competitive advantage of interconnected firms: an extension of the resource-based view. *Academy of Management Review*, 31(3), 638–658.

Lechner, C., & Dowling, M. (2003). Firm networks: external relationships as sources for the growth and competitiveness of entrepreneurial firms. *Entrepreneurship and Regional Development*, 15(1), 1–26.

Malecki, E. J. (2007). Cities and regions competing in the global economy: knowledge and local development policies. *Environment and Planning C: Government and Policy*, 25(5), 638–654.

Malecki, E. J. (2010). Everywhere? The geography of knowledge. *Journal of Regional Science*, 50(1), 493–513.

Massey, D., Quintas, P., & Wield, D. (1992). *High-tech fantasies: Science Parks in Society, Science and Space*. London: Routledge.

Mueller, P. (2006). Entrepreneurship in the region: Breeding ground for nascent entrepreneurs? *Small Business Economics*, 27(1), 41–58.

Nauwelaers, C., & Wintjes, R. (2003). Towards a new paradigm for innovation policy? In B. Asheim, A. Isaksen, C. Nauwelaers, & F. Tödtling (Eds), *Regional Innovation Policy for Small-Medium Enterprises* (pp. 193–219). Cheltenham: Edward Elgar.

Oviatt, B. M., & McDougall, P. P. (2005). Defining international entrepreneurship and modeling the speed of internationalization. *Entrepreneurship Theory and Practice*, 29(5), 537–554.

Perkmann, M., & Walsh, K. (2007). University–industry relationships and open innovation: Towards a research agenda. *International Journal of Management Reviews*, 9(4), 259–280.

Perroux, F. (1955). Note sur la notion de pôle de croissance [Note on the concept of growth poles]. *Economic Appliquée*, 8, 307–320.

Pittaway, L., Roberston, M., Munir, K., Denyer, D., & Neely, A. (2004). Networking and innovation: a systematic review of the evidence. *International Journal of Management Reviews*, 5(3/4), 137–168.

Powell, B. (2007). *Making Poor Nations Rich: Entrepreneurship and the Process of Economic Development*. Stanford University Press, Stanford.

Romer, P. M. (2007). Economic growth. In D. Henderson (Ed.), *The Concise Encyclopedia of Economics* (pp. Indianapolis: Liberty Fund. http://www.econlib.org/library/Enc1/EconomicGrowth.html.

Rychen, F., & Zimmermann, J. B. (2008). Clusters in the global knowledge-based economy: knowledge gatekeepers and temporary proximity. *Regional Studies*, 42(6), 767–776.

Sabel, C. F., and Zeitlin, J. (2004). Neither modularity nor relational contracting: Inter-firm collaboration in the new economy. *Enterprise & Society*, 5, 388–403.

Saxenian, A. (1994). Regional Advantage: Culture and Competition in Silicon Valley and Route 128. Cambridge, MA: Harvard University Press.

Saxenian, A. (2006). The New Argonauts: Regional advantage in a global economy. Cambridge, Mass.: Harvard University Press.

Saxenian, A., & Sabel, C. (2008). Roepke lecture in economic geography: Venture capital in the "periphery": the new argonauts, global search, and local institution building. *Economic Geography*, 84(4), 379–394.

Schuldt, N., & Bathelt, H. (2011). International trade fairs and global buzz. Part II: Practices of global buzz. *European Planning Studies*, 19(1), 1–22.

Scott, A., & Storper, M. (2003). Regions, Globalization, Development. *Regional Studies,* 37(6–7), 549–578.

Storper, M., & Venables, A. J. (2004). Buzz: face-to-face contact and the urban economy. *Journal of Economic Geography*, 4(4), 351–370.

Sturgeon, T. J. (2002). Modular production networks: A new American model of industrial organization. Industrial and Corporate Change, 11, 451–496.

Sturgeon, T. J. (2003). What really goes on in Silicon Valley? Spatial clustering and dispersal in modular production networks. *Journal of Economic Geography*, 3(2), 199–225.

von Hippel, E. (2005). *Democratizing Innovation*. Cambridge, MA: MIT Press.

Weterings, A., & Ponds, R. (2009). Do regional and non-regional knowledge flows differ? An empirical study on clustered firms in the Dutch life sciences and computing services industry. *Industry and Innovation*, 16(1), 11–31.

Wolfe, D., & Gertler, M. (2004). Clusters from the inside and out: local dynamics and global linkages. *Urban Studies*, 41(5/6), 1071–1093.

Zahra, S. A., & George, G. (2002). Absorptive capacity: a review, reconceptualization, and extension. *Academy of Management Review*, 27(2), 185–203.

Index

For Product Safety Concerns and Information please contact our EU
representative GPSR@taylorandfrancis.com
Taylor & Francis Verlag GmbH, Kaufingerstraße 24, 80331 München, Germany